A HISTORY OF INSANITY AND THE ASYLUM

A HISTORY OF INSANITY AND THE ASYLUM
NOT OF SOUND MIND

JULIANA CUMMINGS

PEN & SWORD
HISTORY

AN IMPRINT OF PEN & SWORD BOOKS LTD.
YORKSHIRE - PHILADELPHIA

First published in Great Britain in 2023 by
PEN AND SWORD HISTORY
An imprint of
Pen & Sword Books Ltd
Yorkshire – Philadelphia

Copyright © Juliana Cummings, 2023

ISBN 978 1 39901 214 0

The right of Juliana Cummings to be identified as Author of this work has been asserted by her in accordance with the Copyright, Designs and Patents Act 1988.

A CIP catalogue record for this book is available from the British Library.

All rights reserved. No part of this book may be reproduced or transmitted in any form or by any means, electronic or mechanical including photocopying, recording or by any information storage and retrieval system, without permission from the Publisher in writing.

Typeset in Times New Roman 12/16 by
SJmagic DESIGN SERVICES, India.
Printed and bound in the UK by CPI Group (UK) Ltd.

Pen & Sword Books Limited incorporates the imprints of Atlas, Archaeology, Aviation, Discovery, Family History, Fiction, History, Maritime, Military, Military Classics, Politics, Select, Transport, True Crime, Air World, Frontline Publishing, Leo Cooper, Remember When, Seaforth Publishing, The Praetorian Press, Wharncliffe Local History, Wharncliffe Transport, Wharncliffe True Crime and White Owl.

For a complete list of Pen & Sword titles please contact
PEN & SWORD BOOKS LIMITED
47 Church Street, Barnsley, South Yorkshire, S70 2AS, England
E-mail: enquiries@pen-and-sword.co.uk
Website: www.pen-and-sword.co.uk

Or

PEN AND SWORD BOOKS
1950 Lawrence Rd, Havertown, PA 19083, USA
E-mail: Uspen-and-sword@casematepublishers.com
Website: www.penandswordbooks.com

Contents

Acknowledgements		vi
Introduction		viii
Chapter One	Understanding Insanity and the Pioneers Who Defined Mental Illness	1
Chapter Two	Mental Illness in the Early Middle Ages and the Birth of Bedlam	22
Chapter Three	Caring for the Insane During the Fifteenth, Sixteenth & Seventeenth Centuries	35
Chapter Four	The Age of Enlightenment and the Influence of the Quaker Movement	64
Chapter Five	The Emergence of the Asylum	84
Chapter Six	Women and Children in the Victorian Era Asylum	100
Chapter Seven	Life in a Nineteenth and Twentieth Century Asylum. Daily Living, Patient Abuse, and Those That Pushed for Reform	130
Chapter Eight	Nineteenth and Twentieth Century Treatments for Mental Illness and the Breakthrough of Psychopharmacology	158
Chapter Nine	The Eugenics Movement and the Mentally Ill	205
Chapter Ten	The Closure of the Asylums	225
Bibliography		240
About the Author		246
Index		247

Acknowledgements

I would like to thank my husband and my parents for supporting me while writing this book, along with my extended family and friends.

My sister, who shares my love for bizarre history, was a huge supporter of this book. Jennifer, I love how we can have conversations about the strangest subjects together. There are not many who are as odd as us, are there? Except maybe Dad, because that is where we got our fascination for this stuff.

My best girls, Brenda and Jane, have continued to support me throughout all of my writing. Brenda, again, for always reading and commenting on what I write. Thank you for not being afraid to give me honest feedback! Jane is still my biggest cheerleader and always willing to provide me with her wise advice.

My cousin, Bryan, for being so excited about my books, making me feel special, and always taking the time to check-in. I wish we lived closer!

I want to thank everyone at Pen & Sword for reaching out to me again. I was so honoured to write for you the first time, and when you reached out to me again, I was so thankful. You have all been so supportive and kind. You are all patient and flexible and understood when I needed to add an extra month to my contract due to the pandemic.

Thank you to all the authors who have written on the subject of insanity and asylums. Though there may not be many, it's refreshing to read the words of others who share my love of this aspect of history.

Lastly, I would like to recognise the thousands of patients who suffered and continue to suffer from mental illness. So many of you endured so much pain while medicine made advancements over the past several hundred years. Those who were genuinely stricken with mental illness to those who were completely sane, without your bravery, we would not be where we are today without mental health care.

Introduction

1951. Boston, Massachusetts. McLean Hospital. A male patient is admitted to the psychiatric hospital with the diagnosis of 'schizophrenia-acute undifferentiated reaction'. He is prescribed a course of sub coma insulin shocks without anyone explaining the side effects or risks.

He is barely twenty years old.

By the third day of treatment, the patient is being injected with 20-25 units of insulin three times a day. He reacts with profuse sweating and finds himself ravenous after the treatment because insulin makes one incredibly hungry. He describes the treatment as intense and very painful, and he says hypoglycemia shock was debilitating and torturous. Each treatment lasts between three and four hours until it is ended with a fruit juice or dextrose.

By day six, the patient was calling out, 'I can't take this any longer. It's too unjust. I am not strong enough!'

On the twelfth day, the patient calls out again, 'I can't stand it!'

On day seventeen, the patient is sweating profusely, screaming, 'I can't stand it!' His pupils are dilated, and he is still pouring sweat. Then there is no response from the patient, and he is given fruit juice until he is revived. He remembers nothing.

By day twenty, the patient is getting 90 units of insulin three times a day, every day.

On day thirty-four, the patient has an emotional outburst and cries and shouts as he is dragged to treatment. Screaming while being taken down the hall, he says, 'I must get out of here. I can't stand insulin any longer!'

After 110 treatments of insulin therapy, the patient is physically, emotionally, and intellectually wiped out from the 'safe and effective' treatment.

Introduction

He was released from the hospital in 1953, at age twenty-two.

Unfortunately, this gentleman's story is one of the thousands that have taken place in mental institutions across the Western world during the first half of the twentieth century. It is a story of suffering, not only mentally but physically. But it is also a story of hope.

I have always had a bizarre fascination with the insane asylum. To me, it seemed like a world of yesteryear. One that was hauntingly beautiful and dangerous and one I would never be able to understand. I have always been impressed with their whimsical elegance that is captured so beautifully in photography today. In the buildings that are still standing, I wonder if the creaking floorboards and empty recreation rooms have stories to tell of a time in history that should never be forgotten.

Researching for this book has been a daunting task, as there was so much information that I wasn't aware of. But it has given me great pleasure to learn about the history of insanity and the depth (or lack thereof) of understanding in our ancestors. I was quite moved to learn about the earliest pioneers of the asylum and the doctors who were set on treating their patients. These men should be hailed as superheroes because where would we be without them? Would our mentally ill still be without treatment? How would they fare today in a world dominated by a media that glorifies everything that is wrong with the world?

I was always particularly interested in psychosurgery, perhaps because it bordered on science-fiction. At least to me, it seemed to. But during my research, I found I became utterly fascinated with insulin shock therapy, causing me to start this introduction with the actual account of a patient at McLean Hospital in Boston. Maybe the thought of being forcibly introduced into hypoglycemic shock was really what got my attention. I have hypoglycemia myself, and I can tell you that the feeling you experience when your blood sugar drops is extremely unpleasant. But those of us with hypoglycemia and diabetes are often given no warning. It makes me sympathise significantly with the thousands of patients who had to go through this treatment several times a week, all the while knowing what would happen. I wonder what would be worse, the apprehension or the actual fall in blood sugar.

In writing this book, I will admit that my preconceived notion was that the asylum was a horrible place and that the history of treating the insane was barbaric. And it was in a lot of cases. However, I have come to understand that despite the stigma attached to treating the mentally ill, it was just that, a stigma. I firmly believe that there was a genuine need to help people. From the men that came up with moral treatment (which in some cases wasn't that moral) to the doctors who performed lobotomies, most, if not all, had a deep-seated desire to help their patients.

I hope you, as my reader, are as fascinated by this part of history that has long been misunderstood. I hope that you are able to see into the world of the asylum and try to imagine what every day must have been like not only for patients but for caregivers as well. And possibly, you will be able to look at the asylum with a different lens, one that paints a picture of the importance of institutional healthcare for our mentally ill in society. Because with the shut down of the asylums throughout the United Kingdom and the United States, these people have often been left to fend for themselves in a world that they don't understand and where they were never quite understood.

Chapter One

Understanding Insanity and the Pioneers Who Defined Mental Illness

Insanity, madness, craziness. These are all terms that have been used to describe the array of behaviours that are deemed abnormal mental or behavioural patterns. But what is insanity, and where does its history lay? Who are the pioneers that, throughout time, have helped to get us to where we are today in our understanding of the mind?

According to Oxford Dictionary, the definition of insanity is; *the state of being seriously mentally ill.* Synonyms include madness, lunacy, delirium, and mania. Psychiatry, in modern terms, is the study and treatment of mental illness.

The history of psychiatry and its practices have been hotly contested, and controversy has been raised about interpreting many of its crucial developments. The questions have been asked if the asylum was just a convenient place for inconvenient people. Was Freud genuine, or was he a complete fraud? What were the ethics behind the lobotomy or ECT or the clitorectomy? Are the mentally ill better off without the asylums, or were they a source of security and structure for thousands unfit for society?

And on the flip side of this thinking, there remains the fact that many people choose the field of psychiatry because they have a genuine need to want to help people. Since the dawn of man, there has been an inherent need to help one another. In studying the brain and its emotions, psychiatrists are given the tools to do just that. But it wasn't an easy route, and it still isn't today. Understanding the human brain and all of its incredible capabilities is still a daunting task for even the most brilliant psychiatrists and neurologists.

While man has always been aware that some in society didn't function like the rest, the actual examination and management of the mentally ill in much of Western Europe didn't develop before the end of the eighteenth century. Many people did their best to take care of the mentally unstable, but it wasn't a valid practice that physicians dedicated a field of study to. Before the fifteenth century in England, the insane were often thrown in with the beggars and were referred to as village idiots. Outside of England, the mentally ill were more apt to be cared for in the family home. However, having a mad family member was a shameful thing, and it wasn't unheard of for families to put the ill in with the barn animals or even chain them up. It truly wasn't until the middle of the nineteenth century that mentally ill people in Great Britain weren't looked at with horror and dealt with in a heartless manner.

Mental instability has been around for as long as man has been alive and recognised through history in every society. There are sources that date back roughly 7,000 years ago that show evidence of trepanning, a technique used in antiquity where holes were drilled into the skull to allow demonic spirits to escape. The popular view in ancient cultures is that madness was caused by evil spirits who had invaded the body. But just how this evil had come about is what differs by civilisation.

It has taken the test of time to truly understand mental illness. Like most forms of medicine, the earliest records of understanding mental illness can be traced back to the ancient Greeks and Romans. Their basic understanding was that mental disorders came from the gods and could not be easily explained. And so, the volatile nature of the gods was often the fallback on behaviours that were not yet understood. In turn, many folks also turned to healing gods as a way to find relief from mental instability.

Asclepius was the ancient Greek god of not only medicine but healing. He had several sanctuaries throughout Greece that were important recovery centres in both Greek and Roman times. From the fifth century onwards, the temples of Asclepius became very popular, and pilgrims made the journey to be cured of their illnesses, including mental illness. The healing temples became a prominent part of Asclepius's history.

As described in the Gospel of John, the Pool of Bethesda was deemed to be part of an Asclepion temple by researchers who studied it in 1964. Another of Asclepius's healing temples was on the island of Kos, the birthplace of Hippocrates, the father of medicine. As word of his healing centres grew, pilgrims congregated to them to be cured of their physical and mental ills.

It has been suggested that how mental health professionals approach their work can be tied to Greek Mythology, specifically through Asclepius's daughter, Hygieia. Hygieia focused her work on wellness and cleanliness, and those who followed her movements ultimately tied mental health in as well.

The ancient Greeks were known to associate mental illness more with physical sickness than other cultures throughout history. Greek physicians began to take a more medical approach to mental illness around the fifth century. While folks flocked to the temples for healing, doctors looked for a medical cure. There became an understanding of reasoning with nature, society, and one's consciousness. The idea that one's irrationality existed was becoming a reality. By valuing order and logic, many Greek thinkers could define the problem of senselessness. Greek medicine laid the groundwork for understanding a holistic explanation for health and sickness, including madness.

The Hippocratic Corpus consists of a collection of roughly sixty Ancient Greek medical works. While the collection was not written by Hippocrates himself, it is strongly associated with his teachings. Hippocrates (b. 460 BCE) laid the foundation for medicine, and his practices and guidelines for classifying diseases have been utilised by physicians throughout time. His principles for the diagnosis, treatment, and preclusion of disease are today's standards for medical integrity. Hippocratic medicine was part of the belief system that one could use nature in creating and preserving a sound mind.

The study of mental illness was of significant interest to Hippocrates. He was the first to understand the different types of affliction and to give them separate terminology. Those afflictions included mania, melancholy, phrenitis, insanity, disobedience, paranoia, panic, epilepsy, and hysteria. Several of these terms are still used in today's medicine. A part of his studies of these classifications of mental illness was the need to explain their causes.

Hippocrates looked at mental illness as the effect of nature on man, and he treated them much like any other disease. He insisted that the brain was responsible for mental illness and that one's intelligence and sensitivity reached the brain through the mouth by breathing. According to Hippocrates, the diagnosis and treatment of psychological and physical diseases were based on observation, consideration, the balance of theory, and the four humours.

The theory of the four humours, which was the belief of Greek and Roman doctors, was a significant development in medical knowledge. The Greek philosopher Aristotle was the proponent of the theory that the body consisted of four humours, or liquids; blood, phlegm, yellow bile, and black bile. Black bile was related to cold and dry properties, while yellow bile was related to dry and warm properties. Blood was related to moist and warm qualities, and phlegm was associated with moist and cold qualities.

The theory taught that the body was subjected to development and constant change determined by the balance of the four humours. Hippocrates and those that followed his teachings didn't see disease as a solely organic matter. They believed that the mind and the body were one single entity and that the mind had significant effects on the body during disease. Greek thinker Galen elaborated on this theory. He, too, believed that a lack of balance between the humours could affect one's way of feeling and thinking. Galen associated black bile with those who had a melancholic temperament. Folks with a higher level of yellow bile were often quick-tempered, with enormous vitality, and they angered quickly. Those with a cheerful personality had an abundance of blood and were joyful and pleasant. And folks with a high level of phlegm were known as deep thinkers who were fair and willing to compromise. These humoral balances also explained what would later be called one's psychological disposition. When the four humours cooperated, all was well. Illness, it was believed, resulted when one humour became compromised, and it became easier to understand that mental conditions were an extension of physical ones.

Hippocrates felt that the role of music and art in the treatment of illness in order to improve human behaviour was essential. He felt that healing the soul through music, in turn, healed the body. The same can be said today, as research proves that music therapy is most beneficial for those with mental health conditions.

Asclepius was a pioneer when it came to applying music as therapy to master emotions. He felt that in some cases, the effect of melody that pleases the soul could be as effective as medical treatment and induce a sort of mental catharsis. Ancient Greece theatre acted as psychotherapy for many patients. At the Theater of Epidaurus at the ancient Temple of Epidaurus, patients often experienced a release of their emotions during performances. Perhaps both Asclepius and Hippocrates understood that music acts as an instrument for processing emotions. While it can trigger grief or trauma, it can also be used as a calming agent for those experiencing anxiety. Quiet rooms were also designed at the temple where patients could sleep and dream happily of being mentally stable. It was believed that these dreams would greatly improve their mental health.

Hippocrates also believed in a natural health care outlook where science was met with drug therapy, diet, and exercise. The Asclepieion of Kos, the ancient healing temple and school where Hippocrates taught, offered all patients widespread treatment. This included physical activity, long walks, massage, and the use of dreams for therapeutic reasons.

Greek medicine was clinically grounded in case histories found in Hippocratic writings where mental abnormalities were recorded, often as rambling speech, mouthing illegible words, plucking at one's skin and hair, and having a sense of melancholy.

On the Sacred Disease is a work that comes from the Hippocratic Oath, which originated in the fifth century. In the book, epilepsy was reported as a physiological syndrome and not a mental one. Through this, many Greek physicians began to understand that folks deemed crazy were not crazy at all but suffered from a physical illness. This proved helpful because, before this, most physicians didn't have a very sharp distinction between physical and mental disorders.

One Hippocratic text states:

> Men ought to know that from the brain, and from the brain only, arise our pleasure, joys, laughter, and jests, as well as our sorrows, pains, frights, and tears. Through it, in particular, we think, see, hear and distinguish the ugly from the beautiful, the bad from the good, the pleasant from the unpleasant. It is the same thing which makes us mad or delirious, inspires us with dread and fear, whether by night or by day, brings sleeplessness, inopportune mistakes, aimless anxieties, absentmindedness, and acts that are contrary to habit.

Aretaeus of Cappadocia, who lived during the first century, was one of the most celebrated physicians in Greek history. He wrote several valuable treatises on medicine, including *On the Causes and Signs of Disease*, in which he said spoke on a particular case of melancholy:

> Sufferers are dull or stern; dejected or unreasonably torpid, without any manifest cause, such as the commencement of melancholy, and they also become peevish, dispirited, sleepless, and start-up from a disturbed sleep. Unreasonable fears also seize them. They are prone to change their mind readily, to become base, mean-spirited, illiberal, and in a little time perhaps simple, extravagant, magnificent not from any virtue of the soul but from the changeableness

of the disease. But if the illness becomes more urgent, hatred, avoidance of the haunts of men, vain lamentations are seen. They complain of life and desire to die; in many, the understanding so leads to insensibility and fatuousness that they become ignorant of all things and forgetful of themselves, and live the life of inferior animals.

While little is known about his life, other than he was most likely a citizen of Cappadocia, the works of Aretaeus are considered some of the most valuable medical works ever written. His work showed precise accuracy in the symptoms and character of illnesses. Aside from giving descriptions of many physical diseases, he was also on point with nervous and mental disorders.

Aretaeus not only understood melancholy but mania as well, and he saw it as fury, excitement, and cheerfulness, including euphoria and deliriums. He is credited the discovery of what was later understood as bipolar disorder.

Greek doctors grew more concerned with understanding true psychosis rather than depression or melancholy. They considered a range of behaviours that were deemed inappropriate in public, such as delusions, delirium, or hallucinations. While the term psychosis includes the presence of delusions and hallucinations, physicians believed this to be more of a human condition than one that was an act of the gods. And because hallucinations were relatively commonplace, most people would not have looked for treatment. The philosopher Socrates was said to have heard voices and experienced hallucinations, and his followers were in awe of him, rather than thinking he was mad. Socrates talked of a voice that warned him of danger or making an error. Plato quoted him as saying:

> It is a voice that comes to me and forbids me from doing something I'm intending to do. However, it never tells me what to do, just what not to do.

When the voice, which he called his daemonic sign, spoke to him, Socrates would begin to stand motionless, often for significant parts of the day. Did this mean that he may have suffered from some sort of schizophrenia, or were the voices he pledged to have heard simply divine? If there were no reason to suspect anything was out of the ordinary, then it would have been a moot point.

Greek physician Soranus of Ephesus, who lived during the first or second century, wrote a treatise called *On Acute and Chronic Diseases*, which was translated by Roman physician Caelius Aurelianus. Through his understanding of the works, Aurelianus described three kinds of madness. Phrenitis, which he believed was delirium from fever and a fluctuating pulse, was one type of madness, and today we understand it to mean inflammation of the brain. Mania was a condition that presented with frenzy and anger, along with chaotic thoughts and delirium, but without fever. And finally, melancholy, which closely resembled modern-day depression, included states of paranoia and catatonic stupor. This state was probably closely related to what we know today as schizophrenia, with its main symptom being a withdrawal from reality.

Soranus, though we know little else about his life, other than he belonged to the Methodic school, was one of the most distinguished students at that school. He believed that people should be able to use their minds for philosophical discussion.

Today, we know that mental illness was not caused by unclean spirits or an imbalance in the humours. However, those were justifiable theories in antiquity, as was the unruliness of women.

Cicero (106 BCE – 43 BCE), a Roman Scholar, believed that mental instability was caused by a moral failing or an encounter with a seductress. He stated that insanity was a mild condition that resulted from a failure of will and that rage was more of a serious condition that involved a total lack of reasoning. This rage was often believed to have been caused by a group of bloodthirsty goddesses, which supported his theory that mental illness was caused by uncontrollable women.

However, we also have to wonder whether or not Cicero's seemingly displeasure of women resulted from the fact that he was in a marriage with a very self-confident woman who showed more interest in his political career than he would have liked. Cicero often complained that his wife Terentia had betrayed him, though he never said how.

What is interesting about Cicero is that he was convinced that unruly women created madness. Yet, in letters about Cicero's physical and emotional state, he appeared to have several bouts of suicidal depression. These attacks affected his relationship with his friends and family and quite possibly shortened his life. Following the death of his daughter, Cicero went into a depressive episode that included 'fits of weeping'.

One of the greatest Roman medical writers who lived during the 1rst century was Aulus Cornelius Celsus. In his medical treatise, *De Medicina*, Celsus wrote of female hysteria, saying:

> In females, a violent disease also arises in the womb; and, next to the stomach, tis part is most sympathetically affected or most sympathetically affects the rest of the system. Sometimes also, it so completely destroys the senses that on occasions, the patient fall, as if in epilepsy. This case, however, differs in that the eyes are not turned, nor does froth issue forth, nor are there any convulsions; there is only a deep sleep.

But it wasn't just the Romans who believed ill-tempered women caused mental illness. Hysteria in women has been accurately described since the second millennium BCE.

The Kahun Papyrus, a collection of ancient Egyptian gynaecological texts dating around 1900 BCE, identifies hysterical disorders in the uterus of the female body.

Dating to 1600 BCE, the Eber Papyrus tells of symptoms of hysteria. The Eber Papyrus is one of the oldest medical documents to refer to female hysteria, and there are indications that the uterus should be forced back into its natural position.

Greek mythology also believed female hysteria to play a part in psychiatry. Plato states that the uterus is sad when it does not join with the male. Aristotle and Hippocrates were also of the opinion that it is unfortunate when a uterus does not give rise to a new life. This was in part blamed on the theory of women suffering from hysteria. Hippocrates believed that the cause of female hysteria lay in the movement of the uterus. He assumed the idea of a restless uterus was the cause of stagnant humours and an inadequate sex life. A woman's body is physiologically cold and wet, making the uterus prone to illness. He explains that in virgins, single or sterile women, and widows, this 'bad' uterus will produce toxic fumes and wander around the body, causing anxiety, suffocation, convulsions, and tremors. Affected women are advised to cure themselves by pushing the uterus back into its natural place.

The idea of hysteria in women also goes back to Aretaeus of Cappadocia in his 'wandering womb' theory. He stated that a woman's uterus could move out of place and float around her body. Some of his works, translated in 1856, state:

> In the middle of the flanks of women lies the womb, a female viscus, closely resembling an animal; for it is moved of itself hither and thither in the flanks, also upwards in a direct line to below the cartilage of the thorax, and also obliquely to the right or to the left, either to the liver or the spleen, and it likewise is subject to prolapsus downwards, and in a word, it is altogether erratic. It delights also in fragrant smells and advances towards them, and it has an aversion to fetid smells and flees from them; and, on the whole, the womb is like an animal within an animal.

Although it was Soranus who greatly opposed Aretaeus's wandering womb theory, he preferred the term 'hysterical suffocation' and described the actual suffocation of the uterus. He wrote that the uterus did not froth about like a wild animal aroused by foul odours, but instead, it was drawn together by inflammation. Galen, who lived at roughly the same time as Aretaeus, also disagreed with his theory. Galen supported that the uterus itself did not move but that its inflammation was due to materials being held within it.

Of course, we know today that women's hysteria or any wandering wombs are absolutely untrue. The belief carried on for centuries and would haunt women, especially during the late nineteenth century.

Ancient Romans continued to follow the teachings of Hippocrates and his theory of the four humours. They believed that an imbalance of the humours was responsible for mania, melancholy, fear, or despair. The belief in the humoral theory, which would carry on through the middle of the sixteenth century, is not so far off in principle. Today, we know that the imbalance of the body's many hormones can often contribute to mental instability. Both Greek and Roman medicine offered a wealth of different therapies to treat the mentally ill. Soranus recommended talking to the deranged, while Celsus believed in isolating patients in total darkness and then scaring them in the hopes that they would recover from their malady. Bloodletting and purging were also among the methods used by the Romans to aid in mental illness, along with various herbs and proper diet. Hot and cold baths were used in the belief that they could restore the humoral balance. Other, much harsher methods recommended included being chained and whipped.

However, Asclepiades of Bithynia, a Greek philosopher who flourished in Rome, rejected Hippocrates' humoral theory. Asclepiades instead believed that disease resulted from conditions of solid particles. He thought that fresh air and sunlight, along with diet and exercise, was the correct treatment for mental illness. These ideas got some early recognition. However, with the rise of Christianity and the fall of the Roman Empire, the idea that mental illness was a punishment from the divine or demonic possession began to take hold. It was this thought process that would prevail for centuries.

Christianity in the Roman Empire was recognised in 313 AD, and it was soon denied that man was responsible for madness. Christianity preached that the human will was outnumbered by the spiritual will of God, angels, and saints, as well as Satan and his league of minions.

Jesus Christ, who is often portrayed as one who casts out demons, was an example of Christian association with madness. Stories of the supernatural are often aligned with tales of madness. These tales were a convenient source of power for the Catholic Church, which gave them the support they needed to declare themselves the authority. This deemed authority allowed the Church to interpret the presence of the divine and evil here on earth. The Church used the influence of God and Satan as an explanation for all sorts of strange occurrences. Possession or so-called possession was one of the most common causes of disturbances. Insanity was commonly viewed as a diabolical scheme of Satan and his heretics. Madness is talked about in the Bible through stories of possession in cases where God has used madness as a form of punishment.

Throughout Biblical times, mental instability continued to be seen as reprimands from the divine or the presence of an entity. As Christianity spread, exorcisms and healing became common. The Church believed that if Jesus could cast out a demon, then church leaders should be able to do the same. Often physicians came across cases of madness that they believed were caused by the supernatural, and the patient was referred to a priest. Madness was seen as the Holy Ghost and the devil battling for the possession of one's soul, with symptoms being despair, anguish, and other disturbances of the mind. Unclean spirits were usually driven away through the Catholic Mass or exorcism. Those believed to be possessed or mad often made pilgrimages to religious shrines or houses in homes of relief.

In the town of Geel, located in the Belgian province of Antwerp, there is a shrine that has been there in honour of St Dymphna since the mid-sixteenth century. Dymphna was born in Ireland in the seventh century and possessed the same characteristics as her mother.

Dymphna was a being of great beauty and was known as a joyous child and the jewel of her home. As a young girl filled with grace, Dymphna was filled with the love of Jesus Christ and had taken a vow of chastity in his honour. After losing her mother in early childhood, Dymphna's faith only deepened. Though he mourned her mother, her father wasted no time finding another spouse. After searching many countries to no avail, Dymphna's father decided it was his own daughter whom he wanted to marry.

Understandably so, Dymphna was appalled at the suggestion that she marry her father. After requesting a time of forty days to rest, she begged her priest, Father Gerebran, to help her flee Ireland and her father. The priest brought Dymphna to a small village called Geel in the country of Belgium. While villagers took them in with hospitality, Dymphna's father set out to find her in a fit of rage. Upon finding her, he was confronted by Father Gerebran to rebuke his sinful desires. However, Dymphna's father felt that beheading the priest was a better way to settle the dispute.

Dymphna's father tried to pursue her but to no avail further. Her courage against his offensive threats infuriated him, and he took off her head as well. The crown of martyrdom fell upon her in the fifteenth year of her life, on the fifteenth day of May.

Her body lay in a cave, which was customary for the time, for quite a while. Villagers wished to give her a proper burial, and when workers entered the cave to retrieve her body, they were greeted with a beautiful white coffin that looked as if it were carved by the hands of God. St Dymphna was found in the coffin, clutching a red tile against her breast that bared her name.

Her remains were then placed in a small church, and miracles and cures began to fall upon those who visited. And the majority of those who made the journey to the site suffered from some sort of mental illness. Word of the shrine spread throughout Europe, speaking of its ability to heal those afflicted with unsound minds. People, some brought by relatives, began to flock to the shrine from distant places.

These patrons were at first lodged in the small annex of the church, but soon they began to take refuge in the homes of those who lived in Geel. This act of kindness helped Geel become known as a town that cared for the insane. Geel had become the very model of what the British government hoped to achieve over fifteen hundred years later.

Aside from the ancient Greeks, and roughly 1,000 years later, Islamic doctors brought many exciting and innovative beliefs to the understanding of mental illness. The Arabic term for mental illness is *majnoon,* which means covered. It was thought initially that mentally ill patients could not differentiate between reality and fantasy. This term was gradually changed by Avicenna, one of the most gifted thinkers of Islamic times.

Born in c. 980 in Transoxiana, Avicenna was educated at a centre of learning in Bukhara. He was later educated in medicine and became a physician at eighteen years and was also highly skilled in the Greek Sciences. He defined mental illness as one who suffers from a condition in which reality is replaced with fantasy. Avicenna's most celebrated work, *The Canon of Medicine*, gives descriptions and treatments for an array of mental disorders, such as mania, depression, and sexual dysfunction.

Avicenna gave a noteworthy description of melancholy, dividing it into early and chronic stages. He stated that the early onset of melancholia included unfounded fear, a short temper, tremors, dizziness, and suspicion of evil. Chronic melancholia, he explained, included symptoms of sadness and restlessness, with moaning and atypical fears or delusions. These features were what we today would describe as a manic phase, with uncontrollable laughter, increased sexual drive and energy, and a sense of grandeur. Today, Avicenna's description of melancholia is similar to the symptoms found in the DSM-5. He may have been one of the first physicians to take documentation on the transitional phase of depression to mania.

Like Galen, Avicenna described an overabundance of black bile being present in those who were quick to anger. But Avicenna also viewed melancholy as a disease that affected many of the body's systems, especially the heart. Avicenna's view of psychology put to rest the belief that mental illness was caused by the supernatural. He was also a pioneer in psychosomatic medicine, connecting mental health and physical changes to the body. He understood the importance of the link between the body and mind and felt that a person could overcome a physical ailment by having faith that they would become well again. He also, in turn, believed that one could become physically sick through suggestive thoughts alone. Among his cures were rudimentary fear, as well as shock and music therapy, much like his Greek predecessors.

Ancient Islam is fortunate to have many other brilliant contributors in the world of medicine. Physician and philosopher Muhammad ibn Zakariya al-Razi, was among one of the first in the world to write on mental illness. He was also the director of one of the first psychiatric wards in history. Although in a more primitive form, he also used psychotherapy in his practice.

Al-Razi was born in Tehran in the year 865 A.D, and after studying medicine, he was appointed head doctor of a local hospital in Baghdad. Here, he introduced the idea of a psychiatric ward to care for mentally disturbed patients. He believed that mental illness should be treated no differently than physical illness when it came to care. His patients were provided with medication, diet modification, baths, and music therapy. He considered one's mental health to be a significant factor in their well-being.

His early forms of cognitive therapy were used to help those suffering from obsessive behaviour. Al-Razi believed that part of a compulsive disorder was caused by changes in blood flow to the brain.

He was a firm believer that physicians should be kind and soft-spoken when dealing with their patients, as he felt that communicating on a personal level was key. When delivering unfavourable news, he stressed that gentleness would significantly reduce the patient's anxiety. He also used a positive approach to instil hope in his patients that they would recover.

Al-Razi wrote over two hundred and thirty books during his lifetime, thirty-six of which remain today. One of his most popular works, *Liber Continens*, offered several explanations for mental illness that were common in the tenth century. Reading like a medical encyclopedia, his book brought to light many symptoms of mental illness as well as different methods of treatment.

In the ancient world, the essence of good behaviour was one's self-control. In its earliest forms and throughout history, mental illness was viewed as a deviation from the social norm where one could have been a danger to themselves or those around them. Violence, grief, bloodlust, and cannibalism have been associated with many cultures for thousands of centuries; however, that doesn't make them the victims of mental instability.

In fact, in some societies even today, cannibalism is the cultural norm. Ritualistic cannibalism can be fuelled by the belief that consuming the flesh of the deceased will endow the cannibal with certain characteristics. In most parts of the world, this practice is not usual and, under English law, considered a crime. But throughout the world, there has been hesitation to label cannibalism as a mental disorder even though it can be seen as the epitome of deviating from the social norm.

Psychiatrists or those who studied mental illness throughout time are certainly not few and far between. But some stand out for their contributions to the field for bringing us closer to understanding how the human psyche works.

Perhaps no psychiatrist in history has had a more significant impact on the practice of psychiatry than Emil Kraepelin (1856-1926). The German-born physician is widely regarded as the father of scientific psychiatry. Born in the small town of Neustrelitz, Germany, Kraepelin studied medicine in Munich before beginning his career as a psychiatrist in Leipzig.

One of his most recognisable achievements in his career was the connection between the development of disease and the indication of psychiatric disorders. Leading theories of his time believed that specific symptoms were characteristic of an illness. But Kraepelin opposed this. His observations led him to believe that the symptoms and the manifestation of psychiatric illness could identify a disorder. Kraepelin differentiated between 'dementia praecox' (known as schizophrenia today) and 'manic depression' as two types of psychosis, developing his concept of endogenous psychosis. He firmly believed that schizophrenia was a gradual neurodegenerative disease resulting in the loss of cognitive functions. Alternately, he thought that manic depression was a disorder that came in episodes and did not permanently impair brain function. Kraepelin's hypothesis on the separation of these disorders formed the basis of psychiatric illness for over one hundred years. His understanding of the difference between the two disorders is still enshrined in the DSM (diagnostic and statistical manual) that is widely used in the United States and throughout much of the world.

Kraepelin was also an uncommon pioneer in psychopharmacological research. This is not to say that some of his thinking was not a bit far-reaching. He believed that opponents of the First World War, and those who claimed to be socialists, were mentally ill. He was known for his generalisation of mental illness to social and political circumstances. He also conjected that the Jews had a predisposition to psychiatric disorders. Perhaps this has something to do with the fact that he was not known for having much bedside manner during his career. He was of the opinion that patients should be observed and not listened to.

He moved back to Munich in 1903, where he founded the Department of Psychiatry at Munich University. It was in his laboratory that Alois Alzheimer studied the underlying causes of Alzheimer's dementia, hence giving the disease its name.

Concerning psychotherapy, Kraepelin was highly critical of Sigmund Freud, especially his theory on dream interpretation.

The viewpoints between the two men still cause much controversy today. However, Kraepelin was a brilliant thinker who was one of the first to understand mental illness.

Emil Kraepelin died in 1926 in Munich after having dedicated his last years to work on his psychiatric textbook *Lehrbuch der Psychiatrie* and the development of the *Deutsche Forschungsanstalt für Psychiatrie* (German Research Institute for Psychiatry).

Ironically it was Kraepelin's arch-nemesis that was far more recognisable in the field of psychiatry; Austrian neurologist Sigmund Freud (1856-1939). Freud is often referred to as the father of psychoanalysis, and he believed that much of mental life is at a level outside our consciousness.

Freud was born in the town of Freiberg, Austria, to Galician Jewish parents. After attending the University of Vienna, he became a doctor, where he was appointed associate professor of neuropathology. Having studied with Jean-Martin Charcot, a renowned neurologist, Freud began to take an interest in the practice of medical psychopathology. He was intrigued by Charcot's use of hypnosis, which he often used on his patients in front of an audience. Although, after a bout of using hypnosis, Freud's inconsistent results led him to abandon the method. He concluded that encouraging patients to speak freely about what ideas or memories served them would provide effective relief against mental disorders. He called this technique 'free association', which led him to begin analysing his patient's dreams. He discovered that by doing so, he could reveal the complexity of the unconscious or the psychic action of repression. In 1896, Freud coined his new method, 'psychoanalysis'.

Freud also suggested that unconscious memories of sexual molestation in early childhood often led to hysteria and neurosis. He called this theory 'Freud's Seduction Theory'. He set out to test his theory of psychogenetic origins of mental illness in a number of cases. In 1899, Freud published his works, *The Interpretation of Dreams*, giving detailed interpretations of not only his dreams but those of his patients. Freud's analysis of dreams, as wish fulfillments, became the foundation for the core structure of repression.

His ideas infused American psychiatry throughout most of the twentieth century. He is also responsible for opening up psychiatry to an outpatient service. Before Freud's ideas, psychiatrists were affiliated with the asylum, where they were known as mad doctors. Freud brought about the rise of psychoanalysis, and with that, the field of psychiatry became a rewarding and prestigious career. Current day research continues to support that Freud's psychoanalytic treatments are a solid base for many psychiatric disorders.

In 1938, Freud was forced to leave Austria to escape Nazi persecution, and he died in political refuge in the United Kingdom a year later. Though his escape was over ten years after the death of Emil Kraepelin, one has to wonder if Freud's nationality had something to do with the fact that Kraepelin so openly opposed him, especially when he was convinced that people of Jewish descent were predisposed to mental illness.

Though Kraepelin and Freud were considered two of the most relevant figures in the birth of modern psychiatry, there are equal scores of physicians and scholars that greatly oppose the idea of treating mental illness.

Hungarian psychiatrist Thomas Szasz (1920-2012) is known greatly for his criticism of psychiatry. He said that:

> mental illness was a myth, fabricated by doctors for professional advancement. Over the centuries, medical men have been involved in a self-serving manufacturing of madness by putting labels on people who are social pests, odd or challenging.

Szasz, a Hungarian-American psychiatrist and academic, served most of his career as a professor of psychiatry at New York Upstate Medical University in Syracuse, New York. He became most known as a social critic of both the moral and scientific foundations of psychiatry, even though he was a distinguished member of both the American Psychiatric Association and the American Psychoanalytic Association.

Throughout his career, Szasz argued that mental illness was an image of human problems. He claimed that mental illness was in no sense an illness like that of a physical malady. He argued that there were no acceptable biological tests or necropsy findings that were adequate for verifying DSM diagnosis.

Szasz was adamant throughout his life that he was not anti-psychiatry, only that he opposed forced psychiatry. He greatly opposed involuntary psychiatric treatment. However, he was comfortable with the practice of psychotherapy between a doctor and a consenting patient. He believed that every individual had the right to bodily and mental self-ownership. He criticised the use of psychiatry in much of the Western world and thought Freud and his followers were to blame for the invention of the unconscious.

Interestingly, Szasz took his own life in September of 2012 after suffering a fall and living in chronic pain. In his writings, Szasz argued for the right to suicide.

Paris historian and political activist Michel Foucault (1926-1984) said that mental illness was constructed by medico-psychiatric practices, recasting its heroes as villains. His theories focused on the relationships between knowledge and power and the way they were used as a form of control, specifically through institutions.

After earning a degree in psychology from the University of Paris, Foucault published *Madness and Civilization* in 1961. The book, which was an adaptation of his doctoral dissertation, looks at the history of psychiatric treatment. Foucault believed that psychiatry could not be understood by placing people in institutions. He argued that throughout history, we have simply incarcerated mass populations of people who were undesirable. Because confinement also took aim at poverty, along with housing the insane, Foucault suggests it was merely moral panic. Because whatever the reason, he argued, millions were locked away without any choice.

However, Foucault also disagreed with those who went about dismantling the horrors of Bedlam. He described the heroes of the Quaker movement as those who wanted nothing more than gigantic moral imprisonment. He argued in his book that West European society held a social disconnect when it came to mental illness. In the English-speaking world, the book became an enormous influence on the anti-psychiatry movement of the 1960s. His writings have offered enemies of organised psychiatry a leg to stand on. The world of academia criticised his work, stating that it was not a conventional piece. His book was said to make broad assumptions without anything to solidify them.

Though there were conflicting ideas among some of the most brilliant men in psychiatry, they have all contributed to the foundation needed to understand the mind further. The ancient Greeks, Romans, and the men of ancient Islam should be given much credit for laying the groundwork for the men who followed in their footsteps and those who will continue to do so.

Chapter Two

Mental Illness in the Early Middle Ages and the Birth of Bedlam

There is still much to be discovered about the history of mental illness in early modern England. While Arab cultures had grasped a better understanding of the mind and its inner workings, the Western world fell tremendously behind. The Greeks and Romans had very progressive thoughts towards mental illness and medicine in general, but the English Middle Ages didn't continue this thinking. While we understand prominent highlights in history regarding leading authoritative figures, we have little information about the ideas and experiences of ordinary people throughout history.

Treatment of the mad or insane during the Middle Ages remained a bit of a conundrum as mental illness was probably one of the things that physicians understood the least. If your sanity was at risk, more emphasis was put on how to deal with your lands rather than your illness. This was especially true if you were of noble birth as treatments and dealings considered variably. If you were on the lower rung of society, you could expect little to no treatment for your illness. The belief in demonic possession was so prevalent during the Middle Ages that most psychiatric conditions were blamed on it. You could have been viewed as spiritually bankrupt as well as mad. Whether your treatment was of medical or divine intervention, the outcome was to get you to recover and return to your senses.

In the Middle Ages, specifically in the biblical text, demonic possession was the cause of erratic behaviour in society. An exorcism was the standard treatment applied to ridding the body of demons. There are several cases of this in the writings and tales of the saints.

The writers of these stories were indeed witnesses to their time, and they shared their knowledge eagerly.

Demonic possession was very prevalent in the New Testament. In Greek culture, the word 'Daimon' was used for a spirit, and in the Bible, this word was exclusively used to describe evil beings or demons. In the Gospels, as mental illness was always assumed a demonic possession, the individuals were treated differently, such as in Mark 5-8, Jesus says, 'Come out of this man, you unclean spirit'. The Gerasene demon tale in Mark would have been referred to in later times as one with acute mania, and today, a mood disorder.

The ancient Greek theory of the four humours carried on through the Middle Ages, and the foundation for all medicine still relied heavily on what Hippocrates and Galen wrote of. And in the Middle Ages, if it wasn't the devil making you mad, then it was believed to have been caused by an imbalance of the humours. Writers and scholars of the time continued to elaborate on this foundation in their works of not only physical ailments but mental ones.

Thirteenth-century scholar and member of the Franciscan order, Bartholomaues Anglicus (1203-1272), referred to madness in his compendium *De Propietatibus Rerun*. The highly cited book of the Middle Ages said that madness was because of the ingestion of melancholy-inducing foods, being bitten by a rabid dog, robust wine, or affliction of disease caused by other wild beasts. Anglicus stated these external forces would provoke the disparity of the four humours, producing a state of fear, sadness, or melancholy.

Not much is known about the early life of Bartholomaues, other than he held senior positions in the church. He is believed to have been educated at Oxford, and he later taught in Paris. His works were used for students and the general public alike and gave a plethora of information to scholars of his day. He wrote of music therapy as a form of treatment for depression, as did his Greek predecessors. He also spoke of sleep for relief, as well as a form of binding for frantic patients, both of which would be used over 700 years later.

Trepanation, Bartholomaues believed, could also be used to rid the body of harmful vapours. But research shows us that there may have been a lot more to the reasoning behind why trepanning was done.

Trepanning was practised long before the Middle Ages, in places like ancient Greece, Africa, and the Far East, and is still used today, although for many different reasons. The technique is often used in treating subdural hematomas. This pooling of blood between the brain and its outermost covering is often a medical emergency. Caused primarily by head trauma or certain medications, pooled blood can push against the brain. In severe cases, surgical intervention through a craniotomy is needed. And unlike those procedures of the past, modern-day surgery is done under sterile conditions. The modern method of the operation would not leave a permanent hole in the skull as the ancient form of trepanning did.

The word 'trepanation' stems from the Greek word 'trypanon', meaning to bore or auger. While there might have been slight differences in how people throughout the ages used trepanation, the fundamentals have not changed. Was the piercing of the skull with a sharp object the very first form of psychosurgery? Were the reasons those who went before us found it necessary to perform the procedure linked in any way to why modern brain surgery is performed?

The sources that tell us trepanation was performed during the Neolithic period show evidence of it in the hunters and gatherers. While the reasons may remain unknown as to why it was done, the process of puncturing the skull would not cease with our Stone Age ancestors. It continued throughout ancient Greece and into medieval Europe and would evolve into what it is today.

But why was trepanation done, and did those reasons change over time? There is also evidence of the procedure being done on the skulls of animals in the Neolithic Era. Some historians believe that trepanation may have taken place to save the animal in some primitive form of cranial surgery. And yet others have conflicting theories that perhaps trepanation was used as a practice technique in the form of surgical experimentation.

Hippocrates spoke of the procedure in his texts. In his works, *Places in Man*, he writes that trepanation may have been used for prevention:

> If the skull is broken and there is a fissure-fracture, it is dangerous. You should trephine in this case, to prevent pus from flowing through the fracture of the bone and infecting the membrane; for, since in this narrow place it can get in but not out, it causes distress and madness.

Can we assume that Hippocrates also meant mental illness when he spoke of distress and madness?

But as the procedure progressed throughout medieval Europe, the reasons seemed to vary. Hungarians performed the ritual after death, but other groups seemed to do so when the patient was alive, leading us to believe that it was used as some sort of preventative or abortive method of medicine.

Authors of a 2011 case study agreed that trepanning was used for therapeutic reasons, such as treating convulsions, behavioural changes, and even headaches. It was also said to have been used in religious rituals to free people from the grips of a demon, as was written about by Bartholomaues Anglicus. And perhaps trepanation in the form of a cross was a way of emulating Christ during the performance of rituals. This concept was renewed in the Middle Ages through the figure of St Francis of Assisi and other twelfth century saints that performed exorcisms.

A popular narrative of the life of Saint Francis, written by St Bonaventure in 1262, speaks of the demonic possession of a Franciscan companion. It says:

> One of the Brethren was afflicted with such a horrible disease as that it was asserted of many to be rather a tormenting from demons than a natural sickness. For often, he was quite dashed down on the ground and

wallowed foaming, with his limbs now drawn up, now stretched forth and folded, now twisted, now became rigid and fi d. At times he was quite stretched out stiff and with his feet on a level with his head would be raised into the air and then fall back again with dreadful fashion.

The agitation, foaming at the mouth, and seizures were typical symptoms of believed demonic possession during the Middle Ages. And today, we know them as grand mal or tonic-clonic seizures, medically. The falling to the ground was probably caused by unconsciousness, and the rigid contracting of the muscles would be known as the tonic phase of a grand mal seizure. During the healing, St Francis hands his brethren a piece of ecclesiastical bread, and he is revived instantly. Though witnesses of the event would be sure it was supernatural healing, it was most likely that the phases of the seizure were over. One could also assume that the episode was caused by hypoglycemia. In that case, a piece of bread loaded with carbohydrates would have most certainly made the distressed Brethren recover.

Another tale of demonic possession that can easily be explained away by modern medicine was written by Berceo, a clerk in the monastery of Saint Aemilian. It describes a priest, who the devil himself had invaded:

> The demon made him say really crazy things. Besides the things said, he did other horrible things. The illness had many evil natures, for which the sick man made many evil gestures.

Though the priest's agitation was thought to be the invasion of a demon, the gesture, tics, and face grimacing, are the same actions displayed by one with Tourette's Syndrom. Tourette's Syndrom is also indicative of expletives and blasphemous words blurted out with no warning.

The basic assumption is that mental instability during the Middle Ages was most likely as common as it is today. But psychologically challenged individuals would seek out help from a religious leader as opposed to a medical professional. And evil spirits were more than likely an easy scapegoat for a greatly misunderstood condition. During medieval times, the first asylums were established by religious leaders because of this inherent belief that mentally ill people were considered to be suffering from demonic possession. So, therapy from a religious figure would seem appropriate for the times.

In the thirteenth century, a 'natural born idiot', one deemed insane since birth, whether by an evil spirit or not, was protected by law. During this time, care of the insane was usually left to the family, but if they were unable to care for you, the crown made a provision. And the crown's response to the insane was determined by conditions such as society and culture. A legally insane person's best interest was at hand, and it was the primary care of the realm and the community to see that you were well taken care of. The apparent problem was that there was little to any understanding about mental health in the Middle Ages, and so very few hospitals truly cared for the insane as the crown was more concerned with your lands. Part of the law in caring for one meant that your estate was protected under the kingdom.

During the reign of Edward I of England (1239-1307), under *Praerogativa Regis* (The Royal Prerogative), a distinction was made between a natural-born idiot and a lunatic. As the natural-born idiot was incompetent since birth, a lunatic was declared insane at some point in their life. This didn't mean the crown, or anyone else, had any idea how you may have gotten that way. But, if you had always been mad, your lands were immediately deemed wardship by the crown. They would remain so until you died, and your estates would be passed on to an heir. In the case of the lunatic, the realm still provided for you and your family but did so without taking your lands. The rational thought behind this was that you had acquired your properties during a period of sanity, and so you should be able to keep them once you recovered.

You were taken before a jury of about twelve men and questioned for the king to decide your case. Was the person insane? If so, when did it start, and were there any periods of lucidity? Did the person own any lands, and if so, who was their heir? The alleged insane were given a chance to speak for themselves and answer any questions. These questions were typically put gently, and the person was given a series of quick memory tests and an assessment of necessary skills. Once the mental capacity of a patient had been established, settlements were decided, and your lands were distributed accordingly. The council was more apt to name a natural fool because, of course, that meant more money for the crown, and in roughly 80% of cases, one was deemed a 'natural idiot'. The insane were usually given food, clothing, shoes, and a bed that would be charged to their estate. Because the end result would ultimately benefit the crown, the care of the insane was rooted in who would care for your lands rather than what to do with you. In the case of most married women, they weren't typically given an inquisition as it was assumed that a women's husband would deal with her mental state.

When it comes to the medieval hospital, there remains a great misunderstanding of precisely what a hospital was. The earliest hospitals in the Middle Ages were those of hospitality and shelters for all. The very word, hospital, is derived from the Latin word *Hospes,* meaning host or guest. In the tenth, eleventh, and twelfth centuries, hospitality was an obligation, a duty, and a privilege to welcome not only those sent by the monarchy to recover but to travellers. And, as mentioned earlier, the most primitive hospitals in England were predominantly religious houses.

In the Middle Ages, cases of madness were often treated both spiritually and physically. In these places, taking care of one's soul was just as important as caring for their body. Most of these hospitals were for sick or ageing patients. They were often referred to as almshouses that provided charity to the poor and other folks who needed medical or spiritual assistance.

Settlements of these religious communities were built to house monks, priests, and even laypeople. Together, they lived a life of spiritual discipline based on the Benedictine Rule, which consisted of St Benedict's teachings. Benedictine rule taught about the essential monastic virtues of humility, silence, and obedience. The settlements ranged in size from communities housing several hundred to houses with only a few members. No matter the size, the brothers practised the fundamentals of the Catholic Church in their dedication to the community and the sick. Aside from being houses of prayer, monasteries have been synonymous as places of charity and giving.

After the Norman Conquest, most works of mercy were done in the monastery. Englishmen have always loved to travel and visit holy shrines. Many hospitals were built along the pilgrimage routes and could house thirty people or more. And all were welcome, travellers, invalids, even lepers.

During the reign of Henry III, in 1247, Bedlam hospital was established. Founded initially as the Priory of the New Order of Our Lady of Bethlehem by Italian Bishop Goggredo de Prefetti, it was a centre for collecting alms to support the Crusades. It was never intended to be a hospital and certainly not a place to house the insane.

But because de Prefetti's priory was dutiful to the Church of the Nativity, it would serve as a refuge to the poor. The priory brothers had begun to understand that some patients required a different kind of care, and they recognised the symptoms of mental illness as a separate disease.

By the fourteenth century, the hospital in Bishop's Gate began to specialise in the treatment of lunatics, and it would soon earn its notorious name, Bedlam. The word lunatic was the legal term for people, although Bedlam housed many who weren't insane at all. Like many during the Middle Ages, folks who suffered from learning disabilities, epilepsy, or tumours were mistaken for being insane, as it was believed that madness was a behaviour.

The exact date in which Bedlam began to concentrate on the care of the insane is unknown. But it has been generally agreed among historians that it was some time around 1377. However, the first conclusive record of insane patients was not until 1403, during a visit from the Charity of Commissioners. It was recorded that there were six male patients who were deemed insane. The report also stated that the hospital was in possession of six locks, eleven chains, and two pairs of stocks. Whether or not these were used to restrain patients is unknown.

Bethlem Hospital, as it was initially called before gaining its notorious nickname, like most medieval hospitals, began as a religious order. Those in need of care came here when they had nowhere else to go. It was not for those with mental illness, simply for those who could not care for themselves. However, over time the notion of one who wasn't self-sufficient soon became synonymous with the mad.

Bedlam is believed to have started out with twenty or so small rooms. Conditions were less than adequate with no fireplaces for warmth, and there were more than likely several inmates to a room. Beds, if there were any at all, were probably just straw laid about the floor. The good intentions of the priory at Our Lady of Bethlehem were all but abandoned.

The informal name of Bedlam began to stick after the word entered everyday speech, denoting a state of chaos or madness. It was around this time that the place housing a small number of patients in 1403 slowly began the shift from a simple hospital for the poor into a special place to house the insane. The position of Master or Keeper of Bedlam was one that required very little if any effort and rested with the support of the crown until 1547. Once the city took control, the position then passed through the hands of men with a much more simple status; tradesman.

In 1553, Edward VI passed the responsibility of Bridewell Palace, a home for children and disorderly women, to the city. Bridewell was built for Edward's father, Henry VIII, starting in the year 1515 as a place for celebrations within the Tudor court and home to Henry's illegitimate son, Henry Blount. However, Bridewell's days as a place of pleasantry were short-lived, as it soon became the gathering place for conferences with the Papal Legate, who would oversee the king's divorce from Queen Katherine of Aragon.

After his father's death, when Edward VI passed Bridewell Palace to the city of London, it soon became not only a home for the destitute but a prison used to punish those with petty crimes. Short-lived stays and daily whippings were on the roster for most patients.

But it would not be until almost forty years after Edward's grant to the city that the governors of Bridewell began to show interest in the well-being of Bedlam. The newfound interest in Bedlam is thought to have resulted from the English Poor Laws, passed during the late Tudor era in 1587. The hospital had come under terrible scrutiny, and the governors needed a way to increase hospital revenue. After an inspection of the hospital under the current keeper, it was noted it had fallen into a shameful condition. It was reported that:

> it is not fit for any man to dwell in which was left by the keeper for that is so loathsomely filthy, kept not fit for any man to come into the house.

The inspection also found that several patients had been there for over ten years, and one had been there for almost twenty-five years.

Repairs slowly began to be done, and the visits from the governors became more frequent. A 1607 visit demanded the purchase of clothing and food for the patients as there was a considerable absence of these essential items.

Although records of patients were likely kept until the sixteenth century, Bedlam's horrendous conditions became notorious. One's social status meant little, and if you were sent to Bedlam, rich and poor alike, were hidden away from society to be forgotten about. In addition to those with learning disabilities, the hospital was a place to go for those who were poor and believed to be dangerous. Often, they lacked friends or family who were willing to support them.

The Crown would change hands several times before the keeper of Bedlam was someone with a medical background. In 1619, James I and VI appointed Helkiah Crooke (1576-1648) as keeper-physician of Bedlam. The graduate of Cambridge was of a much higher social ranking than the city-appointed comptrollers of the past. But the Board of Governors wasn't about to give up leadership that quickly, and Crooke was unsuccessful in his attempts to petition the king for Bedlam to become a separate entity from Bridewell.

Aside from his conflict with the Bridewell Governors, Crooke had irregular attendance at the hospital while at the same time greatly misusing its funds. After changing hands once again, the crown began an investigation of Crooke under Charles I. Along with failing to do anything to better the lives of the patients at Bedlam, Cooke also used hospital goods for his own devices. It was said that the patients were likely to starve under his leadership. He was formally dismissed in May 1633.

The year 1634 stands out for Bedlam hospital, as it was a time that marked the official end of the old-style keeper. Using a model taken from royal hospitals, Bedlam now ran on a three-tiered programme. An apothecary, a visiting surgeon, and a non-resident physician were soon in charge. But the conditions at Bedlam had continued to worsen while Crooke was the keeper. English writer Donald Lupton described his observations at Bedlam as 'cryings, screechings, roarings, brawlings, shaking of chains, swearings, frettings, and chaffings'.

Because Bedlam had been built over a sewer that served the hospital and the precinct, it was the target of blocked drains and overflows of waste. The hospital's front was notorious for its filth, reflecting insufficient water supply. Until 1657, the water supply consisted of a single wooden vat to which water was transported. Because most patients chose not to use the community privy, they used the chamber pots, or piss pots, in their cells. Left to their own devices, with pots of overflowing waste, patients would often hurl their own excrement at hospital workers or visitors in defiance.

The patients at Bedlam were given an inadequate diet through most of the seventeenth century, especially during Crooke's time, as many patients were found to be starving to death. Practices of unethical staff also led to patient malnourishment. Patients were only fed twice a day, given a reduced-calorie diet with little taste. The portions were less than generous, as they more than likely reflected the four humours theory, which said that cutting down the rations of food fed to the insane was justified. The avoidance of rich foods, along with purges, would help restore the body to balance.

The treatments of patients at Bedlam became as infamous as its conditions. Laxatives made from bark, syrup, senna, and water were given regularly to patients, as it was believed that the purging of one's digestive system would help cleanse their system. Beatings were also common and were thought to not only be a form of punishment but one of rehabilitation. During the fourteenth and fifteenth centuries, because it was still believed that madness was caused by demonic possession, in many cases, part of the brutal treatment was bounding one and then beating them until administrators were satisfied that the evil spirit had fled the body.

Bedlam had somewhat of an open-door policy, allowing visits by friends and relatives of the patients. But it was also well known to allow the public with no connection to the inmates to observe. One of the most disgraceful parts of Bedlam's history is that they let the mad be somewhat of a public show.

It is assumed that as early as 1598, the Bridewell Governors started charging public spectators as a way to raise the hospital's income. The first documentation was recorded in 1610, as a payment of ten shillings was collected, and the visitor was given the 'privilege of rambling through the hospital to view its deranged denizens'.

After Bedlam moved to the Moorfields in 1676, there was evidence that the number of visitors began to increase. In 1681, the Bridewell Governors wrote about 'the great quantity of persons that come daily to see the laid lunatics'.

Thomas Tyron, an English author, remarked on the 'swarms of people' who visited Bedlam during public holidays. And public holidays and Sundays seemed to draw the most crowds.

Bedlam had become a public spectacle, and some claim there may have been upwards of 90,000 visitors a year. Well-educated, wealthy people were sought out to visit Bedlam as if it were some bizarre model of charity. Showing the mad off like zoo animals was a way to arouse compassion in visitors with the hopes they would leave monetary donations. As the spectacles continued into the eighteenth century, the average income collected from charity was thought to be around 300-350 pounds annually. Viewing the mad was done so with a word of caution as they were displayed as an example of what could happen if people became lax with their morals. Chances are, though, that most visitors came as a form of entertainment value. Bedlam was looked at as a 'rare diversion to cheer and amuse' and became as big a tourist trap as the Tower of London and Whitehall Palace.

Not surprisingly, the visits subjected Bedlam's patients to abuse. They were taunted, poked with sticks or cans, and assaulted both physically and sexually. The mid to late eighteenth century was when Bedlam patients suffered the worst abuse, but thankfully, the abuse ended in 1770. The horrors of Bedlam have led the Western world to believe that all of the insane were treated sadistically, but parts of history tell us that the chains and manacles were reserved for the most violent of patients. Even so, English laymen throughout had come to associate the name Bedlam with the starkest madmen, who were dangerous, murderous criminals.

Bedlam Hospital would continue to change through the next several hundred years. It was moved to St George's Fields in Southwark in 1815 and then to Monks Orchard in 1930, where it still functions today.

While the Middles Ages will never be celebrated for its advancements in medical and psychiatric history, it gave us an idea of how primitive things were for mankind. If anything good came out of Bedlam and its disastrous beginning, it's that over time, doctors used it as an example of how not to treat their mentally ill patients.

Chapter Three

Caring for the Insane During the Fifteenth, Sixteenth & Seventeenth Centuries

When Henry VII took the throne in 1485, English doctors hadn't made much progress in treating one's physical health. Early Tudor medicine still relied on Galen's teachings of the humoral theory, and their understanding of mental illness was still relatively primitive. Adhering to Galen's view, Tudor doctors still believed that almost all mental illness was caused by an abundance of black bile, stating that evil unbalanced humours overcame the brain and resulted in mental illness. The belief that one who suffered from natural melancholy might have been one who hid from society and spent too much time alone was still common. Folks suffering from natural melancholy often felt fear, sorrow, despair, insomnia, and a reduced appetite.

Denis Fontanon, a French professor and physician, stated that mania:

> Occurs sometimes solely from the warmer temper of the brain without a harmful humour, and this is like what happens in drunkenness. It occasionally arises from stinging and warm humours, such as yellow bile, attacking the brain and stimulating it along with its membranes.

Addressing its varieties, Fontanon went into great detail explaining their distinct features and causes. He said it was a:

> good sign if mania involved laughter, whereas when the mixture of blood and yellow bile was burned-that is, it

appeared especially heavy and thickened-there would be brutal madness, and this is the most dangerous of all.

Sixteenth-century physicians, not only in England but throughout Western Europe, felt that balancing a patient's humours was pivotal for good health, along with avoiding certain foods and seeking out merry company. But there was no organised group of psychiatric specialists, and the stereotypical lunatic was still considered the beggar.

Both Islamic and Christian medicine followed Hippocrates and Galen's traditions, and Greek thinking had clearly retained its validity into the Renaissance. But the problem was, fifteenth-century physicians were at a standstill in understanding why mental illness happened or what it even was. The thinking was still archaic, and the ailments that would have deemed you insane were endless. People were quick to judge and doctors quick to diagnose a subject they knew very little about.

Today, we know that epilepsy doesn't fall under the category of mental illness, but that wasn't always the case. Psychiatry wasn't always a distinct profession, and the symptoms of epilepsy were not understood. Although epilepsy itself does not cause an intellectual problem, the disorder can be caused by the same afflictions that may have presented at birth. Low oxygen or birth trauma can cause not only intellectual disability but epilepsy and cerebral palsy. In a time when these things were not yet understood, it is easy to see how epilepsy could have been labelled as a mental illness.

Uncontrolled seizures are most commonly associated with epilepsy. Seizures occur when neurons in the brain misfire, resulting in abnormal movements or behaviours. These activities are often very dramatic, causing violent seizures and loss of consciousness, which understandably could have been perceived as mental illness. A person who experiences an attack can also experience hallucinations and repetitive movements such as blinking or walking in circles, which would have easily been interpreted as a possible demonic possession.

Depression can also be a common affliction in those with epilepsy, along with memory impairment. These afflictions can play a part in the onset of seizures. Epilepsy can also play a role in the development of anxiety and behavioural problems, including fear or stress. Epilepsy can also cause lasting changes in mood and thinking, which can be presented as pain, irritability, or even euphoria.

Cerebrovascular disorders such as strokes could have been mistaken for mental illness. Strokes can cause a confused state, weak and uncontrollable movements, as well as personality changes which would have presented as possible psychosis.

Multiple Sclerosis, as well as other central nervous system disorders, could have been mistaken for mental illness. Multiple Sclerosis presents with fatigue, depression, mania, or psychosis. The earliest documentation of what may have been sclerosis dates back to Holland in the year 1395, where a young woman named Lidwina developed an acute illness with symptoms including blindness, weakness, and pain. Was she genuinely suffering from what we know today to be multiple sclerosis, or was she afflicted with something else? Although we will never know, if Lidwina presented with the depression or mania that often accompanies MS, it's possible she may have been deemed mentally ill.

Tumours of the brain's frontal lobe can cause personality changes and behavioural symptoms. Encephalitis, inflammation of the brain caused by a viral infection, can cause confused thinking, seizures, and problems with movement.

Because of the lack of modern medicine during childbirth during the fifteenth and sixteenth centuries, birth trauma or inadequate prenatal care was responsible for several afflictions that could label one as mentally ill. By definition, birth trauma refers to the damage of tissues or organs in a newly delivered child. These are often long-term consequences resulting in brain damage, which may be displayed as mental retardation. And throughout history, before this was understood, many who may have suffered from mental retardation were viewed as having a mental illness. It wasn't until the seventeenth century that intellectual disability was understood as a structural problem in the brain and dismissed as a mental illness.

Metabolic disorders, like hypothyroidism, though not primarily neurological, presented as such. Hypothyroidism can cause impaired cognition, hallucinations, delusions, paranoia, anxiety, irritability, and delirium.

Narcolepsy, a disorder causing excessive daytime sleepiness, can cause tiredness, hallucinations, and twitching that could have confused psychosis.

The wandering womb was still a widespread belief in the mid to late Middle Ages and was quickly the scapegoat for an unruly woman.

In understanding all of these bizarre assumptions, it's not difficult to picture the challenges a fifteenth or sixteenth-century physician would have encountered. While they knew little about the body, what they knew about the mind was even less so.

The Tudors were still not entirely convinced that fits couldn't be caused by demonic possession, and priests were often called to exorcise patients. Little did Tudor doctors know, but a patient presenting with jerks and stiffening of the muscles was probably having an epileptic fit.

The sixteenth century was a time of deep religious turmoil, and the frequency of possession seemed to increase. To Catholics and Protestants alike, the devil was a genuine threat, and it was believed that possession was an internal struggle in someone's mind and body.

Over time, science changed the way believers approached their faith regarding medicine and the treatment of illness. A rapid change was seen during the sixteenth century as the knowledge of medicine grew. The Church was still quite powerful but did not have as much clout as it did prior to the Reformation. Henry VIII's reformation caused the fall away from the Catholic Church, and soon accusations of madness were used as a form of political power. It became the battle of one Christian denomination over the other as the new Church of England took hold.

It was widely believed that variations in temperament could contribute to mental disorders, and it was said that having a particular personality can make people more vulnerable to illness. Tudor and Stuart doctors believed there was a connection between body and soul. The regimens used to treat mental illness didn't differ all that much from what would have been given to someone with a physical ailment. Bloodletting was still relatively widespread, along with purges and enemas used to expel the body of unbalanced humours. Afflictions of the mind were generally treated with bloodletting by extracting blood from the forehead by tapping the head or veins to draw the corrupted humours away from the sickened brain.

The practice of bloodletting dates back to ancient Egypt, and in ancient Greece, it was used during the time of Hippocrates. Bleeding a patient back to health was believed to be a purge of bad humours.

The Greek physician, Galen, also believed in treating patients through bloodletting after discovering that veins and arteries were not full of air, but were filled with blood, as was the original theory. Galen's concepts were that blood was created in the body and then used. It was not yet understood that blood circulated, so it was thought to idle in the extremities. Galen also believed that blood was the dominant humour and the one most in need of care. And so, to bring the body back into balance, excess or stagnant blood needed to be removed through either bloodletting or purging. As the theory of bloodletting carried into the sixteenth and seventeenth centuries, physicians realised they needed to consider the patient's age and sex, as bleeding could endanger the lives of diseased men and women.

Purging was used under the same premise as bloodletting in the early treatment of mental illness. A typical sixteenth or seventeenth-century laxative for melancholy may have contained aloe, colocynth, and black hellebore. Another may have consisted of myrobalans, rhubarb, and senna to empty the bowels. The expansion of trade during the seventeenth century brought many medicines from the New World, such as tobacco, from the fields of North Carolina.

Tobacco worked tremendously for making one vomit, and purging the gastrointestinal system by either vomiting or elimination was made easier with tobacco. Seventeenth-century doctors believed that applications of both hot and dry tobacco were beneficial. Nasal irrigations and fumigations were commonly practiced as a way to purge the head, or in Latin terms, 'Caput Pungia'.

Used freely in the seventeenth century in England, opiates often eased the torment of mental disorders. They facilitated the misery of insomnia and calmed the anguish of stark madness. The effectiveness of opiates brought relief to many frantic people. These potions usually didn't do anything to help the patient but could at least alleviate symptoms. And perhaps those suffering were cured by their faith in the remedies prescribed to them as if it were a placebo effect. Doctors also regulated their patient's physical environment by controlling diet, elimination, exercise, sleeping, and passion. Encouraging them to seek merry company, play games, dress nicely and visit places to avoid solitude, as well as attend church regularly.

What one could expect as a cure or treatment of madness fell in line with the medicine of the time. It was archaic and not terribly understood, and the mind was still an enigma to seventeenth-century physicians; however medical professionals during the Tudor and Stuart reign did believe there was a way to treat their patients. The methods of physicians, astrologers, and apothecaries may have differed, but they all had the desire to heal their patient's bodies and minds by restoring harmony with the natural order.

During the late Middle Ages, the connection between medicine and astrology was solid. Physicians and astrologers took astral influences seriously when dealing with patients. They relieved heavily on iatromathematics, which was based on the assumption that the movement of the heavens had a significant impact on the health of humans. It was believed that astrological medicine would allow physicians to know the exact time a patient would fall ill. The practice of medical astrology peaked during the fifteenth and sixteenth centuries and was seen as the intellectual foundation of medical education.

Medical practice in Tudor and Stuart England presented a rich and varied approach to healing with the best of intentions. Doctors relied on and wrote treatises on both physical and mental illnesses.

One of the first English treatises on melancholy was published by Cambridge-educated physician Timothy Bright in 1586. His *Treatise of Melancholie* was the most critical work on the subject of melancholy during the reign of Queen Elizabeth Tudor.

Bright was born in Sheffield, England, around 1551 and graduated from Cambridge University in 1574. He was granted his licence to practice medicine soon after. Two editions of Bright's work on melancholy came out in 1586 and a third in 1612. The sad and fearful humour of melancholy was an almost fashionable malady during Elizabeth I's reign. Coupled with sadness and male intellect, melancholic poets show up often in the art and literature of that time. They are famously seen in Romeo and Juliet and Hamlet.

Bright stated that because melancholic humours were cold, they would settle in the spleen, causing vapours to rise to the brain. He was convinced that this was the cause for unreasonable behaviour. He stated in his text that:

> The perturbations of melancholy are, for the most part, sad and fearful, and such as rise of them; as distrust, doubt diffidence, despair sometimes furious and sometimes merry in appearance, through a kind of Sardonian, and false laughter, as the humour is disposed that procureth these diversities. Those which are sad and pensive, rise of that melancholic humour, which is the grossest part of the blood, whether it be juice or excrement, not passing the natural temper in the heat whereof it partaketh and is called cold in comparison only. This, for the most part, settled in the spleen and with his vapours anointing the

heart and passing up to the brain, counterfetteth terrible objects to the fantasy, and polluting both the substance and spirits of the brain, causing it without external occasion, to forge monstrous fictions, and terrible to the conceit, which the judgment takin as the yare presented by the disordered instrument, deliver over to the heart, which hath no judgment of discretion in itself but giving credit to the mistaken report of the brain, breaketh out into the inordinate passion, against reason.

Bright believed that one of the first things that played a role in melancholy was one's diet. He felt that nourishment played a large part in determining the abundance of the humours and the health and tendencies of the person. The method of digesting food took place in stages. It was believed that in the first stage, the stomach produced a white fluid called chyle. It was then carried to the liver, which was considered a hot organ, where a further mixture produced the four humours. Melancholy was believed to have been the heaviest of the humours, with a sludge-like mixture that sank to the bottom, and when these fluids were transported to the heart, the purest blood was transformed into vital spirits which warm the entire body. Bright believed that if the flow of critical energies was restricted, the blood could degenerate into melancholy.

Bright also believed a list of foods would have contributed to melancholy, such as cabbage, acorns, mutton, sodden wheat, and waterfowl, to name a few. Although physicians of the time didn't believe that diet entirely was the only cause of melancholy, they also thought that certain emotional reasons were the culprit.

Scholars have determined that William Shakespeare was very familiar with Timothy Bright's work, and the understanding of melancholy was represented in his work. It seemed very likely that the knowledge of melancholy in Bright's work probably influenced the theory about the suffering that was described in Hamlet. Bright explores the causes and treatments of sadness, fear, and desperation. He suggests that the mind and body may be interdependent, with melancholy affecting not only the bodily sense but also the soul and spirit. And so, in Bright's Treatise, we see the reflection of Elizabethan society.

Fifteenth and sixteenth-century doctors also responded to mental illness by deciding whether or not the sick individual was a danger to others. If they were nonviolent, they were usually left in the custody of their families. But violent victims were often sent to places like Bedlam.

In England, the local government still relied on the community to establish and enforce law and order. Because no official police force existed yet, it was often your neighbours, friends, or the local church who were looked upon to hold a community together. England was, however, experiencing a time of extreme population growth after a shakeup of the feudal system, putting stressors on how best to keep order throughout. While the Black Death ended almost 150 years prior, its consequences were still felt throughout much of Europe. The long-term effects on the country's inhabitants were devastating, and it had taken over a century for population sizes to recover. The addition of new laws would leave the poor vulnerable as England struggled to re-establish social order.

In 1494, the Vagabonds and Beggars Act was passed through an act of parliament. This law seemed to punish the poor for simply being poor. This cruel act stated that:

> vagabonds, idle and suspected persons shall be set in the stocks for three days and three nights and have none other sustenance, but bread and water and then shall be put out of town. Every beggar suitable to work shall resort to the place where he last dwelled, is best known, or was born and there remain upon the pain aforesaid.

This law, along with the future poor laws in England, strived to reinforce that the poor knew their correct place in society. And the poor were often categorised along with the mentally ill and looked at no differently, subjecting them to the same treatment as those in the early asylums.

However, the monarchy had the upper hand in any event. During the reign of Henry VIII, an insanity law that had been in place since the fourteenth century was amended in dealing with 'How treason by a lunatic shall be punished and in what manner he shall be tried'.

Considering it took Henry over thirty-five years to deem it necessary to change such a law, it's possible that the Tudor king wanted to make an example out of people like Lady Jane Rochford. Lady Jane had been arrested for conspiring to adultery with the queen against Henry and went slowly insane during her confinement in the Tower of London while waiting for her trial. The king needed a legal means to execute her, and the Tudor court didn't have a complicated process to determine madness. However, his haste to amend that law two days before Jane's execution most likely meant that it was not of popular opinion to execute the insane.

English law had prohibited anyone deemed mad from standing trial, let alone being sentenced to death, even in the event that they went mad during their imprisonment. As previously stated, most lunatics were allowed to return home or await the monarch's pardon. The main reason for this wasn't that the mad would not have understood their crime but that a criminal deserved to experience their punishment. And if one was mad, they were unlikely to understand why they were being put to death. A criminal would also have a guilty conscience as they knowingly committed a crime. However, an insane person could feel no guilt if they didn't understand their actions. English law regarded one who was mad to have already been punished by their madness alone.

But all it took were the king's words to change a law that had been in place for over one hundred years. Defendants who confessed to treason directly to the king while possessing 'good, perfect, or whole memories' but had fallen into madness while waiting for trial would now be put before appointed commissioners and a jury of twelve. If the insane were found guilty, they 'shall have and suffer execution, their madness of lunacy notwithstanding'.

In the case of Lady Jane, she was the principal lady-in-waiting for Queen Katherine Howard when she began to arrange clandestine meetings between the queen and one of Henry VIII's courtiers, Thomas Culpeper. The king was over thirty years older than his young queen, and no doubt she was flattered to be the object of affection of the handsome courtier with the piercing eyes. When Queen Katherine's affair surfaced and investigations began, both she and Lady Jane now had their lives at risk.

Lady Jane was taken to the Tower and questioned for several months, and I believe it was the utter fear of being held prisoner that played a part in her mental downfall. It's hard for those of us today to understand what it must have been like to be under such psychological stress in the sixteenth century, awaiting a fate she must have known was inevitable. Lady Rochford's husband had been executed by the king only a few years before, and Henry was known for his quick temper.

The king did send his own doctors to examine the state of Lady Jane's mental state, but it was determined that there was no chance she would regain her sanity as she had lost her mind. It was stated that her frenzied fits meant she could not stand trial, and so through an act of attainder, the king condemned her to death.

Despite her insanity, Jane was escorted from the Tower to the scaffold, where she spoke calmly and gently to the crowd as she apologised for her many sins. She was beheaded with a single blow of the executioner's axe on 13 February 1542.

As the population grew in the sixteenth and seventeenth centuries, poverty became a significant problem. Municipal governments experimented with new kinds of institutions like hospitals and workhouses in an attempt to find a solution to the increasing issues of poverty and mental illness.

The English Poor Laws, which had manifested in the late medieval era, began to truly take shape during the Tudor period. Before the Reformation, almshouses and monasteries were still the primary place for poor relief and caring for the sick, but their destruction had left the poor relying on a tax system collected at the parish level. Henry VII's vagabond act in 1494 had offered no real remedy to the issue of poverty throughout England. Along with the lack of treatment, there was still no distinction between the homeless and the mentally ill. You were seen as a sturdy beggar, only to be pushed aside or, worse, punished.

Though it was over five years before the dissolution of the monasteries, Henry VIII made a public decree that whipping should replace the stocks when it came to punishing vagrants. In the 1531 Vagabonds Act, this decree was made law. The poor were given certain places where they were free to beg, though if they were found outside of their area, they were to be imprisoned, whipped if deemed able-bodied, and then returned to their proper jurisdiction.

Due to the collapse of the monasteries, there was a great gathering of the poor in England with nowhere to turn. In 1546, Henry agreed that St Bartholomew's Hospital and St Thomas' Hospital could continue their work as long as the crown was not responsible for their upkeep. St Bartholomew's Hospital was founded in 1123 by the priory of St Bartholomew and had been providing medical care since. The king ordered the citizens of London to pay for their maintenance; however, the city was unable to fund the upkeep, and by 1555 London's poor was growing at an alarming rate.

It was almost two years later, in 1547, when Henry's heir, King Edward VI, established the first housing for the poor at Bridewell before he passed it on to the city of London. However, for those grouped into the able-bodied poor, including some of the mentally ill, things would not improve as the boy king's reign continued. Edward's 1547 Vagabonds Act subjected these unfortunate people to not only several years in prison but being branded with the letter 'V'.

And that was if you were lucky enough to be a first-time offender. If you committed a second offence, you were more than likely put to death under the king's law.

Soon after, in 1552, he passed another poor act, banning begging altogether, leaving the poor and mentally ill vulnerable once again.

The crown would pass from Edward to his sister Queen Mary I and then to their sister Elizabeth I, but she too seemed to have no patience for vagabonds. Elizabeth's Vagabond Act of 1572 instructed that those caught begging be burned through the ear and, if caught again, hung.

But several of Elizabeth's other poor acts also allowed for the chronic beggar and those without work through no fault of their own, to be looked at differently. This distinction would greatly benefit those who may have been unable to work due to mental illness. In 1563, the queen passed the Relief of the Poor Act, requiring those parish residents who could afford it to contribute to collections taken up by the poor. In 1575, she passed another poor act requiring towns to have an ample stock of goods for the poor to work with, like hemp, iron, and wool.

But it was Elizabeth's Act for the Relief of the Poor in 1597 that was the first complete code of relief for the 'deserving poor'. The amendment of the act that followed only a few years later, in 1601, would form the basis of caring for the poor for the next 200 years.

The Elizabethan Poor Law of 1601 would provide care for the different kinds of poor; the able-bodied poor, the impotent poor, and the idle poor. Because the population was still small enough for everyone to know their neighbours, overseers of the poor were usually able to distinguish between the 'deserving' and 'undeserving poor'. The 1601 Act dealt with the folks who had found themselves out of work temporarily and would most likely accept help from the parish. But it also dealt with beggars who were looked at as a threat to society.

After the crown fell under the Stuart Monarchy in 1603, the first adaptation of the 1601 Act was formed in 1607. There was to be a setting up of houses of corrections in each county, and work would be provided for those without paying jobs. There was also a clear distinction to be made between the wandering poor and the settled poor.

However, as the size and complexity of English society increased into the sixteenth century, so did the concern about the nature and prevalence of mental disorders. Population growth and economic change increased the number of insane and suicidal people. Family members of the mentally ill were becoming overburdened, as were the surrounding communities that cared for the sick. Lunatics often roamed around, wandering up and down country roads. This became intolerable to the public, and it was not rare to see the mad chained up in broad daylight. There was great fear among town citizens that the raving mad may resort to violence and angry outbursts.

It was clear that the Renaissance brought no great revelations in psychiatry, and so prior to the eighteenth century, there wasn't a proper study of the illness. Aside from melancholy, several disorders can easily be explained today with science but were looked at as mental illness. Many of them stemmed from the dynamic of the seventeenth-century family dynamic and the stress of caring for a mentally ill family member.

The psychological significance of the family truly reflected beliefs about mad people and the causes of their misery. There were often complaints about anxiety and despair and even marital problems that resulted from the care of a sick family member. The seventeenth-century household was the basic social unit that performed many vital day-to-day functions. The home and those living there had the task of raising and educating children, taking care of sick family, and managing their goods. This social importance of a solid family dynamic was also recognised in caring for mad or troubled kin. Before the English Revolution, only a small handful of the citizens would have been sent into an asylum, as most disturbed people were cared for at home.

Individuals who were cared for at home usually presented with fits of frantic energy or wildly inappropriate laughter. These people would often roam through their homes with moods that were quick to change, perhaps emitting strange laughter or screaming that led to bouts of anger. Uncontrollable rage among the mad was not only terrifying to the family members caring for them but to the everyday observer as well.

And no tale of madness in the sixteenth and seventeenth centuries would be complete without mentioning one of the most notorious healers of the time, Richard Napier. Napier left the modern world thousands of accounts of madness and melancholy in the English language. Whether these accounts are real or imagined can be determined after looking through the abundance of records he kept throughout his life.

Napier, an astrological physician, and Anglican minister, was born in 1559 in Exeter, England. He attended school at Oxford University, earning his B.A. and later, his M.A. Along with the study of medicine, Napier also became a cultured minister for the Church of England. He earned the reputation of being a devout theologian as head of Great Linford Parish in Buckinghamshire.

Napier truly lived on the cusp of two grand eras that flourished during the later years of the Renaissance. The philosophical and religious system developed in the third century was slowly losing its importance as scientific materialism was growing. Because he was a rather shy minister who didn't enjoy preaching all too much, Napier busied himself with theology, alchemy, and astrological medicine. He became interested in astrology in 1597, as many clergymen combined medical care with pastoral care. And for Napier, medicine was the branch of astrology that appealed the most.

Napier's mix of magic, religion, and science also involved seances and priestly magic, which was troubling during a time of significant religious opposition in England. It was a time when Calvinism dominated the land, and the prosecutions of supposed witchcraft were prevalent. Protestants felt very strongly that even if it was done for good reason, anything that involved magic was the work of Satan, and this meant Napier's methods of treatment were frowned upon.

Napier began to treat patients in 1597 and did so for almost forty years. He treated every known malady and worked closely with the poor for little or no money. He earned a reputation as a great healer, and many flocked to Great Linford to consult with him. He treated up to fifteen patients a day, using his methods of questioning and note-taking. He asked his patients a myriad of inquiries and mapped the heavens with the precise moment of his questioning. This allowed him to correspond the patient's symptoms with the great beyond. In this way, the astrological circumstances and disease manifestations could be likened and the proper treatment selected.

Many of Napier's patients were suffering from rather vague and lingering symptoms, and he treated many who fell under the umbrella of emotionally disturbed, frumpy, and simply unkind. He truly felt the disorders of the mind and body could be studied like the movement of the planets. Folks in the seventeenth century were very aware of the dicey cures medicine offered, and for them, Napier gave an alternative. He felt that astrology helped him better diagnose his patients than relying on uroscopy and the humoral theory alone. Most of his patients either didn't know or didn't care that his methods were often perceived as taboo. But Napier lived in the last era where a medical practitioner could combine the use of astrology, magic, and religion. And he did so for a very small fee which was appealing to his patients.

What makes Napier stand out is that even though the medical establishment found him suspicious and unfounded, he was very popular with those he treated. This is clear in the evidence he left behind in his meticulous note-taking. Researchers have spent over ten years digging through thousands of pages of his notes, which has not been an easy task. The documents are full of astrological symbols that are intertwined with his hard-to-read penmanship. Perhaps more interestingly, Napier was known for his outlandishness. He wrote of patients who contracted syphilis and had been 'thrust with a rapier in his privy parts'.

Or patients who visited him for their own strange and ill thoughts. Along with his myriad of diagnoses went his even stranger cures. Aside from the standard prescription for bloodletting and purges, patients were asked to touch a dead man's hands and apply a pigeon to the soles of one's feet. Some of his patients were told of future things, such as the woman who was told she would have a child but 'by some other man and not by her husband'.

Napier's fascinating notes also told of the brutality of life in seventeenth century England. His notes on childbirth and other woman's issues tell of the countless infant deaths he encountered. He wrote intensely on the struggle of mental illness and the horrific treatments used. One older woman, he writes, was 'bound in her bed with cords at night and at daytime is chained at a post'.

Napier wrote of people hallucinating that their family were rats or saw the devil appear in front of them. Before the last decade, historians have unsuccessfully tried to understand Napier's pages of strange stories of angelic visits, and miserable marriages, along with melancholy and disorientation. His works contain significant details of the lives of nobles and lowly cook maids, who have suffered every possible thing under the sun. Napier took on many clients who suffered from suicidal ideology and other harmful thoughts associated with mental illness. Napier believed that these thoughts resulted from possession or a great evil inside them.

If we look into his transcriptions, we see that they divulge into the life of a healer that was almost, if not more, mad than his patients. Historians have spent decades trying to understand Napier's medical ledgers, which are full of stories of bad dreams, delirium, depression, and ghostly visitors. Napier's incoherent and illegible handwriting has, up until recently, been a spider's web of medical notes that baffled doctors for centuries.

Still, in the epitaph written by his fellow curate, he is said to be 'The most renowned physician in body and soul'.

Perhaps the most important of writings during Elizabeth's reign is that of Robert Burton, an English scholar. At the height of Elizabeth's reign, melancholy was becoming the most pervasive of Renaissance ailments. Robert Burton (1577-1640) was an extremely dedicated chronicler of the times, and his book, *The Anatomy of Melancholy*, was published in 1621 under the pseudonym *Democritus Junior*.

The choice for his pseudonym most likely comes from Greek philosopher Democritus, who was said to have been searching for the source of madness. Burton explains that Democritus was not only searching for the reasoning behind madness but melancholy as well. Like his fellow scholar, Burton puts down in writing how 'all the world is melancholy or mad, dotes, and every member of it'.

Melancholy became Burton's life work, and he also learned about the disease through personal experience. He was the son of a noble family in Leicestershire and studied at local schools before going to Oxford. It is believed that Burton consulted with astrological physician Simon Forman in 1597. Burton complained of melancholy and, in his future book, would claim to know it personally.

Burton worked on his book for more than a decade before it was printed. He claims that he lived a 'silent, sedentary, solitary, private life penned upmost part in my study'. However, according to colleagues, he also had a fondness for wenches and was said to be overly cheerful.

Through his book, Burton was able to tap into the knowledge of the past 2,000 years regarding melancholy. The allure and danger of such a condition seem to have always captured people's fascination. One of the first questions posed by Burton was why men who were outstanding in philosophy, poetry, or the arts were melancholic. And these questions were asked long before the time of Ameduaus Mozart and Edgar Allen Poe, whose genius ran parallel to melancholy. Of melancholy sufferer's Burton says:

They will act, conceive all extremes, contrarieties, and contradictions, and that in infinite varieties…scare two of two thousand that concur in the same symptoms. The Tower of Babel never yielded such confusion of tongues, as this chaos of melancholy doth variety of symptoms. Thus melancholy can manifest in symptoms close to modern-day depression or as trapped wind, flatulence, or habitual migraines. It might lead a sufferer towards irretrievable despair; then again, it might make him believe he was a shellfish.

If we look at the melancholy of Mozart and Poe, it becomes evident that Burton was a man before his time. An article published in a 2005 edition of Psychiatry concluded that Mozart suffered terribly with melancholy, especially in the last years of his life. In letters, Mozart spoke about experiencing a constant sadness and depressed mood. He laments about his diminished ability to concentrate and a decrease in the enjoyment he once got from composing. He disliked being alone and had a longing to be nurtured by his wife, often looking for reassurance that he was loved.

Mozart, who was also not known for being good with money, wrote to fellow Freemason Michael Puchberg in 1788 regarding loans. Puchberg says that Mozart was 'deeply depressed during the summer, writing of black thoughts'.

However, on the flip side of Mozart's apparent melancholy, we see fantastic spells of creativity, along with his frivolous and often immature behaviour. While he was often seen drinking too much or throwing temper tantrums, there is no denying that Mozart was an absolute genius. As a child prodigy, he wrote over one hundred pieces before he was fifteen years old. Among many other things, Mozart managed to entirely compose 'Don Giovanni' on the night before its premiere. The piece remains one of the most beautiful musical masterpieces of all time. Mozart's innovativeness and talent proved he had a complex understanding of music that defied those around him.

The mania and genius of Edgar Allen Poe still baffle scholars today. Upon his deathbed, Poe was found in a state of total delirium where he was incoherent and unkempt. Poe's famously dark and gory works seem almost cliché for a person who suffered from lifelong depression and had a history of suicidal tendencies. However, during the time that Poe's melancholy seemed at its worst, he was most successful. The Gold-Bug and The Raven were reprinted dozens of times to keep up with demand during the years that Poe seemed to be spiralling into an unending depression.

While both Mozart and Poe wouldn't produce their masterpieces for over two hundred years, it seemed that Robert Burton was absolutely correct in his connection between the melancholic and those who excelled in the arts.

In addition to believing that melancholy was an overabundance of black bile in the body's four humours, Burton believed that black bile affected those who led more inactive physical lives. He thought that black bile resulted from those who laboured hard in mind with folks such as thinkers, writers, or artists, supporting his questions about why the artists of the day were melancholic. In addition to the humoral imbalances, he saw such causes of melancholy as idleness, passion, misery, and solitude. Burton gave melancholy the definition of being as 'a kind of dotage without fever, having for his ordinary companions fear and sadness, without any apparent occasion'.

Burton theorised that if the body's humours became excessive, one had a better chance of having chronic melancholy. He believed the reason behind excessive black bile could be from a poor diet, grief, lack of sleep, living in a home that faced north, or from too much or too little sex. In his book, Burton dedicated an entire chapter to the melancholy of widows, nuns, and maids. He also stated that the body's effect of ageing might also add to the causes of melancholy.

He declared that the elderly are sad and lonely because their skin has wrinkled. He said that sufferers of melancholy:

> will act, conceive all extremes, contrarieties, and contradictions, and that in infinite varieties ... scarce two of two thousand that concur in the same symptoms. The Tower of Babel never yielded such confusion of tongues, as this chaos of melancholy doth variety of symptoms.

Burton stated that melancholy could manifest as flatulence or migraines and could lead a sufferer to utter despair. But it could also make that same person suffer from delusions. One of Burton's stories tells of an Italian baker who succumbed to melancholy and was convinced he was made of butter. Because of this delusion, he refused to go near his oven or sit in the sun.

Melancholy was quickly becoming an epidemic during the sixteenth and seventeenth centuries, as doctor's case notes told of melancholic men, women, and children. But Burton believed that it wasn't just human beings who suffered from melancholy, and he thought that the same affliction could be found in horses, birds, and even trees.

Along with many of Burton's bizarre stories, he told the story of two trees that longed to be together so badly that their trunks had grown towards each other. Among several stories of Burton's own odd behaviour, one claims he would go to Folly Bridge in Oxford to listen to the bargemen argue. Upon hearing them bicker, Burton held his sides in uncontrollable laughter.

His book's very title page claimed that he would explore melancholy:

> with all the kinds, causes, symptoms, prognostics, and several cures of it ... philosophically, medicinally, historically opened and cut up.

Burton continued to edit *The Anatomy of Melancholy*, adding more and more words until it was more than half a million words by the time he passed away in 1651. Each updated addition to the manuscript had new cases of melancholy, with more insight into causes, symptoms, and treatments. In his first edition of the book, Burton portrayed melancholy to be, in its early stages, as a 'most delightsome humour, to walk alone, and meditate'.

By the last edition, the definition changed to 'a most delightsome humour, to be alone, dwell alone, walk alone, meditate, lie in bed whole days, dreaming awake as it were'.

However, according to Burton, any happiness found with this condition did not last. The more melancholy took hold of one, the more fear and sorrow would override their pleasurable sensations. He explained melancholy as a 'cankered soul macerated with cares and discontents, and impatience'.

The change in Burton's wording clearly reflects the dangerous nature of melancholy, not only with his readers but with himself as well. Democritus Junior, as he continued to call himself as his pen name, wrote of his own experience claiming that:

> to ease my mind by writing, I had a heavy heart, a full head, a kind of imposthume in my head, which I was very desirous to be unladen of, and could imagine no fitter evacuation than this. Besides, I might not well refrain for where there's pain; there's a finger, one must need scratch where it itcheth. I was not a little offended with the malady, shall I say my Mistress Melancholy, my Egeria, or my bed genius, and for that cause, as he was that is stung with a scorpion, I would expect a nail with a nail, comfort one sorrow with another, make an antidote out of that which was the prime causes of my disease.

It was clear that Burton used writing almost as a purge, much like Poe or Mozart did in their works. Burton's language reminds us of the deep physiological roots of the belief of melancholy in the humour system. Before publishing the final edition of his treatise, he inserted the word 'agony' into several places when describing his suffering. Perhaps this can cast a bit of light on the epitaph found on his gravestone, which reads 'to whom Meleanchoy gave life and death'.

Many psychiatrists today may state that Burton's book is something of a fairy tale and offered very little medical insight, but doing so would be to ignore the passion in his work. Burton made the significant connection between those whose literary work resulted from their deep suffering and the genius that often went along with it. He understood that individuals who suffered from melancholy or other types of brain deficiency exhibited extreme promise alongside it. Centuries later, it is still evident that such people are gifted with creativity that only comes from the complexity of some kind of mental illness. Nikola Tesla was said to be mentally compromised and, even more recently, Steve Jobs, who may have suffered from a mood disorder.

There was a healthy appetite for Burton's book in his day, as early copies suggest that many readers engaged actively in it, some taking notes or underlining specific ideas or phrases. A century after it was written, English astrologer Samuel Johnson described Burton's book as 'the only book that ever took him out of bed two hours sooner than he wished to rise'.

The curiosity that Burton encouraged among his readers often became their best hope against the affliction of melancholy.

There is no doubt that Robert Burton was a troubled person who was deeply affected by melancholy. He was also said to have predicted the date of his death with certainty, as it is believed that he may have committed suicide. The crime of suicide was severe during Burton's time as it was considered a civil and religious crime. Victims of suicide were often denied funerals and burials in the churchyard, and families usually went to great lengths to hide the stigma of suicide.

Interestingly enough, in his section 'Prognostics of Melancholy' in his book, Burton explains that suicide is often the outcome of melancholy. Still, he also speaks about classical and medieval arguments surrounding the ethic of suicide. It would appear as though Burton struggled with conflicting views regarding suicide, stating that it is simply the result of mental illness; however, he also said that committing suicide is a poor moral choice. In any event, on 15 August 1639, Burton drew up his will, and five months later, at the age of sixty-two, he was dead. There is still debate about how he died, but Burton scholars have not ruled out the possibility that he took his own life. A reasonably large consensus believed he committed suicide by hanging himself in his private room at Christ Church in Oxford.

Not only were the emotional matters prevalent during these times, but historians believe that the physical environment of preindustrial England was so dangerous that it inhibited the formation of close emotional ties between family members. Both men and women were engulfed with a vast fear of dying. Understandably so, as epidemics, consumption, parasites, dysentery, accidents, infections, and botched childbirth were all things that killed without warning, and age was not a factor. If fear of death wasn't enough mental stress, doctors and clergymen cautioned against excessive mourning and grief. Bereavement, folks were told, was a common explanation for madness and despair. After all, it was Richard Burton who said 'the causes of melancholy were so numerous that they seem to multiply as they are discovered'.

It is hard to imagine enduring the death of a loved one without some form of grieving madness. To think that those who lost loved ones were told mourning caused madness would be even more cause to think one was insane.

The Tudor and Stuart monarchy responded to the growing concern about insanity by refurbishing places to help families deal with housing a madman. Most poor individuals had no property to protect, but still, the monarchy tried to assist them by providing at least some financial relief for families.

The Court of Wards and Liveries, enacted under Henry VIII, did attempt to treat wealthy lunatics with delicacy. These, usually appointed, relatives or friends of mad landowners were expected to see that the land was cared for and their property preserved. Lunacy was seen as a temporary state, and the law said when a madman recovered, he should get his land back, so it was in the best interest of all if the crown had ultimate control. It was believed that a lunatic lacked reason and could not be legally responsible. So who better to manage the affairs of children, idiots, and the insane than the crown?

You were of little importance to the crown if you didn't own lands and were often left to your own devices. This was frequently the case with the poor, who were left to wander the streets and beg. Most peasants were considered simple-minded people, and because your social rank declared your position, it was assumed that those with nobility required more thought to do their job. And because most peasants had little access to a physician, they turned to prayer for healing. If you were considered beneficial enough to be treated by a doctor, your treatments would include diet, exercise, possibly being bled, and most importantly, not doing anything that would cause you to get passionate.

Henry VIII's closing of the monasteries also had a lot of social ramifications. The system that was created extended power from the king's privy council to justices of the peace, allowing them to exercise control over lunatics. Commissions were designed to investigate cases of mad behaviour. Once one was deemed to be suffering from melancholy, local officials only had a few options. If friends and family couldn't take someone in, or if the person was too violent, the local officials had to put them in jail or worse, Bedlam.

While peasants could not afford proper treatment by a physician in the event of mental illness, they were at least given the hope of divine intervention. After his death, Henry VI had been revered as a saint to whom many would pray for a cure to insanity. Many miracles were attributed to the king, and he had become informally regarded as a martyr. The present King of England at the time, Henry VII, had begun compiling a list of the miracles attributed to him so he could start the canonisation process for his predecessor. Several holy acts had been accredited to Henry VI, including curing a young girl who suffered from cervical lymphadenitis. The girl was said to have been healed by the king's laying on of hands. Henry also interceded in the execution of a man who was being unjustly hung. With the king's hands between the rope and the accused man's throat, it is said that he kept the man alive, for he was revived after being left for dead. In a time when peasants sought out divine intervention, miracles, and relics such as the king's offered great hope. Demonic possession was still a real and frightening event, especially to people with little to no education. The idea of an intervention through God was often their only means of survival.

If a member of the monarchy went mad, the kingdom went to great lengths to ensure that they were treated with the best care to assure a speedy recovery. Henry VI succeeded to the crown of England when he was less than a year old. He inherited the Hundred Years War along with setbacks in France and squabbling between nobles in his kingdom. Known for being a melancholy young man who behaved rather childish, Henry suffered his first recorded mental breakdown in the summer of 1453. With what started with a fever, Henry went into a fit while at a hunting lodge in Wiltshire. He went into a state of withdrawal and was found to be physically and mentally catatonic. He found himself no longer able to walk or talk and couldn't even hold his head up. He was described as being slumped over like a rag doll. He seemed indifferent to what went on around him. Three months into his insanity, after several long years of waiting, the queen gave birth to a healthy baby boy. The baby was presented to the king in hopes of recognition and a blessing. But the king hadn't any idea who the child was and could not be stirred from his stupor. He no longer recognised his queen and was being spoon-fed by his attendants. Royal physicians tried a regiment of medications, baths, and enemas along with being bled. But the king didn't stir. His head was shaved in desperation to rid the brain of the black bile that physicians were sure was causing his upset. These symptoms were almost identical to what happened to his grandfather, King Charles of France. Day and night, Henry was attended to, kept free from illness, and given a proper diet by his men.

It wasn't until December of 1454 that the king began to show signs of recovery. He recognised the queen at this point, and when his child was brought to him, he was overjoyed. The monarch appeared to have suffered another attack in the fall of 1455, where he again became detached from reality. He also lost interest in the politics of his kingdom.

During the War of the Roses, Henry would continue to suffer from attacks of mental illness. In July of 1460, the king was captured and then released by Yorkists at the Second Battle of St Albans. But it was apparent to those around him that the king was suffering yet another bout of insanity as he was laughing and singing merrily while the battle raged on. Ousted from his throne in February of 1461, Henry and his queen fled to Scotland. After wandering as a fugitive in the forests, he was eventually seated back on the throne when Edward IV was in exile. But his second reign was short-lived, and he was taken prisoner at the Tower of London once Edward returned to reclaim his throne. In May of 1471, Henry VI was found dead in the tower, believed to have been murdered.

Pretenders to the throne often met a far worse fate. In 1555, William Fetherstone claimed to be King Edward VI, who had died two years earlier. Fetherstone was imprisoned and then released, believing to be suffering from harmless lunacy. But in 1556, he made another appearance and claimed that King Edward was still alive and began sending out pamphlets to tell the people. He was found guilty of treason and drawn and quartered under the order of

Queen Mary Tudor. Legit lunatic or not, one had to have been mad to attempt to overthrow the crown, especially knowing that you'd face death in the end.

In 1609 counties were ordered to establish houses of correction to confine the able-bodied poor and train them for jobs. Still, it would be several decades before scores of entrepreneurs founded private madhouses to care for the insane. It's important to remember that Bedlam was a pioneer of its day, and the concept of the mental hospital was not yet considered.

Despite the interest, the actual management of mental disorders did not change much before 1660. Contemporary ideas about illness were still rooted in ancient science and medieval Christianity. Because of this, popular stereotypes of mental disorders were adapted to fit English conditions. Some municipal city governments began to establish dwellings for the pauper lunatic. However, private hospitals were not built until the last half of the seventeenth century, and places that operated as proper asylums were not founded until almost a century later.

During the course of the seventeenth century religious controversy still prevailed over medical explanations for insanity. Radical Protestants developed new means for casting out devils while the Quakers employed their powers of exorcism and spiritual healing to prove their divine inspiration. Conditions after the English Revolution showed how beliefs about insanity and recovery before the sixteenth century had been integrated into the social lives of ordinary people. Common villagers readily blamed the devil for madness and spirits, and witches were a constant menace to happiness and health. Methods of curing the mind were as diverse as the forces believed to cause them. Many healers devoted themselves chiefly to overcoming the supernatural cause of suffering. Traditionally clergymen were the most respected healers. But Protestant reformers eliminated exorcism from the Church of England's liturgy. But this affected the church's ability to satisfy popular demand for healing magic. For centuries, parish clergy misunderstood the psychological maladies of laymen. The mentally ill were urged to repent their sins and seek God's refuge. They also visited the sick and afflicted and provided advice in times of anxiety.

Late Tudor and Stuart puritan ministers revitalised the practice of 'practical divinity' to reform the beliefs and manners of the English. Some say that the puritans pushing Calvinism enhanced anxieties in people, but the puritan movement had significant consequences for the treatment of the insane. Villages and cities were full of people who could use magical means to relieve mental and physical pain. Sick people often went to the healers. Physicians didn't really deny the existence of witchcraft and possession. But they thought patients hurt by these means were rare. But the sceptical approach of the unseen powers was an excellent excuse for the doctors when their science was ineffective. Demand for religious remedies for mental illness persisted due to the glaring inadequacies of medical science. Medicine had not made a ton of progress since the Greeks, and many still believed that religious remedies cured the disorders of the mind more effectively than medicine alone. Clergymen still did spiritual counsel groups, prayer, and fasting. They visited the homes of people suffering from mental illness to help. Part of their work was to comfort the sad and settle the peace of people's souls. Fasting with the insane or possessed helped people step closer to recovering. George Fox, the leader of the Dissenting sects, had a gift for calming mad lunatics and those thought to be possessed. He believed that the key to healing the insane lay in his ability to communicate his conviction that inner light resides inside everyone.

Religious therapy was a good political weapon of the Dissenters while trying to capture the hearts of the English. The Anglican clergy said that prayer and fasting for the insane violated the church's canons. Throughout the seventeenth century, most English people continued to believe that mental illness was caused by either natural or supernatural forces. Either divine or diabolical. It wasn't until the Age of Enlightenment that things began to change for much of Europe and eventually for those suffering from insanity.

Chapter Four

The Age of Enlightenment and the Influence of the Quaker Movement

The Renaissance offered a period of innovation when it came to treating the human body, and while it did lead to several significant breakthroughs, much of it didn't change at all.

Andreas Vesalius (1514-1564), a renowned anatomist from Belgium, made a considerable contribution to the study of the human body with his book, *The Fabric of the Human Body*, as it offered several new anatomically correct drawings of the human body. Unlike the elementary sketches of the medieval doctor, Vesalius' drawings told a different and more advanced story of how humans functioned.

French barber-surgeon turned physician Ambroise Pare (1510-1590) essentially set the stage for modern surgery with his genius on the battlefield during the 1537 Siege of Turin. He understood the need to include pain relief along with surgical intervention, and he would ultimately replace Galen's tradition of ancient medical beliefs with one that genuinely promoted healing.

And yet, with these incredible achievements in the field of medicine, the Renaissance still lacked advancement in the treatment of mental illness.

Folks during the Middle Ages and Renaissance were still archaic in their thinking regarding great catastrophes. There was an immense fear that the hand of God was responsible when it came to the punishment of sins, which often took form in unpreventable events caused by mother nature. The Bayeux Tapestry, depicting the events surrounding William the Conqueror, shows Halley's comet embroidered on the fabric. The comet was believed by Harold II, King of England, to be a bad omen. Defeated by William I during the Battle of Hastings, he confirmed the fearsome reputation comets earned in the eleventh century.

Nearly 600 years after William's conquest, fear still gripped the English. In 1654, a massive comet, visible in the London sky, was seen as yet another prophecy of doom. And in a way, it was, at least to the seventeenth-century Englishman. Though death did not come from enemy forces, but from another enemy; plague. Bubonic plague had surfaced again and would wipe out roughly a quarter of London's population.

People were still under the impression that disaster was an act of God, and they continued to live in fear. The Catholic Church still dominated much of Europe and had many convinced that there would be great reciprocity for sins. And it was still believed that mental illness could result from sinning or the work of the devil. The Elizabethan era offered little hope in the treatment of the mentally ill. It wasn't until the new dawn of thinking, known as the Age of Enlightenment that things began to change.

The Age of Enlightenment stands out as a philosophical movement that changed the way people viewed the world. While many devoted theologians held firm to the belief that the wrath of God was the cause of much human suffering, some started to think otherwise. The Age of Enlightenment is generally believed to stem from 1685 to 1815 when great thinkers throughout Europe questioned authority and felt that the human race could improve through change. A range of ideas began to form about the mathematical laws of the universe, how different social classes should relate to one another, the separation of Church and State, and the relationship between people and the government. The old ideas were slowly being exposed to the light of rational thinking.

The ideas of the period of Enlightenment circulated through meetings at scientific and masonic lodges, coffeehouses, and the circulation of books and journals. These ideas undermined the authority of the English monarchy as well as the church and paved the way for political revolutions. These ideas also centred around the sovereignty of reason and the evidence of the senses as sources of knowledge. The Age of Enlightenment was marked by the importance of the scientific method, which devised of acquiring knowledge that had the development of science behind it. The Age of Enlightenment also questioned religious authority. The pre-moral times, which ran through the mid-1700s, were still heavily dominated by the Church's influence.

Renaissance humanism had been a time that embraced the study of classical antiquity that made its way into fourteenth, fifteenth, and sixteenth centuries throughout Europe. It was a time that centred around religion and the New Testament. The Enlightenment emerged from this movement as one that undermined the Catholic Church. It paved the way for future political revolutions and a surge in understanding when it came to the treatment of the mentally ill. No longer would they be looked at as outcasts of society to simply be cast aside.

There was an increase in goods coming into Europe, such as tobacco, coffee, and chocolate. From the Americas came new crops, like corn and potatoes. The excitement of this newness made people begin to question life as they had always known it. Europe always seemed to be on the brink of catastrophe, but maybe, that wasn't the case. Travel throughout the world had begun to expand, and it was noticed that other cultures didn't do things as the Europeans did.

Sir Francis Bacon (1561-1626), an English politician whose prime was over fifty years before the beginning of the Age of Enlightenment, was one of the first pre-thinkers when it came to truthfulness and knowledge. While his thinking still fell in line with the medieval theory of the four humours, he also felt that man should not dismiss doubt when assessing the truth. He also wrote of moral principles and the importance of human conduct when dealing with others.

Frenchman Rene Descartes (1596-1650) was equally important to the beginning of the Enlightenment as he was a significant figure in the rationalism movement. Rationalism was based on understanding the world through reason, which would span through the seventeenth and eighteenth centuries.

French historians date the Enlightenment from the death of King Louis XIV in 1715, who was executed on the guillotine. He was considered a victim of the rationalist thinking of the Age of

Enlightenment because he was an outspoken critic of the social and religious hierarchies of the nation. However, there wasn't a single date or time that established the Enlightenment. It was a time to consider the ideas of many great thinkers, whether they were French, Scottish, English, or American. But collectively, they brought about the emergence of questioning authority with rational thought.

French philosopher, Baron de Montesquieu, born in 1689, saw Europe in a critical light. In his *The Persian Letters*, published in 1721, he wrote about European society through the eyes of two Persian visitors. The absurdities of French culture were criticised, with remarks made on things that seemed absurd, such as priests turning wine into blood. As a result, many of Montesquieu's works were banned by the Catholic Church. However, his works received the highest of praises from the rest of Europe, especially Britain. As a champion of liberty, his works had a powerful influence on many American Founding Fathers.

The name that stands out the most for the Enlightenment is Sir Isaac Newton (1643-1727). Newton struggled with the idea of the supernatural with incredible difficulty. Aside from other theologian beliefs that God held you to the earth, Newton helped us understand that it was the pull of gravity that did so. For him, it was the obvious explanation. The whole thrust of the Enlightenment was searching for natural reasoning for things of scientific method, and Newton's law of gravitational theory spoke to many who struggled with the past rationale of the early to mid-sixteenth century.

Newton would argue against the belief that the order of the heavens had been designed to support our life on earth. His investigations into the history of the Church would be central to his life. Despite his upbringing, he had a strong disagreement with the fundamentals of religion. He believed the Holy Trinity to be a wicked form of belief in more than one god. This was probably driven in part by his disdain for the Catholic Church.

Newton was an original thinker no matter what field he chose to study. He felt that everyone had a duty to discover the truths about science and religion. He had his own views on the idea of the human soul, and some of his views exhibited great scepticism.

Francois-Marie Arouet, known his by pen name, Voltaire (1694-1778), was also a critic of the Catholic Church, who advocated for freedom of speech, freedom of religion, and the separation of church and state.

Voltaire was born in Paris in 1694, educated by the Jesuits at the College Lous-le-Grand, and studied law under the pressure of his father. But Voltaire longed to become a writer, and against his father's wishes, began to produce essays on controversial subjects. From early on, Voltaire started to have run-ins with the French authorities after speaking out against the government. His activities would lead to two separate imprisonments, as well as a temporary exile to England. Voltaire's main arguments were for free-thinking and religious tolerance. He stood for eradicating the priesthood and the aristocratic monarchial rule and favoured a monarchy that protected the people.

Voltaire's views on philosophy and politics can be found in most of his writings, and his subjects stretched across the drama, politics, and satirical genres. His works also extensively criticised the Roman Catholic Church and its institutions. He also wrote on the theories of historians while demonstrating his own ways of looking at the past. He preferred to view Europe as a whole rather than a group of separate notions.

Voltaire held firm to the belief that only an enlightened monarch could bring change to Europe. It was a time of much illiteracy, and he felt it was in the king's interest to improve the education of his people. It was during his flee to Britain under political asylum in 1726, that his ideas began to circulate through English Society.

The Enlightenment may have been about honesty, curiosity, and openness, but it also led to tensions between religious establishments and emerging science. The scientific thinkers that lived throughout the Middle Ages and into the Renaissance, were men of the church, formally schooled in theology. Because the Catholic Church ultimately controlled higher learning, the pioneers of new science challenged the church's domination.

David Hume (1711-1776), a Scottish philosopher, was especially sceptical of religion. While he didn't deny the existence of God, he believed in reason along with religion, and he felt that God was seen as mere superstition. People known as deists also thought that God existed but didn't have the influence in everyday life that everyone thought He did. Hume believed that persecuting people for their religious beliefs seemed somewhat cruel.

Hume was one of the most important figures of the Enlightenment, as he believed in the recognition of the difference between fact and value. He thought humanity to be more motivated by emotion over reason. When he published his work, *A Treatise of Human Nature*, Hume argued against the existence of instinct and believed that our knowledge as humans derived from experience. He thought that humans only experienced a small number of sensations and that free will was the only way to true freedom. His views on God's existence and cognitive science were considered controversial for his time.

Jean-Jacques Rousseau (1712-1778), a Genevan philosopher, influenced the progress of the Enlightenment throughout Europe. His work, *The Social Contract*, was the cornerstone of modern social thought. He advocated for the healing of Europe's social problems. He held firm in the belief that man should be free and not repressed by the chains of societal thinking. *The Social Contract* alone speaks of the need for government to establish the freedoms of all its citizens, a point that was argued later by Karl Marx and other communists. But aside from this, Rousseau argued that inequality among society was not natural and needed to be remedied.

The scientific and medical doctrines of the Age of Enlightenment were becoming more and more sophisticated. Less attention was being paid to the supernatural as the cause of mental illness. It became considerable that the ill could have an actual disease rather than a supernatural possession of the mind and soul. The eighteenth and nineteenth centuries brought about the beginning of modern psychiatry and the dawn of the moral era. The mentally ill would soon be removed from the general population and put into groups that could be managed in hospitals under the treatment of a physician. However, because patients were placed in a hospital setting, the treatments didn't change much in their favour.

Dr Benjamin Rush (1745-1813) was an American physician and signer of the United States Declaration of Independence. Along with being a supporter of the American Revolution, he was also a leader in the American Enlightenment. Rush opposed slavery and favoured public schools and the education of women. He also leaned towards a more progressive penal system and was committed to structuring medical knowledge around explanatory theories. He promoted the need for public health and a clean environment, including personal and military hygiene.

As a leading physician, he had a significant impact on the rise of the medical profession not only in America but in Europe as well. These impacts included mental health. In 1812, Rush published one of the first treatises on psychiatric disorders. *Medical Inquiries and Observations, Upon the Diseases of the Mind*, looked at the different kinds of mental illness, their causes, and possible cures. Rush was of the opinion that mental illness was caused by a disruption in the body's blood circulation, specifically in the brain. Because he thought that sensory overload was also partly to blame for mental illness, he often treated patients with devices designed to improve brain circulation, such as the centrifugal spinning board. The spinning board, or spinning chair, also known as a type of rotation therapy, was a bit of a fad during the early nineteenth century. Its founder was Erasmus Darwin, grandfather to Charles Darwin. Darwin felt that excessive spinning of a patient would decrease the amount of brain congestion by way of the building pressure. Another of Rush's methods in treating the mentally ill was the tranquillizer chair, a heavy wooden chair in which the patient was strapped to by the chest, ankles, knees, and abdomen. The patient's head was then inserted into a wooden box. A method of restraint similar to the straitjacket, it reduced the flow of blood to the head.

Though it seems cruel, Rush's intentions for his treatments were well-meaning. While working at Pennsylvania Hospital, he was appalled by the conditions some of the patients were kept in. He advocated extensively for better treatment and more humane conditions. Bloodletting was still a common practice for treating physical and mental ailments alike. Like many physicians of the time, Rush believed that bloodletting and purging with mercury chloride, or calomel, was the ideal medical treatment for the insane. He truly believed that he was helping his patients with forced purging. But because it was often difficult to get patients to ingest calomel, Rush had his own methods for 'tricking' them into it. He said:

> It is sometimes difficult to prevail upon patients in this state of madness, or even to compel them, to take mercury in any of the ways in which it is usually administered. In these cases, I have succeeded by sprinkling a few grains of calomel daily upon a piece of bread and afterward spreading over it, a thin covering of butter.

It's hard for us to imagine that Rush's inventions in the treatment of insanity were favoured at any point in history, but it was the common practice of the time. Along with the standard procedures for bleeding and mercury treatment, Rush believed that restraint in many forms was also the answer to treating the insane, as proven by his invention of the tranquillizing chair. He was an advocate of physical punishment and chaining patients in what were more or less dungeons, as these were the practised treatments of the time. And yet, Rush was a strong advocate for more humane mental institutions and felt that patients be treated like people rather than animals. However, he is quoted as saying:

> Terror acts powerfully upon the body, through the medium of the mind, and should be employed in the cure of madness.

Rush's belief in restraints and confinement caused him to be a pioneer in Moral Therapy, a form of treatment that would soon rise to notoriety in the wealthier mental health institutions throughout Europe and the United States. Moral Treatment or Moral Therapy developed during the framework of the Enlightenment, focusing on the individual rights of mental patients. From the beginning of the eighteenth century, those deemed insane were still viewed as folks with a complete loss of reason and were still considered a mockery to the general public. There were some beginning arguments for a better understanding of the psychology of patients, but for the most part, the conditions for patients hadn't changed.

At the latter part of the Enlightenment, Dr Joseph Mason Cox, an English physician devoted to the care of the mentally ill, popularised a form of treatment that was promised to cure insanity, called 'the swing'. The swing was created as a way to cause vomiting without the use of emetics. The swings ran on different machines that would spin people into a motion so violent that they would vomit. Cox believed that his swing was a way of both morally and medically treating patients. He said:

> Though we cannot accurately explain in what way the best remedies promote relief in madness, yet we have the most unequivocal proofs that those which occasion a degree of vertigo often contribute to correct the morbid state of the intellect, and no one of them is so well calculated to produce this effect as the swing.

Cox's apparatus worked by first strapping a patient into a straitjacket and then into the swing chair. The swing would then spin at such a ferocious rate that the patient would vomit uncontrollably until unconsciousness and shock took over. Understandably they would begin begging to be released from the chair, which was only done if the patient agreed to 'stop their behaviours and obey orders'. Patients were then put to bed, where they would sleep until they recovered. However, if the patient became a problem again, the process was started all over.

In one particular case of an insane man, Cox is cited as saying:

> I was determined to try the effects of the circulating swing as a last resource, into which he was placed as an inanimate lump, with his eyes shut; after a few circumvolutions one eye was observed to be occasionally opened, and at length both, a degree of alarm seemed next excited, then nausea, and retching to vomit; the motion was then suspended, and he was consulted as to his unwillingness to comply with my requisitions, but he still refusing, the gyrations were renewed, when the former effects were soon obvious, and the motion being increased, full vomiting ensued; he now begged to be liberated, and promised compliance with my wishes; he was taken out, put to bed, and slept for some hours, when food was offered, but, as usual, refused; he was reminded of his promise, and threatened with an immediate repetition of the swing; this succeeded, and for some days the prognosis seemed more favourable, but the reluctance to eating returned, and recourse was again had to the swing, two or three times, with the former success, till at length he yielded entirely to my wishes, and by very simple management, both mind and body were at length perfectly restored, and I have the pleasure of knowing that he continues well, and I am confident owes his life and reason to the swing.

John Monro, a doctor at the infamous Bedlam asylum, said in 1758 that 'vomiting is indefinitely preferable to any other' when discussing his choice of cures for insanity. While he prescribed the traditional treatment methods like bloodletting, his go-to was making his patients vomit. As written in his own words, he is cited as saying the following about an older male patient whom he caused to vomit over sixty times in six months.

> the most adequate and constant cure of it is by evacuation ... The evacuation by vomiting is infinitely preferable to any other. ... I lately received from a worthy friend of mine the case of a gentleman, who had laboured under a melancholy for three years; he himself calls it a hypochondriacal, convulsive disorder, from which he was relieved entirely by the use of vomits, and a proper regimen. So very sensible was he of their good effects, that he did not scruple to take sixty-one from the third of October to the second of April following; and for eighteen nights successively one each night; by which means he got rid of a prodigious quantity of phlegm and obtained a perfect recovery. The first seventeen were composed of one ounce of the yin, ipecacoan with one grain of emetic tartar, and afterward, he made use of no more than half an ounce of the wine. And those, who are much used to hypochondriacal people, will find them, in general, less weakened with vomits than purges.

Earlier in the Enlightenment, in 1725, Scottish surgeon Patrick Blair perfected another 'cure' of the insane that he originally learned from a colleague in 1694. Blair's water treatment consisted of dropping large amounts of water onto the head of an insane patient who was first strapped in a chair. Unlike many physicians of the time who were convinced insanity stemmed from unhealthy nerves, Blair thought insanity to be a religious choice. For this reason, he found water treatment effective in stopping an insane man from continuing his behaviour. He often put blindfolds on his patients to instil more fear into them before spraying gallons of water on them.

Both Blair's water treatment and the swing were methods of inducing a kind of torture to bring about a cure for insanity.

It was the illness and treatment of Britain's King George III that may have ultimately led to the consideration of more therapeutic intercessions for the insane. King George began to suffer from serious illness in 1788 and, by 1810, was no longer fit to reign. The king suffered from incoherent speech, irritation, violent outbursts, and sexual misconduct. Though it is thought today that King George may have been suffering from porphyria, a disease affecting haemoglobin production, which can seriously affect the nervous system, there is little evidence in the king's medical records to suggest so.

As was common practice for that time, the king had to be restrained several times when his violent outbursts became uncontrollable. However, during one of his more severe attacks, ordained priest and doctor Francis Willis was called upon to treat the king as he had established a good reputation as a healer. King George was given a bland diet and only a spoon in which to feed himself, as he could not be trusted with a knife. This extract was recorded in Dr Willis's diary on 2 March 1801 and explains some of the bizarre treatments prescribed:

> His Majesty's feet were put into hot water and vinegar for half an hour. Soon after His Majesty put on such an appearance of being exhausted, that his life was despaired of - his pulse too had rapidly increased.
>
> They gave him a strong dose of bark (Peruvian bark contained quinine) which had the effect of composing him and putting him to sleep for an hour and a half, which he had not had for, I think, nearly 48 hours before which time too he had been in a very restless and unquiet state.

Purgatives, arsenicals, tartar emetic, and skin blistering were used to rid the king's body of toxins. Although the king's arsenic levels proved dangerous, Willis's treatment of the English Monarch was seen as a success. Willis put aside any use of restraints or any violence and was given credit for helping the king recover. Willis's monument at Greatford Church says:

> he was happily the chief agent in removing the malady which afflicted his present Majesty (George III) in the year 1789. On that occasion, he displayed an energy and acuteness of mind which excited the admiration and procured for him the esteem of the nation. The kindness and benevolence of his disposition were testified by the tears and lamentations which followed him to the grave.

Willis used what was becoming known as moral treatment, which is based on humane care for patients. It began to replace some of the more abhorrent methods of care at the time, including bloodletting, toxic medications, purging, and physical restraints.

English Quaker William Tuke (1732-1822), who would go on to discover some of the eighteenth-century's first asylums, became one of the founders of moral treatment, where a daily work routine was established with chores, allowing patients to feel a sense of community. Patients were ultimately told they would be treated in a way that was a reflection of their behaviour.

With moral therapy came the notion of actually curing people, which was considered a part of good enlightened thinking. During the second half of the eighteenth century, physicians had more confidence to help the mentally ill, and enlightenment thinking began to spread all over Europe.

Along with the thinkers of the Enlightenment through Western Europe came the early thinking of trying to better understand what caused the insane to be the way they were. For the most part, the nonsense of demonic possession had been widely debated with the Enlightenment, and some wanted a better understanding of human psychiatry.

There was a new theory arising that would be coined, *the nerve theory*, which would become commonplace through the early 1900s. Doctors began to suspect that one's mental deficiency may lie in the physical malfunction of the nerves. Having a biological foundation for an illness allowed doctors to have hope in treatment. The theory of nerves causing mental illness became widespread in the seventeenth and eighteenth centuries. Hysteria, hypochondria, fatigue, or dullness were often diagnosed as nerves. The problems of anxious wealthy women were blamed on vapours of the nerves coming from the uterus to derange the brain. As it was, various disorders of the human nervous system had fallen under the umbrella term of nerves. Nervous malady became almost fashionable in wealthy societies, and the profession of nerve doctors grew rapidly

One physician that was particularly concerned with these nerve disorders, especially among Britain's elite, was Dr George Cheyne (1671-1743), from Scotland. In Dr Cheyne's work titled, *The English Malady*, he claimed that a significant portion of England's upper class was suffering from a nervous disorder that he named the English Malady. He believed that the luxuries and abundance of food were factors in this problem of the well-to-do. He thought that women especially were subject to weak nerves, which caused fainting, and it soon became the chic behaviour of many housewives. And it also became chic to quickly diagnose women with simply having nerves. One of the treatments often prescribed to nervous women was chicken soup and a hot bath, as it was believed both were calming for the soul. They weren't wrong there, as this treatment is still a source of comfort today. Other nerve treatments included hypnosis and the 'rest cure', which was strict enforcement of six to eight weeks of rest and isolation accompanied by a diet rich in fatty milk. However, most of these treatments were for the upper-class elites, and those deemed the ordinary folk could expect to be given a nerve tonic.

The nerve tonic was made from the recipes of medical entrepreneurs who saw the rise of nerve disorders as an opportunity for profit.

As time went on, the majority of these tonics used additives that were poorly understood and often addictive, such as lithium salts, cocaine, and morphine.

While we understand today that psychiatry has a biological and psychosocial component, the biological theory was dominant during the Age of Enlightenment. In 1758, English physician William Battie (1703-1776) believed that muscular spasms led to laxity of the brain, causing weakness of the nerves, hence, the nerve theory. Italian physician, Vincent Chiarugi (1759-1820), felt that the nervous system was also the cause of mental health. Perhaps Battie said it best. During his career, he stated 'Madness, though a terrible and at present, a very frequent calamity is perhaps as little understood as any that ever afflicted mankind'.

The early doctors of psychiatry had a gut feeling that the primary cause of mental illness was organic. They also understood that hereditary played a part as well. Battie was part of a long tradition of British doctors who thought deeply on the inheritability of madness. Philippe Pinel (1745-1826), who was also a pioneer in the humane treatment of the mentally ill, and his French colleague, Jean-Etienne Dominique Esquirol (1772-1840), were also keen on the idea of hereditary being a factor. This generation of doctors understood that people with illness in the family stood a great chance of becoming ill themselves.

The advancements in higher thinking that the Enlightenment also brought discussions about formalised care for the insane. William Battie was one of the first to talk about the therapeutic benefits of institutional care. During his lifetime, he was one of the most eminent psychiatrists in Britain. He was the founding medical officer at St Luke's in London, which opened in 1751. Battie hoped that his new asylum would bring about an unparalleled standard of care that would be a great competition with Bedlam. His treatise, *Treatise on Madness*, was a pivotal turning point in psychiatry. His was the first that was written specifically on madness. Psychiatry was still far from being established, and Battie hoped to do away with some of the antiquated ideas on madness. Battie promoted the idea that the insane should not be locked away to protect society. He believed they could benefit from therapeutic time spent in a psychiatric institution. He thought madness to be a manageable disease. He said:

> Madness is as manageable as many other distempers, which re equally dreadful and obstinate, and yet are not looked upon as incurable; such unhappy objects ought by no means to be abandoned, much less shut up in loathsome prisons as criminals or nuisances to the society.

Because so many of the eighteenth-century medical manuals said that madness came from irritated nerves, physicians naturally felt a calm setting was in order. Johann Christian Reil (1759-1813), a pioneer in German psychiatry, thought a pleasant environment with no bars on the windows was adequate for patients. He believed that baths, exercise, schedule, activities, and more of a patient and doctor relationship were ideal. Reil demonstrated new ways of treating the mentally ill and spoke of the madman as sick folks who needed medical care. He passionately advocated for the introduction of public insane asylums and the caring treatment of the ill.

Italian physician Vincenzo Chiarugi was pivotal in the introduction of humanitarian reform to the care of people with mental illness. During his time as director of Santa Dorotea hospital in Florence, he outlawed using chains to restrain psychiatric patients. While at Bonifacio Hospital, he implemented new rules regarding the conduct of the staff, record keeping, and custody and care of the patients. Chiarugi was adamant that patients be treated with respect and not be harmed physically in any way. He insisted that patients have access to the hospital grounds to take walks and exercise and that they must be bathed regularly. In his treatise, *On Insanity*, he said that patients with mania should be confined to a secure, quiet room with nothing dangerous or overstimulating. Chiarugi, along with Tuke, was one of the first to encourage moral therapy, though his writing was almost unknown in England.

Among some of the more notable facilities that practiced the same ideas as Reil and Chiarugi was a facility in Kent that was founded by Dr William Perfect (1734-1809) in the 1760s. During this time, he had become a crusader throughout Great Britain in trying to eliminate smallpox through the development of inoculation. Dr Perfect also had a particular interest in mental illness and opened a small asylum that he operated out of his home. He welcomed patients into his house and became quite successful at a time when it was not considered possible to treat people suffering from insanity. Dr Perfect used gentleness and common sense in his approach to helping the insane. Although his practice was small, it remained the principal private asylum in Kent for years.

During the late eighteenth century, people in France, England, and the United States strongly began to advocate for the mentally ill. In the French Hospital, Bicetre, Dr Pinel instituted what he called 'treatment moral'. Like Chiarugi, Pinel did not believe that people needed to be chained and beaten. His ideas were revolutionary as he felt that patients should be treated as a person who was suffering from a disease and not looked at as an outcast from society. Pinel believed that patients should be given a diagnosis and a respectable therapy for it. He embraced kindness and patience, along with recreation, as part of a treatment plan. He believed in fresh air and walks for patients, allowing them to engage in pleasant conservation. He believed that mad people were truly suffering from an illness out of their control and should be approached with dignity and compassion. Pinel was credited with defying the concept of ethical treatment on the mentally ill. His ideas would help with the development of other institutions in Europe that focused on that very thing.

During this time, there was only a basic series of common laws designed to confine a person who was disordered in mind. In 1763, a committee of the House of Commons was set up by a Whig politician and barrister, Thomas Townshend (1733-1800). The committee's purpose was to study unlawfulness in madhouses and focus on cases like those of women who were committed solely on the word of their husbands. It was common for asylums to admit anyone as long as they were paid accordingly. People in these asylums were treated as if they were insane, but agents agreed that most of the people they admitted were not insane at all. There were never physicians to attend to these patients, and there were no records of their attendance being kept at any of the facilities. The committee soon discovered that these things were a common occurrence, and legislative intervention was desperately needed.

The Madhouse Act of 1774 was an act of Parliament that set out the legal framework for regulating asylums throughout Britain. In 1773, a bill was introduced to Parliament by barrister Thomas Townshend after hearing too many stories of atrocities in private madhouses. Townshend sponsored the bill to regulate private madhouses and involved the Royal College of Physicians in the care of patients. The bill was presented to the House of Commons, where it was amended, revised on 20 May, and received royal assent. The act would set limits on the number of patients who could be admitted into a madhouse. Licences and regulations would also become law for madhouse proprietors, and both had to be renewed once a year. The city of London would now carry out official inspections of madhouses and require medical certification for the incarceration of lunatics. Penalties were set for keeping any insane person without a licence. On 20 November 1774, the act became officially known as the Madhouses Act of 1774. It was continued by the Madhouse Continuation Act of 1779 and then by the Madhouse Law Perpetuation Act of 1786.

While Pinel was calling for his reforms in France, William Tuke (1732-1822), the English Quaker and philanthropist, was troubled by the violations of human decency when it came to the treatment of the insane. Tuke rejected traditional medical intervention and instead emphasised the importance of rural, quiet retreats where patients could engage in reading and conversation.

In 1732, Tuke was born into a prominent Quaker family, and he would adhere to the principles of simplicity, peace, integrity, community, equality, and stewardship throughout his life. In 1791, Tuke was affected by an incident surrounding a Quaker widow who passed away while a patient at York Lunatic Asylum. The asylum, known today as the Bootham Park Hospital, was established in 1772 to house fifty-four patients. With the help of Dr Alexander Hunter (1729-1809) and architect John Carr (1723-1807), the Archbishop of York intended to create a lunatic asylum that would prevent the mentally ill from being left in unsuitable conditions.

York Lunatic Asylum was completed by 1777, and while it may have been physically attractive with Tuscan columns and elegant Venetian windows, that was the extent of its beauty. The building was thought of as a waste of money as it was soon discovered that underneath its grand façade was a place where patients were still treated horribly as well as being kept in utter squalor. The Asylum soon fell under great scrutiny. Tuke also witnessed some unsettling conditions during a visit to St Luke's Asylum, where he saw a naked female patient chained to a wall. Tuke considered that the intent of the conditions was not to be cruel but perhaps there were no other alternatives that had been effective. At the time, the ill-treatment of patients was still widely accepted throughout Europe. The mentally ill were still believed to be sub-human-like animals who were insensitive to cruel treatment methods, such as beatings and starvation. The original founders of moral medicine still didn't truly understand the cause of mental illness, and their treatments were still empiric. The York Retreat was soon founded as a result of these attitudes.

William's daughter, Ann, came up with the idea to form an institution for the insane run by Quakers themselves. In 1790, after purchasing eleven acres of land, William Tuke established the York Retreat, and it was here that the mentally ill would be treated with Christian charity, humanity, and kindness. He believed that all patients must be kept under the direct supervision of a physician to ensure proper care.

In 1796 the Retreat officially opened in the vast countryside of York and operated under the philosophy that a quiet place where patients could live and work would be best. It started with less than ten patients, and the use of chains and physical punishment was not permitted. Patients were instead given walks and jobs working on the farms in the quiet surroundings of York. Patients were also encouraged to engage in different skills and to read books. They could wander about the grounds and gardens and interact with the domestic animals that also took up residence on the property. The patients at the York Retreat were treated with kindness and thought of as people who had great potential to recover if given the correct tools. Traditional treatments for the insane, such as bleeding and purging, were replaced with much gentler methods, like warm baths. Tuke also insisted that proper diet and exercise would greatly benefit patients. This doesn't mean that the York Retreat wasn't without some form of restraint. Straitjackets were used at times as either a threat or a last resort. However, it was agreed that using fear tactics on patients could make things worse. It was better to be observant and kind when treating patients.

The York Retreat ran on the foundation of the Quaker beliefs of compassion and respect, along with self-control. The Retreat truly marked the beginning of the move away from the brutal use of restraints such as chains. The kind nature of doctors became the foundation of more compassionate care. Physicians believed that the ill could now be rehabilitated by gaining a genuine acceptance of morality, along with the desire to work and contribute to society. Tuke's approach to mental illness would begin a series of reforms and a greater understanding of the importance of establishing a peaceful, home-like environment for England's mentally deficient citizens.

Chapter Five

The Emergence of the Asylum

The early nineteenth century and well into the Victorian era was the beginning of rapid change when dealing with the mentally ill. But perhaps the ideal lunatic asylum was built over 700 years before the Quaker influence. If the family-like asylum that still stands in Belgium today wasn't the perfect place, it indeed served as a model in the minds of well-meaning physicians. After the shrine to St Dympha was erected in the city of Geel and pilgrims began to flock to it for healing, an annexe was added in 1480 to accommodate the growing number of people. As mentioned earlier, the townspeople came to welcome the pilgrims into their homes, and by the Renaissance, Geel became known as a place for the mad to go and receive spiritual help. They came by the masses, drawn to the hope of a cure, and the townspeople welcomed them as an act of Christian charity. As attitudes towards mental illness continued to be transformed throughout the nineteenth century, Geel remained somewhat of a beacon of what was to come. For generations, the system in which the insane were dealt with was a system of neglect and abuse. During the Middle Ages and beyond, people who suffered from mental illness often spent their lives locked away from the rest of the world. With the progressive ideals that began to take shape, the standard of the Geel asylum was one that reformers attempted to model. The emergence of the nineteenth-century asylum was about to take place.

In 1808, Parliament passed the County Asylums Act, which set the foundation for a nationwide network of insane asylums throughout the United Kingdom. These publically funded asylums would accommodate paupers and those remaining in the hostile communities of the workhouses. The act surfaced after a series of legislation in the previous century was put forth to curb the abuses that had been going on in Britain's asylums since the fourteenth century. Bedlam was still a place for people to come and gawk at the mentally ill but was also becoming the epitome of how the insane should never be treated.

The 1808 County Asylums Act gave magistrates the ability to build an asylum in every county in the country. While the act intended to provide people with a care system, there were several deficiencies, and it wouldn't be until the mid-nineteenth century that the mass construction of asylums began to occur. Nevertheless, the 1808 act and the national network it created would be a crucial move forward in seeking asylum care.

Prior to the act, several private asylums had already begun to open throughout Great Britain. In 1806, Brislington House opened as one of the first purposely built insane asylums in England. Psychiatrist Edward Long Fox (1761-1835) established the operation on the theory of moral treatment pioneered at York Retreat. Fox already had a successful private practice in Bristol and was able to pay the cost of opening Brislington Estate. Fox's goal was to attract wealthy patients, as he separated all patients at Brislington according to their social rank. It had even been suggested that King George may have spent time at Bristlingon during one of his many episodes of mania. In addition to the wealthiest of patients, Brislington received paupers through funding of local parishes, though these patients were kept furthest from those in high society, per Fox's preference.

Each separate block of Brislington had patient access to large landscaped areas for patients to walk and perform outdoor activities such as gardening and farming. The idea was to allow patients to get fresh air with the protection of being in a closely enclosed space.

With the passing of the 1808 Country Asylums Act, a vast undertaking would begin as plans to carry out the act were set in place. The architecture and building of Britain's new insane asylums was not something to be taken lightly. The design of the asylum generally followed one of five models throughout Great Britain.

The Radial Plan was rooted in the works of the eighteenth-century British theologian Jeremy Bentham (1748-1832). Bentham's designs for institutional buildings were called the panopticon. The concept was to allow all prisoners or patients of an institution to be observed by staff without realising it. While Bentham conceived his ideal to be applied to prisons, the plan was also applied to the asylum. The architecture of the radial plan consisted of a large circular room with a central observation area that contained several levels. Because the design was based on a prison system, there were cells with barred doors and windows that would allow an inmate or patient to be seen at all times. Few counties used the radial plan because it may have been considered inhumane due to little sunlight and poor circulation, but many asylums constructed did use it.

St Lawrence's Hospital in Cornwall opened in 1815 in the form of a star-shaped building with a central block and wings that radiated outward.

Exminster Hospital, which opened in Devon in 1845, was commissioned by London architect Charles Fowler. The asylum was designed with beautiful gardens with countryside views to provide a therapeutic environment for the patients. The building also had a ballroom to aid in social interaction along with the treatment of mental illness. The semi-circular design was built with six radial arms that branched out like the spokes of a wheel. At the end of each radial arm, there stood service areas that were used depending on the gender of the patients. Near the main site of the building stood a large kitchen and an administrative block. The number of patients admitted to Exminster rose steadily, reaching its peak of 1,421 in 1915. The hospital became known as Devon County Lunatic Asylum in 1920.

The Corridor Plan was used primarily between 1830 and 1890, and it was laid out with the administrative offices in the centre and the wards of the asylum bordering it on either side. This allowed for easy separation of gender, and it made it easy to communicate throughout the asylum.

The City of London Lunatic Asylum opened its doors in 1866 after using the corridor plan. The building, which represented the structure of a castle, spread out over extensive grounds. The administration building was complete with offices, a chapel, and a great hall. Each wing of the hospital had wards and single cells, one to house male patients and one to house female patients. A water tower stood in the centre of the site, acting as a focal point. The two-storey pavilions contained the laundry facilities, the morgue, the bakery, and several workshops. The pavilions were joined to the main building by seemingly endless hallways, and both had bedrooms on the upper floors. Patients could enjoy the outdoors but were always kept separate from the opposite sex. The hospital initially had accommodation for only 220 patients. When new wings opened in 1875 and 1892, private patients were granted admittance. They were kept in separate, more respectable wards from the paupers and received better food. The facility continued to grow in size, and by 1948, it could house over 640 patients.

Oxford County Pauper Lunatic Asylum opened in 1846 using the corridor plan as well as The Lincolnshire County Lunatic Asylum, which opened its doors in 1852.

Horton Road Hospital, also known as Gloucestershire First County Asylum, opened in 1823, under Sir George Onesiphorus Paul, 2nd Baronet, who was involved in the reform of the mentally ill. Though he divided patients by social class, he believed that no person should be disadvantaged due to their place in society. Paul thought that both the poor and wealthy should be treated as equals, and he was one of the primary voices in the creation of the 1808 Asylums Act. Horton Road Hospital began as a three-storey crescent facility that housed the wealthy, paupers, and charity patients. The county eventually took over management of the hospital in the late 1850s, and it was used exclusively for paupers.

The Pavilion Asylum plan was laid out in a semi-detached block formation, consisting of three types of layout. The Standard Pavilion was made up of a long corridor on either side of the administrative block. The water tower was either centrally located or remote. Hellesdon Hospital and the Anne at Lancaster Moor were examples of this structure.

The Dual Pavilion structure was composed of both the administration and service blocks lined with long corridors and ward blocks. This design was made to make the separation of more difficult patients easy. Walley Asylum, Calderstones was designed to house different classes of patients. Either side of the administrative block was for physically sick inmates, followed by acute and epileptic patients. Working inmates were placed in wards where they could work in the laundry or workshops depending on their gender. The hospital, which was designed for 2,000 patients, was lined by visiting rooms on either side of each corridor. Behind the facility's recreation hall were the kitchen and water tower. Male patients were kept to the east of the main building, and female patients were kept to the west.

The Radial Pavilion design was rare for an asylum. It was more of a go-between for the Pavilion and the Echelon plan, consisting of a semi-circular corridor with services in the middle. Cane Hospital in Coulsdon and St Luke's Whittingham remain two of the only examples of this type of rare architectural structure.

The Echelon Plan gained popularity in the 1880s due to the arrangements of the wards and offices and its large corridors. The Broad Arrow was the earlier of the two types of Echelon plans, consisting of the wards being spread out across a large area. It was a set up of pavilion blocks interconnected with shorter corridors branching off a sizeable main corridor.

The Compact Arrow Echelon Plan revolutionised the design of asylums throughout Great Britain. It was also the most practicable, leading George Thomas Hine (1842-1916) to become one of the most recognised architects of the time. Hine's output included new county asylums for Worcestershire, Lincolnshire, Surrey, and many others. The Compact Arrow design kept the longer corridors of the broad arrow plan; however, the wards were moved closer, eliminating short connecting corridors. This design also gave the building a feeling of fresh air and sunlight, which was deemed necessary for the patients' mental health. The plan also allowed the staff to move about quickly through the conjoined buildings.

Perhaps one of the most infamous asylums featuring the echelon plan was Highroyds in West Yorkshire. The estate for the asylum was purchased in 1885 by the West Riding justices and was initially known as the West Ryder Pauper Lunatic Asylum. The hospital was intended to be primarily self-sufficient with its own surgical suite, library, pharmacy, bakery, butchery shop, and its own gardens. Patients were expected to earn their keep, working on the farm or in the various facilities of the hospital.

Today these buildings stand as important reminders of when medicine surrounding mental illness was in its elementary forms. They are breathtaking examples of architecture that moulded much of what the Victorian era insane asylum was.

Though he didn't contribute to the architecture of Britain's asylums, I feel I would be doing a disservice to the history of psychiatric medicine if I didn't mention Thomas Kirkbride. Kirkbride was the man behind the intriguing Kirkbride insane asylums that are spread all over the United States. The Philadelphia doctor had a great love for architecture and how it could be used to help cure those deemed insane. He was a devout Quaker who firmly believed that mental illness was a condition that could and should be treated. But he thought that should not be done by simply locking people away for the rest of their lives. Kirkbride was moved by England's moral treatment philosophy and believed that patients should be given adequate sleep, food, and exercise. After working for several years at the Friend's Asylum in Pennsylvania, he became superintendent of the Philadelphia Hospital for the Insane in 1840. Kirkbride envisioned a place where patients could be treated in a loving and structured environment. He had several designs in mind and began to document the things he learned along the way over the years.

Thomas Kirkbride's idea of the perfect asylum was very specific, especially in the shape of the building. His asylums were shaped with a V formation, similar to how a flock of birds would appear in the sky. Each side of the V consisted of two separate wards where patients were separated by gender and then further separated by condition. Kirkbride designed his buildings so that each pavilion would be set back from the previous, ensuring that there was maximum sunlight and ventilation. He wanted his buildings to be surrounded by nature so that whenever patients looked outdoors, they were greeted with beautiful greenery and a bright blue sky.

When Thomas Kirkbride's book, *On the Construction, Organization, and General Arrangements of Hospitals for the Insane With Some Remarks on Insanity and Its Treatment*, was released, the number of insane asylums throughout the United States grew significantly. Architects were given the foundation to build a fully operational, state-of-the-art insane asylum, and these buildings soon gained the name 'Kirkbrides'.

Like many asylums throughout the United Kingdom, Kirkbrides were built on grounds that stretched for acres. Most contained working farms, both dairy, vegetable, and livestock, along with bakeries, all of which provided some type of job to the inmates. While Mr Kirkbride felt that hard work was part of moral treatment, he also felt that patients should have their amusement too. Most of the asylums had bowling alleys, ballrooms, and baseball diamonds. The corridors and walls were usually painted in pastels, as they gave rooms throughout the hospital a calming atmosphere.

The General Lunatic Asylum of Nottingham, also known as Sneinton Asylum, would be the first to open after the County Asylum Act of 1808 was passed. The architects that built Sneinton studied the methods used by the Quakers at the York Retreat and Brislington House. It officially opened its doors in October of 1811, and the first patients, six paupers from St Mary's Parish, were fully admitted in February of 1812.

John Storer (1747-1837) was the leading figure in getting Sneinton built. He was one of Nottingham's most successful physicians and had long been interested in the welfare of the mentally ill. Sneinton also divided its patients into classes, those who could pay for themselves in full, those who could pay partly, and the paupers, who were generally funded by their local parish. The idea was built on the Quaker theory, where patients were treated with kindness and restraints and beatings were limited. More disruptive patients were placed in different blocks, and in some cases, padded rooms were used. The diet at Sneinton was one of a rather dull repetition, consisting of bread, meat, milk, cheese, and beer. Some patients were able to work in the gardens, which would provide them with extra food. The water supply and adequate piping system helped to prevent any significant epidemics. The Lunacy Commissioners who visited the facility regularly found it to be a clean and pleasant atmosphere for patients. Attendants were said to be keen on keeping the patients healthy. Nurses and attendants kept patient rooms clean and provided proper exercise and amusement.

Norfolk County Asylum, later known as St Andrew's Hospital, opened its doors in 1814. The asylum, also dedicated to housing pauper lunatics, was revolutionary for its time. Norfolk was the third hospital of its kind to open in response to the County Act of 1808. The county of Norfolk located an ideal site close to the village of Thorpe St Andrew. The asylum, which sat north of the River Yare, was opened to house 100 inmates. The building consisted of a series of two-storey wings for both male and female patients centred around a central administration block. The ward of the building was built on the corridor plan, and by the mid-1850s, further alterations would be needed. The ward block soon expanded with wings that jutted out. Because the farmland surrounding Norfolk was beneficial, a bridge used for patients to access the land was built in 1856. A laundry and water tower complex was added near the female wing, and a chapel was constructed south of the main building in 1860. Plans to relieve the ever-pressing problem of overcrowding that soon affected most of Britain's asylums, including developing an auxiliary building to house over 250 inmates, both male and female, were put in place. The central administration would soon manage cases including imbeciles, lunatics, and others who were not considered treatable. Most of the hospital's patients were allowed in the day rooms and outdoor courts for exercise. Those deemed capable of work could find themselves tending to the farmland or working in the laundry or kitchen areas. Norfolk County Asylum would continue to grow over the next eighty years before it was incorporated by the NHS in 1948 and would eventually shut its doors for good in 1998.

One of the more famous early English mental institutions was West Riding Pauper Lunatic Asylum at Wakefield, which opened in 1818. The magistracy of West Riding took dramatic steps to build the asylum after a meeting of the General Quarter Sessions of the West Riding in Leeds agreed to move forward. It was the first of four public asylums in the West Riding of Yorkshire and would later be known as Stanley Royd Hospital after being taken over by the NHS in 1948.

In March of 1815, twenty-five acres of land was purchased, and the design team got to work. When completed, the asylum stood on over twenty-five quiet and peaceful acres surrounded by plantations in Wakefield and Stanley. The hospital would play its role in bettering the treatment of the insane and, like the others of the time, it was meant to be a safe space for them. Like its sister hospital High Royds, West Riding was a self-sufficient hospital with its own gardens and farm land, dairy cows, bakery, and its own butcher. There was also a laundry service and outdoor picnic areas for patients to relax. The hospital was meant to house 150 patients. However, like many of Britain's asylums, it suffered from significant overcrowding, and by 1844, there were over 430 patients. By the 1860s it was home to more than 1,000 patients. West Riding acquired international attention as it was a true pioneer in treating the mentally ill. A visitor in 1832 described it as 'the best madhouse in Great Britain'.

Dr Charles Ellis (1780-1839), thirty-seven years old, was the first superintendent of the facility and was known to be a champion of humane treatment. Along with his wife, Mildred, the two would become instrumental in making their hospital the best place for pauper lunatics in West Riding.

In November of 1818, the hospital accepted its first group of patients; three men and four women. To be admitted to the asylum, the patients needed a reception order. A reception order was a certificate from His Majesty's Justice of the Peace that had the demands from the patient's doctor. The certificate usually stated that the patient was unfit for society and would greatly benefit from staying in one of Britain's asylums.

West Riding Pauper Lunatic Asylum has been known for the colourful tales surrounding its many patients. One of the first patients to appear in the hospital records was a Mr Thomas Arundel, thirty years old. Thomas suffered from depression caused by his outlandish views on religion. The original notes from Mr Arundel's stay state that he was doing well physically and was to be given a cold shower bath every other day. However, at the end of May 1819, Mr Arundel chopped the middle finger of his left hand off with a kitchen knife. Thomas stated that he did so to see if he had any blood in him. Slowly he became a violent and burdensome patient who attempted escapes and often had to be restrained. In November of that same year, Thomas escaped over the wall surrounding the airing courtyard and tried to stab the keepers with a rake. The following year, he ran again before being brought back to the hospital where he was noticeably more depressed and was prescribed a head washing with cold water three times a day.

In 1821, Elizabeth Coulson, just twenty-six years old, was admitted to West Riding for depression. Her diagnosis was that her mental condition was brought on by 'disappointment in marriage'.

Elizabeth's days at the asylum included warm and cold baths, and she also spent time in the spinning chair until she had emptied her stomach through vomiting. In May 1821, hospital notes on Elizabeth state that a regimen of warm baths would be given three times a week along with cold showers. Ms Coulson hated the baths and was known to beg the nurses to omit them as long as she promised to be more cheerful. By this point in her stay, her menstruations had ceased completely.

Ellen Foley was admitted to West Riding in 1861, at the age of twenty-two. Her case notes from her stay indicate that she suffered from 'excited manners-talking and laughing and wandering about the ward breaking the windows'.

In April 1821, thirty-seven-year-old Isabella Whiteley was admitted due to mania brought on by the death of her mother. Isabella would eventually be discharged but would return in June 1824 with another high state of mania. She was treated with opium, zinc sulphate, and other medications until her manner improved slowly. However, she was admitted again in June 1826 for more violent and maniacal behaviour. And twenty years later, in 1845, she was admitted yet again for violence and insanity. Sadly Isabella's pattern of mania would repeat itself until she passed away.

Perhaps one of the most notorious cases was that of William Buckley, who was admitted to West Riding in 1823. Mr Buckley had been locked up under the stairs by his own father for over ten years, causing him to slowly go insane. He was discovered by neighbours and admitted to the asylum. He had dementia and didn't know his name. In 1824, Mr Buckley suffered a fit in the middle of the night and was given porridge with brandy. However, he died the next day. Dr Ellis was moved by Mr Buckley's case, which caused him to push even further for prompt and appropriate care of the mentally ill. He said of Buckley's case:

> Cases of the most distressing nature are coming to light. The unhappy sufferers have been hidden from public view and permitted to remain without those help by which

alone their cure could be effected, nor is this charge to be made against the parochial officers only; indeed, during the present year, fewer cases of negligence have appeared to occur on their parts than in any former one. But to the disgrace of human nature, it must be stated that in some instances, the detention had been with the friends and relations of the patient. One man was discovered who had been confined for 11 years in a hole under the stairs, which was too low for him to stand and too short for him to lay straight. His limbs had become so contracted from their continued bent position as to make any other painful to him. It will scarcely be credited that his father was his keeper. This case alone is sufficient to show how many necessary it is that the unfortunate object who laboured under this most afflicting disease should be placed under the control of the magistracy of the county who will take care to provide whatever is proper for tier recovery and will withhold nothing that is necessary for the conform.

West Riding Asylum was later the site of many outbreaks of disease, many of them deadly. In 1849, an outbreak of cholera killed over 100 patients. In 1984, a bout of food poisoning from salmonella led to nineteen deaths, and over 400 patients and staff were seriously ill.

By 1817, issues of patient abuse and mistreatment raised in a select committee report led to further reform for the mentally ill through an Act of Parliament. The need for reform was also needed due to the fact that the nine functioning county asylums faced the growing problem of overcrowding. The County Asylums Act of 1828 was put in place not only to address any issues with the administrations of the asylums but also to address the issue of the slow development of county asylums throughout the country.

The act also required magistrates to send yearly records of patient admissions, discharges, and deaths and allow the Secretary of State to send a visitor to any county asylums. Counties were now allowed to borrow money to build or expand upon an asylum, and newly appointed commissioners could now license and supervise private asylums. The Act of 1828 also set in place the requirement that each asylum had a residential medical officer. Staying with the practice of moral therapy, it became the responsibility of this medical officer to justify the restraint of a patient.

By 1834, the cost of caring for the poor had grown considerably more expensive, and it was a tremendous tax burden on the middle and upper class. Suspicion began to grow that the people were simply paying for the poor to avoid work and be lazy. However, in that same year, a new Poor Law was introduced to lower the cost of caring for the country's poor. Parishes would now be grouped into unions, which had to build a workhouse if they didn't already have one established. Unfortunately, this forced the poor to receive help only if they left their homes to go to a workhouse.

The workhouse conditions were unforgiving and soon became notorious for its long working days, forced labour, and consistent abuse to the workers. The diet was less than desirable, and families were almost always split up into different parts of the building. Reports began to surface that people were being starved and were at the mercy of the masters and matrons who greatly abused the rules.

The workhouses not only contained the poor but the old, sick, orphans, and the insane. Because many of the workhouse inmates were disabled or mentally ill, the Poor Act led to more pressure to establish asylums. It is uncertain whether the deplorable conditions of workhouses may have led to or at least exasperated the symptoms of mental illness. It's hard to imagine how one could keep their wits about them while struggling to survive in Britain's workhouses. However, by the late 1830s, moral treatment was given more encouragement by discovering that even poor lunatics could be held without restraint.

Mental hospitals were put in place to keep the insane in custody; however, most keepers were little more than guards, and patients were still known to be held in restraints, including chains in some cases, though this was varied from one hospital to the other. Despite William Tuke's push for more humane conditions in Britain's asylums, there were still several justifications for using restraints during the early nineteenth century. Constraints kept patients from harming themselves or others. It wasn't uncommon to see patients strapped into their beds to prevent self-harm. In some cases, patients themselves asked to be restrained in the fear that they may not be able to control themselves. Securing a patient could also prevent them from lascivious actions. Violence was often used by keepers or attendants when dealing with an uncooperative patient, and introducing restraints seemed to increase the level of aggression in these cases.

Lancaster County Lunatic Asylum opened its doors in 1816, the fourth of the asylums under the 1808 act and the first in Lancashire. The first superintendent of the facility talked about the importance of moral treatments but still used a restraint system with patients. He was eventually asked to leave his position after refusing to give clothes to a patient in 1824. The following hospital administrators weren't much better as restraints were still being used. Hospital reports over the years showed evidence that numerous patients were being kept in handcuffs, leg irons, and straitjackets, and in some cases, being chained up. But despite this, along with the conditions of the hospital, such as patients not being adequately clothed and a defective ventilation system, county reports found the hospital to be satisfactory as restraints were accepted as a part of asylum management. Lancaster soon became overcrowded, leading to physical health and suffering, including a 1:6 ratio of patients coming down with cholera or some other highly contagious sickness.

In 1840, magistrates elected two new physicians to run Lancaster County Lunatic Asylum. Samuel Gaskell (1807-1866) and Edward de Vitre (1806-1878) brought about a remarkable change to the facility. While not much is known about Dr de Vitre, we know that Samuel Gaskell showed a preference for medicine at an early age and spent much of his time studying independently before beginning his medical training. After spending several years working at the Manchester Infirmary and Lunatic Asylum, he was appointed superintendent of Lancaster, where he was intent on humanitarian reform and the minimisation of restraints.

Both Gaskell and de Vitre hired new medical officers and instituted the removal of iron bars in 1842. With a newly emerging system of moral disciplines, patients were slowly being classified into groups. New rules were set for quieter patients, and they were to be kept from the noisier ones. Games were introduced, along with workshops and exercise. Reading was encouraged among the patients, and the staff was retrained to be considerate of the patients.

At Lincoln Asylum in Lincolnshire, a patient by the name of William Scrivinger was found dead in his room in 1829. Overnight, Mr Scrivinger had been strapped to his bed in a strait jacket causing him to die from strangulation. The death of Mr Scrivinger prompted authorities at the hospital to do away with any physical restraints. The decision by Lincoln Asylum was a significant influence in the future of asylum reform in the nineteenth century, along with a shift in the attitude of how patients were treated. Both Lincoln and Lancaster Asylums would be influential in the movement for yet further reform for the mentally ill.

It wasn't until the Lunacy Act of 1845 that mental health provisions changed significantly. Despite the County Asylums Act of 1828, growth was still relatively slow regarding the development of the asylums. The Lunacy Act of 1845 resulted from this slow process and was led by Anthony Ashley Cooper, 7th Earl of Shaftsbury (1801-1885), a politician, philanthropist, and social reformer. The act, made up of eleven commissioners, entrusted them with establishing and carrying out provisions, which included furthering the construction of asylums in every county. Regular inspections would become mandatory, along with house regulations and a qualified physician on the grounds. Every county was to make provisions for the mentally ill, and its legal members were now engaged in monitoring the nationwide asylum system.

The Lunatic Act of 1845 ensured that local authorities were required to make adequate provisions for pauper lunatics, and by the 1850s, most were in well-built asylums that were maintained at the public's expense. The expansion of the county asylum was the cause of a momentary conviction among reformers. They said the asylum could do more than house paupers; they could also cure them if treated kindly. By the 1840s only five county asylums abandoned restraints, but by 1854, most others fell in line, and the system was rapidly making headway.

The enactors of the 1808 County Asylum Act were hopeful that asylums would be built throughout the United Kingdom. But it had taken almost fifty years of several amendments for the dreams of the Quakers to be fulfilled.

Chapter Six

Women and Children in the Victorian Era Asylum

Historically, Western medicine has not been kind to women. Throughout the Middle Ages and the Renaissance, making it through childbirth was a perilous endeavour, and if you did survive, you prayed to God that you didn't die from a postpartum infection. Women also vastly outranked men among the levels of distressed people throughout the sixteenth century and beyond, with little to be done offering any relief. The rights of women, if any, were few and far between. Things didn't improve much throughout the Elizabethan Age, and it seemed that with the Victorian Age, they weren't about to change then either. Despite having another strong reigning woman as queen, the Victorian era women were not envied.

During Queen Victoria's reign, women still had few rights. They could not vote or own property if they were married, and any property a woman had was given over to her husband. Women, however, were able to fully participate in the workforce, and by the later years of the Victorian era, the women's suffrage movement was moving forward. Women were primarily seen as belonging to the stereotypical domestic lifestyle, where they were expected to provide a clean and proper household for both their husband and children. When a woman was married, her rights were automatically given to her husband, and he was in ultimate control of all the family's money and property. In addition to this, Victorian women themselves became their husband's property, and in turn, so did their bodies. Women were expected to be producers of offspring, participate in domestic labour, and consent to sexual intercourse whenever their husbands desired. This often led to a very dismal life as a married woman, as they were seen as servants whose sole job was to please her husband.

Single women could also be seen as failures as you didn't amount to much if you weren't married. Women who lived in the Victorian era were at a significant disadvantage both sexually and financially, where one's marriage became a sort of contract that was almost impossible to get out of. The Victorian woman certainly didn't have any rights regarding her health, physical or mental. They could easily have been put into an asylum for simply behaving in a way that the male-dominated society didn't agree with.

During the first half of the nineteenth century, evidence suggested that women were less susceptible to mental illness than men. But this would change drastically towards the second half of the century. The nineteenth century was a new era in mental illness as new diagnoses led to more admission. The rapid construction of large public asylums was now underway in England, allowing both men and women to be committed under one roof. And because a woman could be placed in an asylum for almost anything, county hospitals began to fill with women. And there are many arguments throughout history that state that more women than men were hospitalised.

An 1871 census stated that for every 1,000 male lunatics, there were 1,182 females, and for every 1,000 male paupers, there were 1,242 women. In March 1879, Middlesex's County Asylum at Hanwell in London housed 728 males compared to 1,098 females. Statistics also showed that females remained in asylums longer as they were often deemed incurable. At Hanwell Insane Asylum, also known as St Bernard's Hospital, and the Hanwell Pauper and Lunatic Asylum, men stayed an average of 3.7 years while women were there roughly six years. The sex ratio often determined the layout of the building as there were strict regulations involving segregation. When St Luke's Hospital for Lunatics was remodelled in the 1830s, they did so with the notion that there would be more women patients.

Most homes for the mentally ill that were run by women usually only admitted women. Licensed, privately run homes had more females because, until the 1840s, women were often the proprietors of them. It showed as these homes often held a décor that catered to females and would remind women of a lovely home, with fashionable bedrooms and pretty curtains.

The predominance of women being treated for mental illness first showed up among the pauper lunatics. Poor law administrators were reluctant to shell out a weekly dole to women left by their husbands or those that were widows. Wives of prisoners and mothers of illegitimate children fared no better when it came to relief. As Poor Law relief was decreasing, the asylum's need for help was increasing. Women faced with poverty and economic stressors were often recognised as mad as financial instability made women feel anxious and insecure. Social class and income were significant factors in one's care, and the increase in female patients called for the expansion of places to house them. Mothers of large families often suffered malnutrition. To save money, one might continue to nurse their children well past infancy. Many of the poorer women in asylums were senile, epileptic, or suffered mental retardation.

The Victorian Age was also not without its fair share of prostitution as it was a reasonably significant problem in Britain. A 'fallen woman' was one who disregarded the proper values of grace and virtue and could often be found held up in brothels or simply walking the busy city streets. They were considered a kind of social disease, and the ultimate goal was to have them removed until they could be cured. Placing them in asylums seemed the obvious solution.

Magdalene Asylums, which came to be in the mid-eighteenth century, were designed to house these so-called fallen women, whether they were prostitutes or unwed mothers. Magdalene Asylums were, in actuality, more of a laundry workhouse with gruelling conditions. Women were put to work in stifling heat and forbidden from speaking to anyone about their past and essentially expected to work in complete silence. There wasn't anything particularly rehabilitating about Britain's Magdalene houses at all.

Women who had contracted a sexually transmitted disease were often sent to Lock Hospitals, a hospital or wing specifically for those with venereal disease. Since the Middle Ages, syphilis was one of the most prevalent sexually transmitted diseases throughout Europe, and it continued into Victorian England. In a time before the discovery of penicillin, syphilis was quickly spread by sexual contact.

Today, the dramatic symptoms of syphilis seem to be a thing of the past, and perhaps it's not the first thing to come to mind when patients are diagnosed with acute or chronic psychiatric illness. Still, the end stages of the disease took a terrible toll on one's mental state. Conventional history tells us that the history of syphilis began with King Charles VIII of France during his invasion of Naples in the winter of 1495. The king's army consisted of men with little moral restraint who spent their free time enjoying the attention of women in brothels. Years earlier, Columbus's first voyage to the Americas had taken place, and it is believed that the disease was picked up in the New World and spread to the French soldiers during the invasion of Naples. As Charles and his soldiers returned home, the condition began to spread throughout Europe. First known as the great pox, syphilis was described as being 'so cruel, so distressing, so appalling that until now, nothing so horrifying, nothing more terrible or disgusting, has ever been known on this earth'.

Not only did syphilis cause pus-filled sores around the genitals and legs, along with extreme pain in the limbs, but it also produced psychosis in the later states. When left untreated, as before the discovery of penicillin, syphilis often caused mania, depression, and dementia in patients. After presenting as a sore on the genitals or mouth of the diseased, many experienced a rash on the torso that eventually spread over the entire body. Some people found themselves with muscle aches and flu-like symptoms. Syphilis can last in the body for years, and a small number of people without treatment will develop tertiary syphilis, which affects the nerves, the brain, eyes, blood vessels, joints, and the heart. The end stages of the disease caused people to wind up in the mental asylum. Paranoia, personality changes, loss of the ability to speak, mood swings, and dementia were signs that one had reached the latter and usually deadly stages of the disease. The disease was seen in just as many men, if not more, as it was in women. However, for the sake of explaining the Victorian woman and the asylum, I've focused more on the prevalence in women.

The story of Hannah Chaplin of London highlights the devastation of syphilis in its later stages. During the 1880s, teenage Hannah travelled to South Africa, where she may have worked as a prostitute and contracted syphilis. After becoming pregnant, Hannah returned home to an old boyfriend, Charlie, and they were married in 1884. She would deliver her second child, famed English actor Charlie Chaplin, five years later. But Hannah reverted to her old ways and left her husband for another man.

Hannah suffered for years with excruciating headaches, and in 1898, she had a complete nervous breakdown. She was diagnosed at Lambeth Infirmary. Hannah had developed the third stage of the disease and would have to endure the dreaded complications. She suffered from delusions, psychosis, and destructive behaviour. She stopped practicing proper grooming habits, and her speech began to suffer. Hannah was sent to Cane Hill Lunatic Asylum in Coulsdon, where she would eventually be released but was subsequently readmitted twice. Her hallucinations had become so terrible that she was often placed in a padded room to prevent self-harm. Her now successful actor son brought her to California to live with him in 1921. However, in 1929, she passed at the age of sixty-five after a long and miserable battle with a terrible mental illness.

Women who behaved aggressively, in defiance of their husbands or fathers, or those who were overtly sexual, were quite vulnerable to accusations of insanity. Female patients were often rowdy or restless and seen as more troublesome and abusive in nature. But men expected that women were quiet and immobile. Victorian society stressed female purity as a woman was a wife, mother, and keeper of the home. The home was looked at as a place of morality, and as caretakers of the home, women were more emotional and gentle by nature. Unfortunately, this view of women also led to the conclusion that they were more susceptible to having problems with their mental health.

Most nineteenth-century upper and middle-class women were entirely dependent on their husbands or fathers. Their role was depicted as a respectable wife or daughter who had very little control over her own independence. It was pretty typical for Victorian women to struggle when balancing all the things in their lives while constantly owning up to gender ideals. The routines of asylums were often designed to encourage behaviour according to Victorian stereotypes. Male patients were usually allowed to garden or work the farms while women were kept inside to do mundane chores such as cleaning and laundry.

Psychiatric textbooks from the Victorian era focused on analysing middle-class women and their disorders. The psychiatric symptoms of women were often interpreted according to their gender. It was believed that disorders of the uterus and the reproductive system were the cause of madness in most cases. Any expressions of unhappiness or low self-esteem were never viewed as a reflection of one's life. It was expressions of sexual desire, anger, or aggression that were seen as ghastly digressions from the average female personality. For these women and their families, the asylum was a convenient and socially acceptable solution. The asylum could offer a place for those suffering from disgraceful behaviour that may have been an embarrassment to the family. A woman was not simply viewed as being immoral if she was diagnosed with a recognisable medical condition. It was believed that a stay in the asylum would save the reputation of both the woman and her family.

The same was not said for lower-class women, often referred to as destitute, such as prostitutes who had betrayed their true womanhood by giving into sin. If left alone, women were believed to have been vulnerable to temptation and immorality. Asylums were looked at as a way to save these women from themselves and return them to society in an acceptable manner. Older women servants or caretakers for small children were often some of the largest groups of lunatics to be found in asylums. Social isolation of the ageing governess and their lack of support led to the need to be institutionalised.

It didn't help that nineteenth-century women were often portrayed as mad in literature. They were often depicted as people who had nerve disorders, suffering from constant fainting, agitation or hysteria. Many novels of the time expressed the unhappiness of married women and the trope of melancholy that was often used to explain the limitations Victorian women had.

Emily Dickinson, a reclusive American poet, has often been the topic of conversation regarding mental illness. Scholars have often wondered whether or not she herself suffered from mental illness or had a form of depression. Her mood swings were known to fluctuate with the seasons, as she made several references in her work to winter chills and 'heady' summers. A 2001 article in the *American Journal of Psychiatry* said that Emily may have had a type of manic depression known as Seasonal Affective Disorder. Ms Dickinson went through long periods when she was unable to write due to her depression. It was in the spring and summer that Emily produced most of her works as the bright sunlight filled her with vigour. However, in the darkness of winter, she was bound with sadness, describing the winter as a type of death.

Charlotte Brontë, an English novelist born in 1816, was a writer of classic English literature. It is thought that her clinical depression influenced the character Lucy Snowe in her novel *Villette*. Lucy shows clear signs of mental illness, including a breakdown. Perhaps Brontë saw Lucy as a culmination of her own fears, being a woman that could not escape her own tarnished self.

Emily Brontë, Charlotte's sister, the author of *Wuthering Heights*, was also suspected of mental illness due to family illness and stressors. In her book, Emily depicts the oppression of women from mentally unstable individuals.

Mary Braddon's 1862 novel, *Lady Audley's Secret*, plays extensively on Victorian-era anxieties regarding the domestication of women. While the home was supposed to represent safety and refuge, Braddon's protagonist turns to violence against her family. This was unsettling to readers because it didn't reflect the perfect lady of domestic happiness that the era called for.

It also wasn't unheard of for creative people themselves to be mentally ill and be sent to live in an asylum. Much like Mozart and Poe suffered from mental illness, lesser-known artists of the eighteenth and nineteenth centuries also suffered.

Musician and author Hersilie Rouy spent the latter portion of her life confined to a French asylum. Hersilie was a teacher and pianist in London and Paris who tutored highborn families. In September of 1845, while caring for her ill father in his Parisian home, she was taken against her will by a physician and placed in the Imperial House of Charenton.

Hersilie's father, Charles Rouy, was unfaithful to his first wife, the affair resulting in four illegitimate children. A half-brother, Claude Daniel Rouy, was Hersilie's only sibling considered legitimate. Claude was also the administrator of the Lariboisiere Hospital, from which the doctor who committed Hersilie came.

Hersilie was considered born of 'unknown parents' because her father was unfaithful, which was in defiance of the French Law of 30 June 1838, also known as the Law of the Insane. The Law of the Insane was declared during the reign of King Louis-Philippe and dealt with the asylums and care of the mentally ill.

Ms Rouy's situation left her utterly unaware of why she was removed from her father's home and wrote this of her experience of what was ultimately a kidnapping:

> I do not know by whom, or how, through the paths of which I have kept no memory, so much emotion invaded me when I heard the door close on me. And that I no longer

> needed all my energy to appear calm and to respond to this stranger, who, without having seen or questioned me, had my fate as he pleased. This state, moreover, lasted only the time of the journey. As soon as I stopped and found myself in a quarter closed on all sides, the feeling of my position came back to me; I was able to look around and see where I had been taken.

On the instructions of the admitting doctor, Ms Rouy is registered using her mother's surname, Chevalier, to protect the privacy of her half-brother, Claude Daniel. During her admission to Charenten Hospital, Hersilie was in dispute with Claude Daniel over inheritance rights. And because of his sister's confinement, Claude Daniel was able to take full possession of the inheritance.

Hersilie was examined once she was admitted and given the diagnosis of a monomaniac. She exhibited an obsessive enthusiasm for one particular thing; her 'self-importance', according to doctors. Her absence of marital sexual relations, fatigue, the practice of spiritualism, and disappointed ambition was among the other ailments added to her diagnosis. Asylum doctor, Louis-Florentin Calmeil, prescribed for Ms Rouy the popular treatments of water therapy.

> He prescribed me one hour bath, which is proof that he did not find me too crazy, the madness being measured by the length of the bath in these establishments.

Hersilie Rouy was adamant that she continued to use her proper surname. However, the more she used it in referring to herself, the more she was subjected to worsening treatment, consisting of hydrotherapy and isolation in a dark cell and targeted mistreatment. Ms Rouy continued to denounce her illogical confiscation and the deceitful ways of her half-brother. She spent a lot of time writing while she was locked away even though she was discouraged from doing so and often had her writing materials taken from her. But Hersilie used whatever scraps of paper she could find and sometimes used her own blood when she had no ink. It was these writings that would eventually become part of her personal memoirs.

Her agitation continued to worry the physicians at Charenton, and she was transferred to Salpetriere Hospital in 1854. It was at Salpetriere that Ms Rouy's diagnosis of mental illness would deepen. She was said to have suffered from madness of pride, and lucid madness, according to the head physician, Ulysee Trelat. After being unable to convince her that she was insane, doctors transferred Ms Rouy, and she was then sent from one hospital to the next.

Dr Edouard Le Normand des Varannes, the head physician at the last establishment Ms Rouy would stay at, decided to observe her personally for an extended period. He ultimately agreed that she suffered from no disorder whatsoever and saw no reason to keep her confined. However, in Victorian Europe, a woman's release from the asylum was not that simple.

After reports were sent to the Minister of Justice, it took five long years before Hersilie would be released in 1868. The Interior Minister took full ownership of the errors made regarding Ms Rouy, and the French press soon got word of what became known as the 'Rouy Affair'. It was of great interest to the press because it was very rare for women to be cured and released from an asylum in the 1800s.

After her release, Ms Rouy was renewed with a sense of vigour about her life and promised to dedicate the remainder of her time writing her memoirs, *Memoires d'une alienee*, and fighting for her compensation. Much of Ms Rouy's book details her imprisonment and the legal proceedings that followed her release.

Many feminist historians would later use Ms Rouy's book to point out the suffering many women endured at the hands of alienist medicine. Her book has also been used as a primary historical source of writing regarding the history of psychiatric care for women.

As with many women writers of the time, she expressed the unfairness of being a woman in a mans' word. The so-called aim of moral therapy was to gently convince the woman patient of their insanity and remodel them to fit a male-dominated society. But the asylum greatly oppressed women in the same way that society did. The writings of Hersilie Rouy are a fine testament to the strength of women in Victorian France.

It certainly wasn't difficult to label a woman insane during the nineteenth century, and Ms Rouy's case proves that. Any woman who didn't particularly feel inclined to obey her husband's word or to have a difference of opinion on social or religious matters was seen to be misbehaving. And it was not uncommon for a woman to be placed with the other 'deviants' in the asylum, where she could be cured or just out of the way. In both the United Kingdom and the United States, it was perfectly legal for a man to commit his wife without her say in the matter.

Another perfect example of an entirely sane woman being admitted to an asylum is the case of the American woman, Elizabeth Packard. Elizabeth, born in Western Massachusetts, was a well-educated and bright middle-class woman. In 1839, at just twenty-three years old, she married Calvinist minister Theophilus Packard at her parents' insistence. Theophilus was fourteen years older than Elizabeth and was said to be an unfriendly and authoritative person. However, the couple seemingly had an uneventful, peaceful marriage that would produce six children.

Because Elizabeth was a spirited and brilliant free thinker, she questioned her husband's religious beliefs, his thoughts on finances, children, and slavery. The couple had been married for several years where they now resided in Jacksonville, Illinois, where Elizabeth worked as a teacher.

The state of Illinois opened its first state mental hospital in 1851, and state legislature required a public hearing before any patient could be admitted, unless voluntarily. However, if a woman's husband felt that she needed to be committed, he could do so without any trial. Soon after the opening of the Jacksonville Insane Asylum, Elizabeth Packard's husband deemed her insane due to her excessive thinking and had her committed in 1860.

Elizabeth would spend three years being wrongfully imprisoned, and she refused to agree that she was insane. In 1863, doctors considered her incurable, and she was released. When she returned home, her husband locked her in the family's nursery and nailed the windows shut. Through the help of a friend, she was able to deliver a letter to a judge who issued an order to Theophilus to bring not only himself but Elizabeth, to his chambers. The judge then moved the case of her sanity to trial. It would take the jury only seven minutes to rule in her favour and find her entirely sane.

When Mrs Packard returned home, she discovered that her husband had sold all of her goods and took all of her money and notes, as well as her six children, and left the state of Illinois. Because married women had no recourse, her appeals to the Supreme Courts of Illinois and Massachusetts were denied. Elizabeth would not go down without a fight and spent the next several decades campaigning all over the United States for women's rights as well as calling out the injustices of the American insane asylum. She once again petitioned the legal courts of Illinois and Massachusetts, and in 1869, legislation to allow married women the same rights to property and children was passed. It was then that Elizabeth's children were allowed to return to their loving mother.

Elizabeth Packard would go on to found the Anti-Insane Asylum Society and write several books regarding her beliefs. However, due to the thought process of the time, she was widely criticised by medical professionals for her work. It wouldn't be until 1930 that she would gain the appreciation she deserved.

What exactly were the reasons behind the high admittance rate of women to asylums in the nineteenth century, and what were some of the treatments they could expect? We've already looked into the confinement of women due to 'domestic problems'. Insanity from domestic troubles was always an easy excuse for a husband to admit his wife to an asylum. Perhaps it may have been for the husband to take a break from the marriage or to teach an opinionated wife a lesson.

Nathan Bailey, an English philologist and lexicographer who died in 1742, wrote in his *Dictionarium Britannicum* (Dictionary of the English Language) in 1736 said that madness in women was rooted in the womb. The wandering womb theory of the ancient Greeks was still seen as a principal diagnosis for women.

> the fury of the womb, a species of madness peculiar to woman, exciting them to a vehement desire of venery, and rendering them insatiate therewith

Victorian era women were often diagnosed as having hysteria. Hysteria was seen as having eccentric, nervous, or erratic behaviour, sexual desire, insomnia, or irritability. Physicians thought that stress felt in the life of a typical female could cause them to be nervous and develop faulty reproductive organs. Psychiatric caregivers during the 1800s were obsessed with the notion of female hysteria, a condition that fell under the umbrella of the female nervous system. Female hysteria, recognised for over one thousand years, was the assumed result of improper sexual health. Improper sexual health could have been several things, from being a virgin for too long to having fits and anxiety. The asylum offered a socially acceptable excuse for unruly and potentially scandalous behaviour. It seemed the diagnosis of hysteria was a way to repair the reputation of women who may have been thought of as immoral or ill-behaved.

French neurologist, Jean-Martin Charcot (1825-1893), is looked at as one of the world's pioneers in neurology. He is also wildly regarded for his work on hysteria. He first began studying hysteria after creating a psychiatric ward for females with 'hystero-epilepsy'.

He believed that hysteria in women could either be minor or major. Charcot viewed the condition of one that could be caused by trauma and would photograph women amid their hysterical fits to use as teaching material at the La Salpetriere Asylum for the Insane. Hysteria was based on a long list of complaints, including insomnia, headache, forgetfulness, excessive vaginal bleeding, sweating, anxiety, swollen feet, and other fairly common complaints among women.

There was a tremendous amount of anguish caused by women's gynaecological disorders, conflicts with family and neighbours, as well as problems in their marriage. Thomas Wright, a seventeenth-century English writer, said:

> the emotionality of women to their unableness to resist adversities or any other injury offered and this explanation for their inclination to mercy and pity is also the best explanation for vulnerability to anxiety and gloom.

The 'emotionality of women,' no doubt, wasn't helped by the fact that they were almost always at someone else's beck and call. The housewives of the Victorian era were expected to spend much of their time in the home. A woman of that time pleased God when she loved her husband, had his children, and brought them up. And most certainly, if a child died, which was very common, there would be a tremendous amount of grief to be had. And although folks were cautioned against excessive mourning, a source of such profound distress, like losing a child, could only increase emotional disturbances. Along with this, the psychiatrists of the Victorian era also believed that depression over death should only last a certain amount of time. Anything considered excessive would get you committed.

Treatments for hysteria were usually bizarre and sometimes painful. Charcot used a device called an 'ovary compressor', where pressure was applied to the patient's abdomen in the hopes that a hysterical episode may occur. Physicians during the late 1800s and early

1900s also administered pelvic massages for women using clitoral stimulation for the treatment of hysteria. The use of early electronic vibrators would eventually bring women to a state of orgasm, and it wasn't considered erotic or distasteful. Physicians firmly believed that clitoral stimulation was purely medical and that only vaginal penetration was sexually stimulating for women. If a woman's face became flushed during a pelvic massage and she experienced release, that meant the treatment had been successful and would soon rid the woman of her hysteria.

Before the use of medical vibrators, water therapy was used. Hydrotherapy spas were located in bathhouses in the mid-1800s, and treatment involved pointing a powerful jet of water at a woman's thighs and genital region. According to the health specialists, women felt extreme relief from hysteria and felt like they had had a few drinks.

Doctors attributed the high rates of hysteria to the behaviours of women who were intellectual and maybe attending school or working outside the home. In 1869, the first patented medical vibrator was devised, and physicians used the device to replace their laborious task of manual clitoral stimulation.

American physician George Taylor introduced the 1869 Manipulator, a device where patients sat on a padded table with a hole cut to expose their lower stomach. A vibrating sphere then massaged the woman's genitals. Because the devices were cumbersome and expensive, physicians often used the device out of their homes for their patients.

In the 1880s, the first portable battery-powered vibrator was invented by physician Mortimer Granville, though he insisted the device was for treating only male muscle fatigue. He believed that women might mimic the symptoms of hysteria to gain access to an easy orgasm.

Another problem with women acting in a non-feminine manner was masturbation, or what was called 'self-abuse'. Masturbation was considered a deviant act and could quickly get you committed as it was a sure sign of one's insanity. Masturbation could also be used to accuse a woman of having too much sexual desire. During Victorian England, nymphomania was considered a dangerous ailment that immediately needed to be cured in the asylum. The very meaning of the word nymphomania speaks of a woman with uncontrollable sexual desires, one who is sexually aggressive and both scares and arouses men. In the nineteenth century, a diagnosis of nymphomania was based on a woman's behaviour. Both European and American medical journals describe it as not only a disease but a symptom and a cause. Medical reports speak of women who would insert strange objects into their vaginas or have an orgasm from simply looking at a man.

German psychiatrist Richard Freiherr von Krafft-Ebing recognised nymphomania in the case of a mother who desired her own son. Other doctors saw the disorder as one that only affected young women with blonde hair, while others were convinced it was a disease of widows or virgins. In any event, it was very easy to classify any woman who deviated from the social norm as being diseased. Middle-class Victorian women were expected to be sexually passive. Any woman deemed 'out of control' was quickly classified as a nymphomaniac.

While uterine fury was often linked to women's madness during medieval times and through the Renaissance, less attention was paid to that in the nineteenth century. Doctors were convinced that there was a link between the brain and the genitals, explaining why hysteria and nymphomania were prevalent diagnoses. Disorders in menstruation or problems with the ovaries could lead to an injury of the nervous system and almost always, at least in the nineteenth century, mental illness.

Doctors and gynaecologists of the time were still very unfamiliar with the complexity of female disorders. They felt that they needed to have a particular sign or symptom to diagnose nymphomania properly. Any itching or redness of the genitals, an enlarged and malformed clitoris, or labia was noted to indicate nymphomania.

The usual mental illness treatments, moral therapy, cold baths, purging, and diet proved ineffective in curing a woman of nymphomania or hysteria. And because doctors often lay carpet blame on a woman's sexual organs for all her disorders, there had to be a way to stop all this madness. Because some believed that menstruation was connected to nymphomania, the consideration of removing the ovaries was on the shelf. Towards the end of the century, it was said that removing ovaries in such large numbers was done simply to make money. Critics agreed that disorders might have been made up so that surgeons could set a price for their cure. In the eyes of many, the procedure was fashionable for the times and was no different from spaying or unsexing an animal.

One of the most brutal methods of treating hysteria or nymphomania in women was the removal of the clitoris or labia. Beginning in the 1860s, the clitoridectomy was becoming an acceptable treatment of mental illness and a threat for women exhibiting unruly behaviour.

Dr Isaac Baker Brown, born in 1812, was a well-known nineteenth-century gynaecologist, surgeon, and respectable member of London's medical establishment. In 1845, Baker Brown was one of the founders of St Mary's Hospital in London, and in 1848, he became a member of the College of Surgeons. He began developing new ways to treat ovarian tumours and cysts. Dr Baker Brown founded the London Surgical Home for Women in 1848, where he studied advancing surgical procedures. Some of Baker Brown's operations are still used today, such as the cystostomy. He was also the pioneer of the barbaric procedure known as clitorectomy. His book, published in 1861, *On Surgical Diseases of Women*, included his interpretation of the condition, 'hypertrophy and irritation of the clitoris'. This condition was nothing more than masturbation and was also referred to as the 'peripheral excitement of the pubic nerve'. Baker Brown felt that this could significantly affect a woman's nervous system and possibly lead to sterility. He also felt that masturbation was the cause of epilepsy and mania and felt that something needed to be done; the surgical removal of all or part of a woman's clitoris.

Baker Brown believed that the symptoms of female insanity began at puberty. He said girls became 'restless and excited and indifferent to the social influences of domestic life'.

He practised the procedure on girls with a whole host of problems, ranging from digestive disorders to disobedience to simply not being polite enough. He operated on children as young as ten years old, and he urged the procedure for women seeking a divorce. Baker Brown insisted that his approach was 'humane and effectual' and a proven answer to mania, hysteria, and nymphomania.

Baker Brown's fifty-five-bed private clinic was filled with patients from all walks of life. During his career, he went beyond the clitoridectomy to the removal of the labia as well. In his treatise, *On the Curability of Certain Forms of Insanity, Epilepsy, Catalepsy, and Hysteria in Females*, he believed in a 70% rate of curability using this treatment. He said he had a patient who would attack her husband like a wild animal, but she became a proper and respectful wife after the procedure. A supporter of Baker Brown wrote that he knew of a young idiot woman who could study her Bible and obtain a job after the operation. The matter of consent for the procedure did not fall on the women themselves but their husbands or father. Though Baker Brown stated that he often didn't need the husband's permission because it was the wife who begged him to perform the procedure.

Dr Baker Brown began to receive negative feedback in 1866 from the medical community. Several doctors greatly opposed the use of female mutilation, and they questioned the authenticity of his procedure. It was suggested that while he treated women of unsound mind, the surgical home in which he practised was not licensed for his operation under the Lunacy Act of 1845. He was also accused of performing these surgeries without the consent of his patient or their families. He was eventually expelled from the Obstetrical Society of London. His clinic was closed, and he found himself bankrupt until he passed in 1873. Baker Brown's clitoridectomy was no longer considered an acceptable form of treatment in the United Kingdom.

Still, some major medical congresses praised the so-called effectiveness of gynaecological surgery on women to cure mental disorders. One particular doctor stated that 75% of women seen in mental hospitals suffered from some kind of pelvic malady. According to Victorian doctors, the female life cycle was the key reason that morbid emotions would appear in patients, often dooming them from the start. Scottish physician Thomas Clouston said:

> The risks to the mental functions of the brain from the exhausting calls of menstruation, maternity, and lactation, from the nervous reflex influences of ovulation, conception, and parturition, are often enormous if there is much original predisposition to derangement and the normally profound influences on all the brain functions of the great eras of puberty and the climacteric period are too apt, in these circumstances, to upset the brain stability.

What Victorian doctors called a 'predisposition to derangement' was seen more in women. It was believed that beginning in puberty, girls were already doomed. Late or irregular periods were seen as dangerous conditions. Female adolescence was seen as a state of miniature insanity where girls were plagued with worry, fear, deceit, and a desire for mischief. Edward Tilt, an English physician, and writer said:

> menstruation itself was so disrupting to the female brain that it should be put off as long as possible, and he advised mothers to prevent menarche by ensuring that their teenage daughters remain in the nursery, take

Above: Image of Bedlam

Right: Richard Napier

Robert Burton's Book

Right: David Hume

Below: York Retreat

Claybury Hospital

Above: Hysteria

Right: Child in the Asylum

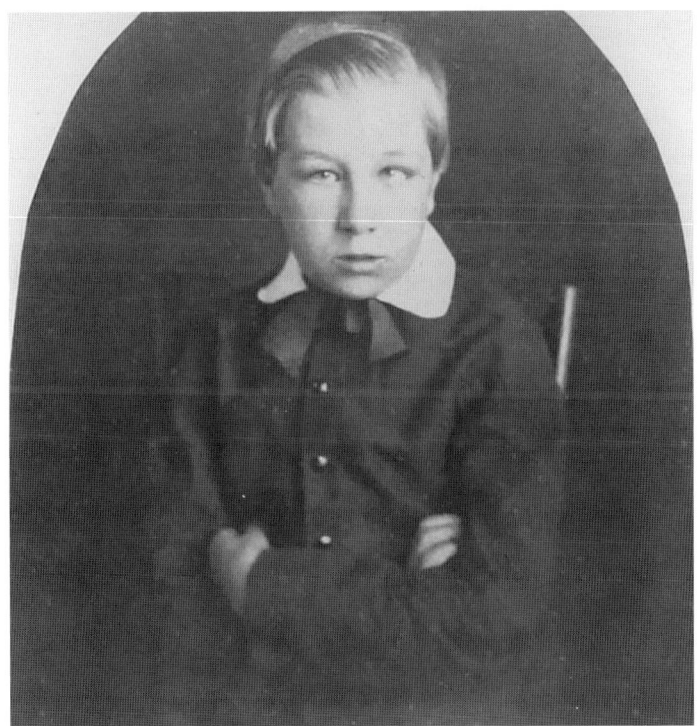

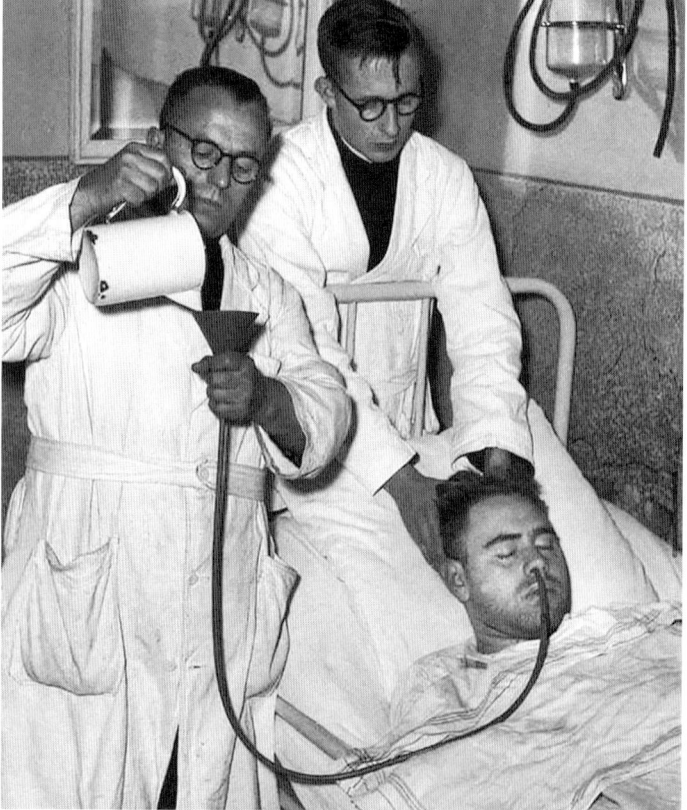

Above: Sewing Room in a Victorian Asylum

Left: Insulin Therapy

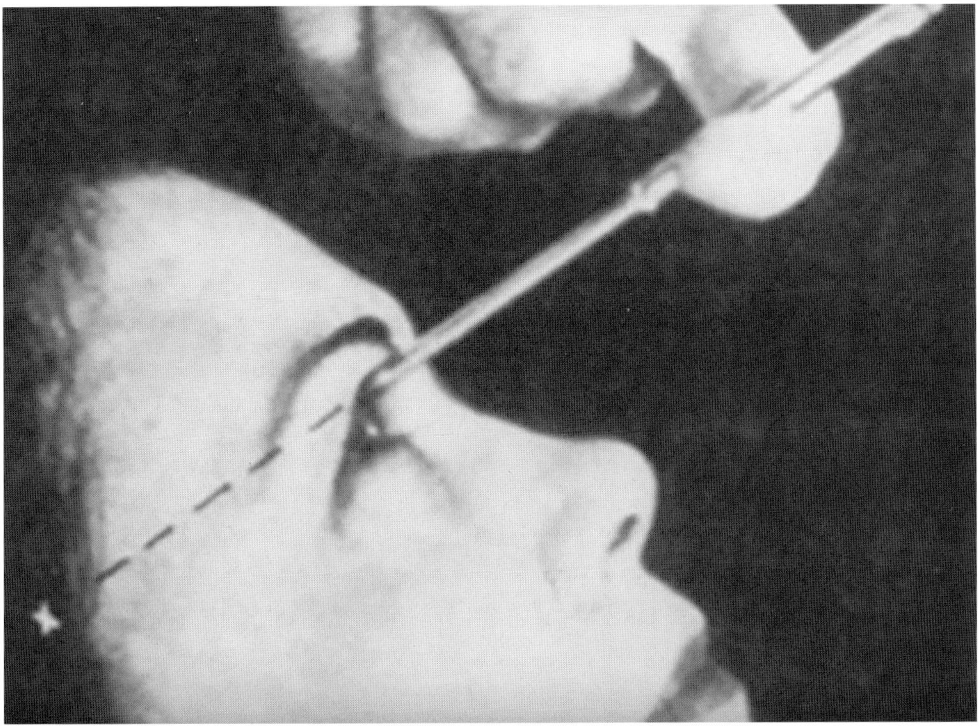

Lobotomy

Aktion T4 Children

Closure of the Asylums

cold baths, avoid featherbeds and novels, eat low-protein diets, and wear drawers. This nursery regime was the principal cause of the pre-eminence of English women, in the vigour of constitution, soundness of judgment, and rectitude of moral principle.

The shaming of the menstrual cycle in women is nothing new. Roman philosopher, Pliny the Elder, spoke of the dangers of menstrual blood in his treatise, *Natural History*, written in 79 AD.

Contact with it turns new wine sour, crops touched by it become barren, grafts die, seeds in gardens are dried up, the fruit of trees falls off, the edge of steel and the gleam of ivory are dulled, hives of bees die, even bronze and iron are at once seized by rust, and a horrible smell fills the air; to taste it drives dogs mad and infects their bites with an incurable poison. Even that very tiny creature, the ant, is said to be sensitive to it and throws away grains of corn that taste of it and do not touch them again.

Victorian physicians had yet to understand menstruation, despite some of the medical advances of the time. It was still believed that menstruation was a disease, and a dangerous one at that, and could easily lead to madness. Dr William Rowley of Oxford University, wrote of menstruation that 'The tongue falters, trembles and incoherent things are spoken; the voice changes; some roar, scream or shriek immoderately; others sign deeply, weep or moan plaintively'.

Women who suffered from heavy menstrual periods were considered dangerous, and the standard treatment was purging and being drugged with opiates. It was claimed that attacks of hysteria would occur after a menstrual flow and that the madness that came from menstruation was one of violence and savagery. Women were believed to be unstable, and the majority of treatments included sedation of some sort. And yet, at the same time, any kind of suppression of menstruation could also have one committed.

Puerperal insanity, which today would probably be known as some form of postpartum depression, accounted for about 10% of women who were admitted to the asylum in the nineteenth century. A postpartum patient who would physically or verbally harm either herself or others, sometimes resulting in suicide or infanticide, was one who suffered from puerperal insanity.

Childbirth was still believed to be linked in some way to insanity and mania. Medical text regarding puerperal insanity first appeared around the 1820s, and it was highlighted as something doctors needed to familiarise themselves with.

There are several reasons why there seemed to be an excess of cases in nineteenth-century asylums. Perhaps the difficulty of dealing with a new baby at home put not only stress on the mother but the father as well. Sending your manic wife to spend some time in the asylum after childbirth was probably a convenient out for many new fathers. Even though symptoms of puerperal insanity didn't always appear immediately following delivery, it was often used as a timely diagnosis for psychiatrists in new mothers.

From a clinical standpoint, the disease started in the first or second week postpartum, where women were said to become highly excitable and irritable. They presented with a furious madness and were often violent and difficult to control. Many also had insomnia and refused to eat. Patients of all walks of life, even highborn women, were documented as soiling their bed or destroying their bedsheets.

Some women may have been genuinely sick due to infection and delirium from high fever. In Edinburgh, 1873, following delivery, a patient at a maternity home became maniacal with a dangerous temperature of 103 degrees. The patient was said to have tried to jump out a hospital window and had to be restrained for her own safety. Sadly she died days later from what was described physically as an infection in the peritoneal cavity as determined by postmortem examination. But because she presented with mania as well, puerperal insanity was listed on her death record. Between 1886 and 1888, between 10-20% of women admitted to insane asylums throughout the United Kingdom were given a diagnosis of puerperal insanity. Physicians, as well as the family of the committed, found puerperal insanity to be a devastating disease as it was heartbreaking to see a new mother so mentally sick. The maternal mortality rate was still relatively high, with most deaths being from haemorrhaging or mia, a type of dangerously high blood pressure during pregnancy that could result in death if not treated. However, between 1-3% of postpartum deaths during the nineteenth century were listed as puerperal insanity. When death did occur with puerperal insanity, the patient usually presented with a high fever and rapid pulse, which tells us it's possible that the woman suffered from some comorbidity, such as typhoid or pneumonia.

But not all maternal deaths from puerperal insanity could be linked to something organic. In 1855, a twenty-three-year-old patient was admitted to Warwick County Asylum with a diagnosis of puerperal mania. The patient presented with a rapid pulse, talking endlessly, shouting, and overcome with restlessness. She passed after a few days, and there was nothing to suggest a physical cause to her untimely death.

England's own queen, Victoria, was said to have taken a dislike to pregnancy. Throughout her reign, she gave birth to nine children in the span of six years, and she was furious upon finding herself pregnant just weeks after her marriage to Prince Albert.

> It is spoiling my happiness; I have always hated the idea, and I prayed God night and day for me to be left free for at least six months, but my prayers have not been answered, and I am really most unhappy. I cannot understand how one can wish for such a thing, especially at the beginning of a marriage.

Victoria also said that if she delivered a 'nasty girl' she would drown it. After giving birth to a daughter, that she thankfully did not harm, Queen Victoria found herself pregnant again. She wept at the thought and suffered from terrible depression and headaches. She was delighted to have given birth to a male heir, but felt no joy at holding her baby. She suffered terribly from postpartum depression for nearly a year. She spoke of weakness and insomnia, and hallucinations. Prince Albert was so concerned that he told her doctor he feared that she was losing her mind.

She gave birth to a third and then a fourth child after a long and brutal labour. Her fifth and sixth children were soon born, and the sixth left her again weeping and miserable after a difficult delivery. After a seventh child and then an eighth, she suffered again from postpartum depression, and she and her husband began to fight violently to the point where he was often unable to calm her down.

Her ninth child was born on 14 April 1857, and by this time, Prince Albert had quite tired of Victoria's constant sad state surrounding the birth of their children. In a letter, he wrote to her:

> I, like everyone else in the house, make the most ample allowance for your state. We cannot, unhappily, bear your bodily sufferings for you. You must struggle with them alone. The moral ones are probably caused by them, but if you were rather less occupied with yourself and your feelings and took more interest in the outside world, you would find that the greatest help of all.

While Albert failed to understand that surge of hormones surrounding childbirth, he also felt that his wife no longer lacked reason. However, Victoria understood that her feelings of mania would come and go and that they bothered her most during pregnancy. We can assume that she had the best of care and the most prestigious royal physicians to tend to her, but that didn't excuse her from suffering from something so prevalent. If Victoria were not Queen of England, there is an excellent chance she would have ended up in the asylum as well.

With puerperal insanity often came infanticide being the result of 'a woman distracted by her wits who wanted to kill her children'.

The notion of infanticide has a history that goes back long before nineteenth-century England. The seventeenth-century mindset was that the mere thought of infanticide had to be caused by the devil or witchcraft. While seventeenth-century infanticide was clearly a product of a severe mental illness, it was also a product of the economic and social circumstances of the time. The terrible choice to murder your own newborn was not unheard of, especially in unmarried women. Many who did take the lives of their babies were servants who found themselves in a terrible predicament once the pregnancy was obvious. The economic and domestic situations of seventeenth-century servants made servants most likely to have children they could not support. Babies, whose deaths were caused by their mothers, were often victims of the mother having no economic plan in place. It was socially impossible for many young, pregnant women to imagine themselves as a mother. The mother of an illegitimate child often gave birth in secret, as it was a shameful situation to be in. To conceal the result of the pregnancy, a baby, stillborn or not, could easily have been buried or tossed in a river. However, most mothers who were accused of infanticide would never confess to actually killing their child. While seventeenth-century women weren't the usual suspects for violence and homicide, they were for the death of a child. And this often led to accusations, whether true or not, of infanticide. A young mother, by the name of Sarah, when accused of murdering her child, began to 'curse and swear and said they were all lying whores and thieves' when speaking of those who accused her.

This was a troublesome and distorted bounty between a mother and child, and it was considered a crime to neglect one's child. Primarily when the neglect resulted in death. Hiding and denying a pregnancy or birth can be explained partly by the medical term 'dissociative reaction', meaning that a woman is mentally unable to acknowledge either her pregnancy or the delivery of her child. It wasn't uncommon for a woman to give birth in a privy and leave the baby as if it were waste and not a child. These women who suffered from a dissociative reaction seemed unable to recognise that anything had ever happened. This denial of pregnancy or birth was sometimes seen as a sign that the young mother didn't have her wits about her. Women in their right minds who kept their pregnancies or births a secret would be unable to simply abandon or conceal a dead child. Disposing of a child's body posed a deeply emotional disturbance that was unfortunately not that rare of an occurrence.

Into the 1800s, many children were still sadly not wanted, and infanticide was still a common occurrence, and often with women who suffered mentally. Early statistics from 1838-1840 showed that seventy-six children were victims of infanticide. Children were often beaten, smothered, given large quantities of opium-based drugs, left for dead through deliberate neglect, starved, not given medical attention, or not so accidentally dropped.

The end of women's reproductive life was almost as bad as the start of it. In psychiatric literature, menopausal women were harshly discussed and ridiculed. One such doctor put it as:

> the death of the reproductive faculty is accompanied by struggles which implicate every organ and every function of the body.

Husbands of menopausal women were advised to withhold any sexual stimuli. Treatments for menopause consisted of injecting iced water into the rectum or the vagina as well as placing leeches on the labia or cervix. It was believed that menopause would cause an electric shock to the brain, and those harsh treatments were needed to stop it. Because public institutions faced intense scrutiny from the public, hospital administrators felt the need to be open-minded and innovative in their treatments, especially when they involved women. But sadly this often led to controversial and dangerous procedures being carried out on women.

In mixed asylums, sexes were kept separate, with everything from different eating areas to different morgues, but that didn't mean they were equal. Dietary allowances were lower for women, and women were watched more than male patients. Female patients had their mail gone through and needed more protection from staff as there was always the fear of pregnancy. Religious excitement or religious deviance was another common reason women were committed to the asylum. The meetings of small church groups or reading too much on religion were believed to cause mass hysteria. Sadly many cases of judgement on religious excitement were made by the patient's family, and the admitting doctor's simply followed suit. It was often used as a way to punish women who were elite thinkers. Religious insanity flourished in a world where medicine was basically unregulated. If religious excitement caused a breakdown, then surely the calming environment of the nineteenth-century asylum would offer the best way to restore one's sanity. Society just did not accept the idea that women could have different beliefs regarding religion, or God and doctors certainly wouldn't entertain the idea that there may be other points of view when it came to Christianity.

By the end of the nineteenth century, doctors unfortunately still thought that women were physically flawed and emotionally masochistic beings. But as Britain moved into the twentieth century, there was a small ray of hope that women and men would be treated equally.

It's hard enough to imagine what women went through in the asylum but harder still to think that children were not exempt from the authorities that ruled them. During the Victorian era, children were admitted to the asylum for much the same reason they might be permitted today. They were often unable to be managed by their parents or the community, and these problematic behaviours were the primary cause of admission.

Before the Mental Deficiency Act of 1913, most young children identified as idiots or imbeciles had minimal experience in institutional care. The 1913 Act was pivotal to the treatment of the feeble-minded as it proposed an institutional separation so that those working in workhouses could expect some other alternative. There are instances where children were described as being idiots after several years of quite normal development. One of the first children admitted to Devon Asylum in Exminster was a six-year-old girl registered as idiotic even though her insanity was only noted in the previous ten months.

It could just as easily have been disruption of the family's household when a decision from authorities came to remove the child and perhaps place them in the asylum. The incapacity of parents to control their deviant children was a fairly common reason for action. One child, John William, had been confined to his room alone for the better portion of his life. Nine-year-old Ethel Pile was chained up by her father to control her destructive habits. Another boy, John L, was so disposed, according to his mother, that she felt she needed to tie him up like a dog. The unwanted public behaviour of a child could also draw attention to the family and bring shame to the household. One child, John Z, was sent to Devon because he had a habit of wandering from home and often wound up in terrible conditions. Adolescent children were usually identified for their violence towards other children in the community. They were a common nuisance to the public, and the asylum was seen as the best place for them.

Children not only came from homes and other institutions but from the workhouses and sometimes, from prisons. Children who were sent to the county asylums from workhouses were usually portrayed as a threat to the running of the workhouse from where they came. Many children under Poor Law care were described as deficient but weren't eligible for the asylum. The county asylums offered custody for only a small number of children known as idiots or imbeciles. This poses the question of why some children wound up in the asylum over others. The vagueness and inconsistency surrounding children in the asylum are attributed partly to the tension with the state's provision for the treatment of lunacy in society. Any child sent to the asylum first had to qualify as a pauper lunatic. This depended on the workhouse staff or family proving that there was a desperate need to have the child committed. These children may have been violent and disruptive in behaviour, including being noisy at night while others were trying to sleep, not being adequately toileted, and other filthy habits. One boy was removed from a workhouse for tormenting and stealing from the pockets of elderly men.

About one-quarter of child admissions were workhouse residents. In some cases, many of these children were examined by the poorhouse physician and had been housed in the poorhouse for some time. Several children were orphans whose parents may have died, and there were no relatives to take care of them. Often the medical officer would have suggested that the orphan be placed with a careful, quiet person before being admitted. Still, if this failed to happen, children could easily be sent to the asylum.

The majority of children were admitted to the asylum because of epilepsy, some form of mania, and being an imbecile or idiot. Puberty and gender weren't usually linked in any way to diagnosis, even though some individuals were considered to be suffering considerably during pubescent changes. More respectable physicians seemed to be reluctant to isolate a case of lunacy as it was often attributed to a physical illness, such as blood poisoning, typhus or scarlet fever, and childhood accidents contributing to the child's condition. More than half of the children admitted had some form of epilepsy recorded on their intake. However, epilepsy could be a wide range of symptoms. Most terms used to classify adults, such as mania and melancholia, were rarely found on the intake forms of children—more certifications of admitted children were taken by physicians who had very little understanding of psychiatry.

There was also no age limit on the admission of children to the asylum. The notice of child-specific psychiatry did not exist, and it would be several decades before the concept unfolded. There are public records of pediatric patients hospitalised at Devon County Asylum between 1845-1915, and the children range from as young as eight years old to age sixteen. Very few young children were sent to the asylums, and there was a clear majority of boys over girls when it came to admissions. This seemed to be a trend, especially around the 1890s, as adolescent males were the largest group entering the asylums. As for girls, it was usually girls who were approaching puberty who figured more prominently.

Unlike women, the process was usually a more extensive series of meetings between the child's family and the asylum. These meetings reflected the weight of the family as much as the physician attending the child.

On 27 May 1896, eight-year-old Frank Jones was brought from the Barton Regis Workhouse to the asylum as a congenital idiot who suffered epilepsy. Because of his aggressive nature, the workhouse could not keep him under control. While in the asylum, Frank often bit those who came close to him and threw powerful fits around feeding time. He passed away in 1905 at the young age of seventeen.

At the age of ten, Frank Wyatt was admitted to Devon County and then released in 1877. However, he was readmitted in 1880. He presented with several behavioural problems, some quite severe. In the summer of 1883, he put his head through two panes of glass. Over the years, he also chewed his clothing to pieces and tore his bed apart, along with many other incidents that caused him to be monitored by staff at all times. Frank was given a regular schedule of sedatives, such as hyoscine, to calm his behaviour.

The rate of admitted children increased considerably with age, as did their chances of recovery. In 1896, Elizabeth Nelmes, sixteen years old, was admitted to the asylum with a diagnosis of mania. She was described as volatile and incoherent. Elizabeth presented weighing only ninety-one pounds and refused any food. It's entirely possible that she suffered from a form of eating disorder, much like we see in young people today. When people are severely malnourished, they suffer from brain fatigue and cannot make decisions. Elizabeth was force-fed with a gastric tube over several weeks, and as her weight increased, she was eventually discharged.

Alice Collins may have also suffered from some kind of eating disorder. She was admitted to the asylum at age sixteen in 1893 for refusing to eat and stated she wanted to be in a coffin. Alice gradually improved over the next few months, gaining over ten pounds and growing one and a half inches in height.

At sixteen years old, Eliza Hill was admitted to Devon County Asylum after suffering from epilepsy since the age of ten. Aside from epilepsy, she was almost completely blind, with poor hearing and very little sense of smell. Ms Hill spent nine miserable years in the asylum and eventually died at the age of twenty-five after a series of terrible fits.

It seems as though most children admitted to the asylum didn't fare well on the other end. Many were kept for decades and never discharged, while some died as a result of institutional care. Whether they were women, children, or male patients, life in the asylum was a reasonably controlled undertaking, and you were expected to follow the rules regardless of your background.

Chapter Seven

Life in a Nineteenth and Twentieth Century Asylum. Daily Living, Patient Abuse, and Those That Pushed for Reform

When one hears the word insane asylum, a particular image may be conjured up. One may imagine an ominous, impressive-sized building with several vast wings spread out over acres of land. Long hallways that echo the sound of nurses' shoes may come to mind. Perhaps one may envision an airing court where patients roam about under the watchful eye of hospital guards. Preconceived notions of the asylum may be imagined as drugged-out patients shuffling throughout the building with sadness in their eyes. Or maybe, due to the horror stories we may have read, the asylum makes us imagine a world where patients are beaten into submission and shunned from society.

In part, these were all true at one time or another. The Victorian era asylum resulted from decades of medical reform in the attempts to treat the mentally ill more kindly and humanely. It was much like a grandiose dream that had been planned out in the minds of nineteenth and twentieth-century psychiatrists. They dreamed of a place that seemed to spread out for miles and was an area of refuge for Britain's most vulnerable. A haven where the care came from well-intended doctors and nurses who had devoted their time to caring for the mentally ill. But what was life honestly like for the staff and patients in these monstrous compounds that housed the insane? Were they actual places of rest for the mentally ill, or was there something more ominous going on in the day-to-day operations?

The majority of asylums were built between 1811 and 1914, but it was in the 1860s that a true building boom began to take place. Many of Britain's newly built asylums displayed the newest and most desirable architecture of the day. Beautiful woodwork gave way to elongated windows that spread throughout the buildings. Impressive fireplaces stood as the centrepieces of several of the rooms.

St John's Asylum in Lincoln, built in 1852, is a prime example of a magnificent Italian-style building. The corridor-style building was designed using bluestone, a sedimentary rock, and Mansfield Stone. St John's was built using slate, hipped roofs, with many stone stacks. Honeycomb vaulted ceilings were used throughout the building in an effort to reduce noise levels in patient rooms.

Stone House Asylum, in Kent, was designed and built starting in 1862 and used the impressive Tudor Revival architecture that seemed to resemble the brick façade of Hampton Court.

The British insane asylum was much like a small city in itself, as its buildings were spread over vast acres of rich farmland and rolling hills. The asylum was ideally away from public roads but close enough to a large town so that the staff could come and go as needed. To utilise sunlight, the main entrance of the asylum would face south, southeast, or southwest. Construction of the buildings primarily used the block principle, and most asylums were two storeys with an abundance of sunlight and good ventilation throughout the facility. The structure and urban planning of the asylums were done to help in the recovery of patients. Along with the lines of moral therapy, green open spaces and sunlight were thought to calm patients' nerves.

Formal gardens and pathways intertwined throughout the buildings, along with benches and plenty of shade for resting out of the hot sun if desired. Gardens provided a safe space where patients could benefit from the therapeutic effects of being connected to nature. Asylum buildings were often linked to the gardens using verandas and trellises, so there was easy access to them. During the Middle Ages, monasteries that cared for the sick incorporated courtyards where patients could gather to get fresh air and enjoy the gardens. These green care ideals were seen in Geel at the shrine of St Dymphna, where patients were cared for among the beautiful land that surrounded them.

E.R. Johnston, an American horticulturist who worked with mentally ill children in the late nineteenth century, said:

> In the garden, every sense is alert. How the eye brightens at the masses of gorgeous color and the beautiful outlines – how many things, hot and cool, rough and smooth, hard and soft, and of different forms are to be grasped and held by trembling uncertain hands whose sense of touch is hardly yet awakened

The asylum thrived on agriculture, and many were equipped with farm animals and land for growing food. Because they were self-sufficient, asylums relied on the work of their patients to keep things moving. Agriculture has long been considered a form of treatment and rehabilitation for the residents of asylums. Farming was a useful tool in keeping patients out of trouble and also providing them with a hobby. A Report of the Commissioners of the Scotch Board of Lunacy, states:

> It is impossible to dismiss the subject of asylum farms without some reference to the way in which they contribute to the mental health of the inmates by affording subjects of interest to many of them. Even among patients drawn from urban districts, there are few to whom the operations of rural life present no features of interest, while to those drawn from rural districts, the horses, the oxen, the sheep, and the crops are unfailing sources of attraction.

In 1870, when the London Asylum for the Insane opened, its administrators were in huge support of agricultural programmes.

They believed that patients would greatly benefit by participating in things that reflected the norms of society. Stables and barns were built for the livestock, a chapel for prayer, engine houses, and laundry rooms were just a few of the buildings on the premises. Asylums were truly ample, as they supplied their own food and meat, washed their own clothes, and produced their own fuel and water. Labour and leisure in the open were seen as harmonious, and it was felt that everyday life should be organised to achieve the therapeutic effects of the asylum.

The asylum buildings were divided into different wards designed to meet the needs of their patients. Some of the patients needed more supervision than others, such as those who were sick or may cause injury to themselves and others. Male and female patients were kept separated for the most part, although in some cases, they were able to share the dining hall. The windows throughout the wards were often a modification of French casement with iron bars to keep patients and staff safe.

The sleeping quarters of the asylums were typically split into dorms that housed between eight to fifteen beds, each with washbasins filled with fresh water in the event of an accident. Single bedrooms were rare and usually kept for patients who posed a risk to others. Each sleeping quarter was also complete with toilets and bathing areas.

Wards were divided by class of diagnosis as much as possible, and the Victorian era asylum had its fair share of diverse patients. A person diagnosed with mania may be unable to sleep or may speak frantically and use wild gestures and foul language. Dementia patients had a loss of rational thought, forgetfulness, and incoherence and were very childlike. Many with dementia forgot their basic hygiene and had a loss of bladder. Those with melancholia were withdrawn, unable to cope with life. Idiots and imbeciles had an absence of mind, and the understanding of how they came to be was usually not there. Some were considered mentally defective, sometimes mute, deaf, or blind—some incapable of eating or bathing. Imbeciles usually presented with large heads or disproportionate limbs. Those afflicted with Mongolian Syndrome, as it was known at the time, were labelled with the idiots and imbeciles.

Mongolian Syndrome got its name in 1862, as children with Down's syndrome shared similar facial features to those described as the Mongolian race. It has long been recognised that the term referred to those who had a specific type of mental deficiency. Modern medicine today has helped us understand that the anomaly is known as Down's Syndrome, and the term Mongolism is no longer used, as it is deemed offensive.

Airing courts, used for patient exercise, were lined with high walls and a dry ditch, giving patients the freedom to see over the wall without escaping. The courts were typically laid out with gardens, walkways, and shaded areas where patients might find reprieve from the summer sun. Often a small shallow pond for birds or fish would have been placed for the enjoyment of the patients and staff.

The main building of the asylum, typically called the administrative building, would often be in the central position of the asylum, with a grand staircase being the focal point. Administration buildings were where you might find the chapel, family waiting room, supply offices, and dispensary.

The Medical Superintendent was required by law to live onsite and usually had a detached house for himself and his family. It was meant to keep his family and private life away from the patients, but at the same time, he would always be available in the event of an emergency.

The asylum chapel would hold Church of England services and was usually large enough to house half the inmates at one time. In many cases, a massive clock tower would proudly stand over the main building, like a beacon, keeping a watchful eye over the acres of land.

Staircases constructed through the asylum were made of stone with wooden rails, and oak floors polished with beeswax would be the foundation for rugs spread out over high traffic areas.

Fireplaces were an excellent source of heat but not always the most practical. They were often fitted with tubular firebacks and combustion stoves to warm the larger rooms. The hospital's greatest challenge for proper warmth was usually in the infirmary, where temperatures needed to be kept stable for the sick patients housed there. In the separate units for infectious disease, opening in the cornices of the rooms allowed for fresh air and ventilation.

The insane asylum was still a hospital and dealt with not only mental sickness but also physical sickness. Throughout the eighteenth and nineteenth centuries, tuberculosis had become an epidemic throughout Europe. By the early twentieth century, it had become one of the United Kingdom's most urgent health problems. Tuberculosis was and still is very contagious. When a person with the disease sneezes, coughs, or even speaks, the bacteria linger in the air for several hours. Those who breathe in the bacteria can quickly become infected. Because a cure for tuberculosis wasn't discovered until the middle of the twentieth century, the condition spread throughout insane asylums with ease. As admittance numbers increased in the asylums, separate wards for tuberculosis patients were becoming more common. Infected patients posed a grave risk to others and were immediately put into isolation in the hospital infirmary.

Lighting throughout the asylum was achieved by gas and, more importantly, by natural sunlight. With the myriad of windows throughout the structures, it was felt that the streaming sunlight could purify the atmosphere. It promoted a healthy and hygienic environment and was considered essential to the recovery of patients. Psychiatrists believed that avoiding darkness was essential in fighting the gloom of melancholy. They understood that the asylum had the stigma of being a dark place and emphasised that light was equated with knowledge and healing.

Psychiatrists throughout western Europe believed that colour greatly affected one's mental state. For this reason, the calming shades of pastel blue, pink, and yellow were frequently seen on the walls and ceilings. Doctors wanted to create a warm and therapeutic environment that didn't overwhelm patients and felt that soft colours displayed an aura of comfort. Dark, bold colours such as grey, black and red were purposely avoided. Red or black could have been associated with trauma in a patient's life, and the goal was not to induce any extra anxiety in patients throughout the asylum walls.

The hospital kitchen usually had a cellar to store extra goods, and the kitchen itself had different areas, such as the scullery, bread room, vegetable room, and dairy room. Most kitchens were equipped with several large copper ranges. Dining rooms would usually accommodate all of the patients in a ward, though those that wished may have been able to eat in their rooms with permission from the staff.

Day rooms were provided for each ward so that patients could socialise without coming into contact with others whose needs differed significantly from their own. The day rooms were designed with warmth and comfort in mind, with more soft pastel colours and large windows to let in sunlight. The staff strove to give the patients a domestic feel, with different seating and plants or bird cages. Bookcases could be found throughout the asylum for the reading pleasure of both patients and staff.

The Recreation Room or Ball Room was a massive 70 x 50-foot work of art, complete with a stage for performances. The room's semi-dome apse was made of marble and ornamented mosaic that, in most cases, was breathtaking. The York County Lunatic Asylum boasted an open ceiling with decorative corbels, beautiful woodwork, panelled doors, and architraves.

In the late nineteenth century, the York County Lunatic Asylum underwent renovations that included an American bowling alley with panelled walls and doors and a stunning coffered ceiling with roof lanterns.

Daily routine for patients was essential to their well-being. The balance of bathing, eating, work, and leisure time could be very stressful to patients in the asylum, and it was easy for them to feel overwhelmed. Hospital staff understood that creating a daily routine and setting specific times to perform everyday tasks would allow patients to focus on their physical and mental health. Having a daily routine also helped patients socialise and form peer relationships.

Designated recreation time was often spent in the dayroom or outdoors in the airing courts and walkways. Dayroom activities may have included accessing the asylum's reading materials, Bible study, or card and board games. Less social patients were most likely drawn to watch the activities of the asylum grounds from the many elongated windows throughout the room. In pleasant weather, outdoor games such as cricket or tennis was enjoyed by patients.

The asylums prided themselves on offering entertainment for their patients with musicals and dances in the grand ballroom. It was a way to bring the patients together and offer a form of dance therapy. Fridays were the typical day for a weekly concert or dance to achieve the desired feeling of community. Annual balls were also held in the asylum where members of the public and the press were invited to participate.

Asylums often had bands that were made up of staff and local musicians. The music usually consisted of polka, or quadrilles, which was a very fashionable dance in eighteenth and nineteenth-century Europe, in which people danced to a medley of opera songs. Minuet dances were also popular, primarily in England and France, beginning in the seventeenth century, though their popularity carried through.

Sunday was considered a day of rest, and patients were given the opportunity to go to church. Some patients were also active participants in the choir.

There was an array of staff that could be found throughout the asylum. The Medical Superintendent was the director of medicine and the head of staff. The Assistant Medical Superintendent was a junior superintendent who attended the Superintendent in their daily tasks. There was almost always a chaplain, who was a trained priest or pastor, and he offered pastoral care to the patients and the staff.

The clerks and stewards consisted of administrative staff and those in charge of raw materials, such as food or fuel. The housekeeper and attendants worked closely with the patients. There tended to be a high turnover rate as they often worked sixteen hours a day. Engineers dealt with the heating systems, and the bailiffs managed the farms and gardens. Indoor servants such as cooks, laundresses, kitchen maids, carpenters, and mechanics added to the overall functioning of the asylum. A lot of responsibility was placed on the staff, and they were expected to be on their best behaviour at all times.

Most patients were woken up around 6 or 7 am and brought to use the bathroom before getting dressed for the day. The dressing and garments of patients in the asylum mainly were an issue of medical authority overriding personal choice as there was great importance on attire. The Lunacy Act of 1845 ensured that basic standards were met for patients with clean, good-quality clothing. Patients were typically issued standard clothing depending on their social class. Paupers were outfitted more with county-issued clothing, while wealthier patients may have been found in more personal effects.

Different types of attire were issued to different patients, often depending on their expected daily tasks. Women were required to have neatly pinned hair, and often dishevelled hair was seen as unruly as was a patient without any clothes at all. Most clothing issued was meant to integrate the patients into a shared sense of identity to not spark conflict between social classes. Proper clothing was seen as a sign of one's respect for the asylum. Clothing issued to patients was expected to provide adequate warmth, especially in those suffering from feebleness, as these people often displayed signs of loss of body heat. Warm flannel coats and trousers and warm socks and undergarments were provided.

Some unruly patients could remain in their sleeping gowns during the day, making them more manageable. The soiling of one's clothes was seen as a sign that patients could not care for themselves, often reflecting daily grooming habits such as hair brushing and shaving.

Clothes and bedding would have to be closely monitored for suicidal patients, and belts were almost always removed from these people. The Lunacy Act of 1890 refers to straitjacket-like garments that were buttoned up the back instead of the front. In violent and maniacal patients, these could be worn for up to twelve hours a day.

Patients travelled in groups to breakfast, which up until the mid-eighteenth century was less than desirable. Conventional fourteenth and fifteenth-century thinking believed it was ill-advised to feed the insane anything to break their fast, and they usually had to wait until supper. But by 1730, more foods were added to the daily fare, and in some facilities, pancakes and fritters were served. Holiday menus became more cheerful, and butter was becoming a common sight. A meal of starchy foods would have been served around noon time. Foods high in fat and starches provided the best energy for the patient mid-day. Patients could also expect some form of sweets if permitted in the form of pastries, pies, or fruits. In recognition of patient and staff safety, special consideration was taken regarding cutlery at all meals. The last meal of the day, which would have been much lighter, typically consisted of tea and some kind of bread and probably resembled tea time. This meal would have been served around five or six in the evening.

Because asylums ran on a tight schedule, it was expected that most events for the day would be brought to a close around 7:30 pm. Facilities and activity rooms were locked, and patients were brought to their rooms. Nights were usually reserved for bathing, and most patients were on a bathing schedule.

As they slept, the patients had the comfort of knowing that attendants would be keeping a watchful eye on them, especially those patients with a form of epilepsy or fits. Those patients that were thought to be capable of inflicting self-harm or harm on others would have been closely monitored at all hours of the night.

Aside from recreational activities, patients were encouraged to work as part of daily life at the asylum, and they were often rewarded for doing so. Due to their conditions, those who could not work were still given basic jobs such as shredding old newspapers to reuse. This was easy and required no supervision, and it was also an excellent job for destructive patients.

Those with more skill could clean and wash floors or polish fixtures and fittings. Furniture and woodwork could also be polished, and rugs could be taken outside and beaten to rid them of dirt and debris. Outdoor work was usually done by male patients. Those capable could work on the asylum farm tilling the soil, spreading manure, or harvesting grains such as barley or oats and wheat. During harvest, when several patients were gathering crops, a tremendous sense of community was felt. Kitchen work like cleaning fruits and vegetables could easily be done by some patients. Others were given seasonable building work, weather permitting. Male patients could also lay gravel and tar or perform needed brickwork.

Patients were always supervised, and certain garden tools were not safe for all patients. However, a sense of independence was established by being given a job to do. Lawn and tree work was standard work among male patients, as the asylum's landscaping was meant to be a pleasing sight. With proper supervision, certain patients were allowed to use garden sheers or cutting tools to trim garden shrubs or grass. Walkways and garden paths were to be weeded and adequately maintained to keep the grounds looking their best. Some patients may have even been asked to assist with draining the main cesspool to the asylum.

Those patients considered gentle in nature were allowed to assist with livestock. Even something as mundane as encouraging cows to graze was seen as a way to be included. Patients who enjoyed working with animals could be taught to milk the cows and churn butter. Chicken coops could also be cleaned by patients, as well as gathering eggs for the kitchen. Bedding for pigs and sheep needed to be changed and could be done by certain patients. If a patient was a trained blacksmith, they might have been asked to trim horses' hooves or fit horseshoes.

Patients known to be handy could assist with painting trim or woodwork or whitewashing the asylum's walls and ceilings. Many patients came to the asylum knowing a trade, and they could be counted on to help dramatically. Every asylum needed experienced shoemakers, tailors, and others who could perform quality artisan work.

Female patients were usually expected to use their domestic skills, such as working in the laundry room. However, not every patient would have been suitable for the laundry room. It was often a noisy atmosphere from the many wash racks being used. The laundry room was also a hot environment due to the heat given off by the drying cabinets. The smell of soap was strong, and it may have irritated the respiratory tracts of more sensitive patients. There was a sewing room and a head seamstress, and if some patients were not a threat to others, they might have been able to attend with sewing. They could perform basic repair to garments or linens or tend to the lace trimming on dresses.

Kitchen work would have been expected of some women patients, though not all. Being around boiling water and the fire from stoves was all risky work. Many of the patients would simply wash and dry dishes.

There is no doubt that the Victorian era asylum was a thriving place that functioned much like a small town. And it's important to remember that the asylum would not have functioned in the way it did without the help of its patients. These people were worthy and added tremendous value to running the asylum smoothly.

However, as the asylums of Britain moved into the late nineteenth and twentieth centuries, they had begun to rapidly deteriorate into what were essentially overcrowded prison-like places for the assumed insane. The admissions protocol for the asylum was lax and problematic.

It was evident by the number of patients being admitted that abuse of the system in England was already taking place. To avoid this, the 1853 Lunatic Asylums Act was passed to set guidelines for admission. Paperwork was required in order to be admitted, along with a medical certificate by a doctor who had previously examined the patient. Some detailed information about the patient was required, including their name and marital status and details on their mental status. Though sadly once admitted, the patients had no chance at appeal. Patients could only be discharged to the family along with the promise they would be continuing the patient's care.

However, despite the regulations, abuse of the system continued to worsen. Asylums had become a place to put the undesirables of society, and they had also become a place to abandon unruly women. Many patients were admitted for ridiculous reasons and often forgotten about, forcing them to spend decades in an asylum. The majority of patients were admitted with chronic dementia or some form of mania. Many were simply diagnosed with heredity or ill health, menstrual problems in women, or traumatic injury. There seemed to be a broad brush with which patients were painted, which led many to be inappropriately admitted.

Requests from asylum administrators looking for a solution to the problem were increasing. A February 1882 *Journal of Mental Science* issued references to Maryborough Asylum in Ireland:

> the asylum buildings were so overcrowded that the medical superintendent had to place his patients under canvas.

A February 1896 issue of the *British Medical Journal* states problems at the Royal Edinburgh Asylum on the high rate of admission.

> Dr Clouston hoped the negotiations now in progress would lead to a diminution of the overcrowding of the rate-paid wards, and consequently to their difficulty in admitting the poorer private patients who applied for admission.

The need for more asylums was multiplying, and with this, the need for more staff and new extensions to existing buildings. There was also increasing pessimism about how well the therapeutic asylums were working. The increase in patients made treatment more difficult and caused the facilities to drift away from the moral treatments. The need for more accommodations also angered taxpayers and cut into the quality of care. Asylum authorities found they were swamped with old chronic patients in limited space for newer patients with a better prognosis of being cured.

A lot of responsibility fell on the attendants and nurses, working long hours in often unpleasant conditions. It became increasingly hard to find good staff. There was very little training and recruitment in the mid-Victorian period. Effective medical therapies had yet to emerge, and the refusal of the upper level of the staff to do administrative duties led to a decline in care. The amount of paperwork was becoming burdensome, and the staff was unable to tend to the needs of the patients. The failings of the asylums led to them being institutions that were of little humanitarian aspiration. Moral treatment had declined into mere custodial care.

By the First World War, asylums had become warehouses for the chronically ill. The dreams that early doctors had of the saviour-like asylum were slipping away. Many patients that were being admitted weren't even mentally ill. The progressive and humane aspirations of physicians were doomed to fail under the pressure in numbers, and Britain seemed to be at the forefront.

In France, state medicine had established itself in hospitals by the seventeenth century, but the same could not be said for other parts of Europe. Germany had become the world leader in psychiatry in the nineteenth century, and along with their competitive nature, they had a history of innovating, reforming, and distinguishing themselves. While Britain resembled Germany and France with its divided regions and counties, a lack of centralisation put them behind on healthcare.

By 1911, dealing with the lack of beds had become the permanent job of almost every mental health authority in Britain. William Battie's former hopes of institutional therapeutic care were shattered by the number of patients.

During the nineteenth and twentieth centuries, there was also a reallocation of illness. People with significant conditions were moved more and more from being cared for at home to being committed to the asylum. The increase in the numbers was also because people in prisons and workhouses got sent to asylums.

Another cause of the rise in numbers was insanity due to alcohol. Alcohol dramatically affects the nervous system and can lead to hallucinations. Severe withdrawal from alcohol can cause psychosis, fits, and tremors. Interestingly, overindulgence often led to admittance to the asylum, yet at the same time, during the nineteenth century, alcohol was used as a form of treatment in those very same asylums.

Perhaps one of the biggest reasons for a high admissions rate to the nineteenth and twentieth-century asylums was the 'discovery' of schizophrenia. While the illness has been around for centuries, the first mention of something resembling it were case reports, both from 1809, from Dr Philippe Pinel and Dr John Haslam.

Haslam's case report of London tea broker, James Tilly Matthews, is one of the first documented cases of a patient believed to be suffering from schizophrenia. He was admitted to Bedlam in 1797.

Emil Kraepelin's classification of dementia praecox would follow in the late nineteenth century.

However, the term schizophrenia was coined in 1908 by Swiss psychiatrist Eugen Bleuler (1857-1939). Bleuler was born in the small town of Zollikon, Switzerland, and would pursue his medical studies in Zurich, Paris, Munich, and London. While giving a lecture to the German Psychiatric Association in Berlin, Bleuler spoke of schizophrenia. He insisted that Emil Kraepelin's dementia praecox was not associated with dementia or advanced maturity. He believed that the splitting of psychic functioning was one of the main symptoms of schizophrenia. In 1911, he wrote:

> I call *dementia praecox* schizophrenia because, as I hope to show, the splitting of the different psychic functions is one of its most important features. In each case, there is a more or less clear splitting of the psychological functions: as the disease becomes distinct, the personality loses its unity.

Bleuler would introduce what he felt were the main symptoms of the schizophrenic patient, known as the four As. They were known as abnormal associations, autistic behaviour and thinking, abnormal affect, and ambivalence. He explained the loss of association between thought, emotion, and behaviour was key. He also believed that with these fundamentals of the disease, a patient could easily manifest delusions, social withdrawal, and a lack of motivation.

Bleuler spent much of his time closely observing his patients to the point where he would spend days with them as he documented their behaviours. His published monograph from 1911 would be translated into English in 1950.

Schizophrenia seemed to be a new type of illness, especially in young people, that would progress to insanity. Historian Edward Hare (1812-1897), a clinician at both Bethlem Royal and Maudsley Hospital, argued that the increase in mental patients, especially during the second half of the nineteenth century, was due to what was recently termed schizophrenia. Like Bleuler, he argued that there was a strong genetic component to the disease.

Some scholars didn't agree and believed that the asylums themselves caused mild symptoms of mental illness to progress. They thought that schizophrenia wasn't new and had been around since the pre-modern era.

In any event, though there were scarce nurse's notes from the 1790s with descriptions of symptoms that mimicked schizophrenia, it seemed to be more of a recent illness in that it significantly increased the numbers of patients in the asylums.

By the early twentieth century, psychiatry had hit a bit of a dead-end. British doctors seemed to be losing contact with the advancements of medicine. While they had prided themselves with the removal of restraints and the introduction of moral therapy, they came to a bit of a standstill. While most of the Western world advanced—Britain continued to struggle to keep up with other European countries when it came to medicine. And in fact, some found it hard to believe how backward England still seemed to be in the dawn of the new century.

Staff doctor, William Stoddart, at Bethlem, in 1904, said 'English psychiatry is far behind that on the continent that there exists in England no school of psychiatry'.

Because of little public funding, an increase in diagnoses, and a lack of staff, asylums had now become sad, hopeless places, overrun with patients. The profession of psychiatry was now at a historic low.

However, in 1907, Dr Henry Maudsley set out to change that. Maudsley was an English psychiatrist, born in 1835 in the North Riding of Yorkshire. As part of his education in medicine, he worked for several months at West Riding Asylum in Wakefield. He was also employed at the Manchester Royal Lunatic Asylum as medical superintendent as well as a physician at the West London Hospital.

In 1866, he married and took over the running of his father-in-law's private asylum, Lawn House. Over time, he had acquired a reputation for being a brilliant psychiatrist and writer of three medical textbooks. Maudsley adhered to the degeneration theory, a concept during the eighteenth century that believed human beings shared a common origin, but over time had degenerated to biological changes, specifically hereditary.

Maudsley wanted to establish a new kind of psychiatric hospital with acute care and an outpatient option. He tried to model his facility after the successful German hospitals, with an institution that could treat easy cases of mental illness, in the hopes of preventing patients from being sent to county asylums. Due to the needed treatment of First World War veterans, the buildings Maudsley commissioned were instead used to treat servicemen from 1919 to 1920. However, Maudsley Hospital was officially opened as a psychiatric facility in 1923, with Dr Edward Mapother (1881-1940) as medical superintendent. Henry Maudsley had passed in 1918, but Dr Mapother would be a significant figure in the hospital's future. Like Maudsley, Dr Mapother wanted to mirror the German clinics. As a result of this modelling, the hospital would become a prominent centre for the research of psychiatric illness in Britain. The young doctors at Maudsley Hospital were encouraged to entertain the new ideas of biochemistry, genetics, and psychology. The doctor's team and several supporting staff would go on to treat 157 patients in the hospital's six wards.

The success of Henry Maudsley's hospital is still felt today, as it remains one of the most highly regarded places throughout many English-speaking countries, and its research is considered more than worthy.

However, despite Henry Maudsley's efforts to change the face of the Victorian asylum, some cases of patient abuse were still being documented. While the nineteenth century had witnessed a tremendous shift in how insanity was regarded, the relationships between staff and patients remained in question. Despite the well-meaning attempts of psychiatrists, the doctor-patient relationship often became strained as the boundaries within the asylum walls were blurred.

Because British asylums were given minimal oversight at the beginning of the nineteenth century, there is little historical literature from the time. But it's not hard to imagine that physical intimacy, whether wanted or not, may have taken place. Intimacy between staff and patients certainly would have been questioned during the nineteenth century. Accusations of actual rape against asylum doctors were almost unheard of until the 1840s, but it did happen in some instances throughout the rest of the century. Patients were already vulnerable in the sense that they had their disorder, but they were also kept from family behind hospital walls. Day in and day out, staff was in contact with patients who suffered a myriad of disorders that seriously disrupted their sense of reality. This meant that patients could easily accuse a staff member of wrongdoing that may have only occurred in the patient's mind. But just because several patients were delusional, it didn't mean that abuse didn't occur.

Asylum notes from two separate accounts of patient abuse during the nineteenth century have surfaced. The documented case of Philip Parry Middleton, from when psychiatry was still in its earliest stages, shows us the power that physicians had during that time.

The year was 1815, and Middleton was one of three superintendents at Hanover Park Asylum in Carlow, Ireland. Middleton was accused of abuse with a married patient, Mrs Hester Hinds, resulting in a pregnancy. He did not deny the accusations, and Middleton moved Mrs Hinds to live in the private home of Dr Rodgers of Wicklow. Mrs Hinds delivered her child in the Rodger's home and was visited by Dr Middleton, who showed her great affection.

The eventual prosecution of Middleton, along with an abundance of trial evidence, did much to expose the sexual appetite exhibited by some members of the asylum staff at Hanover Park, including one of the other superintendents, Charles Delahoyde. But the jury could not reach a verdict, and Philip Middleton's case was dropped. The staff returned to their positions, even though they had broken the trust of their patients.

Divulsions into Middleton's earlier years revealed that he had a tumultuous past. He spent time in prison after encouraging several Englishmen to leave for the Americas during the American War of Independence. He was accused of paying debts in counterfeit coins in 1802 and also found himself wrapped up in other court cases. In 1814, Carlow Castle in Ireland was leased to Dr Middleton, and he intended to use it for a private lunatic asylum. He thought a speedier process of converting the castle would be to use blasting powder. The error of his ways proved itself after the eastern half of the castle collapsed. He eventually travelled to America to pursue his studies, and upon returning to Exeter in 1830, he passed away.

The case of Dr John Campbell, almost eighty-two years later, told the story of a respected and competent asylum superintendent who would find himself at the other end of the mental health spectrum. The role of hospital superintendent was incredibly demanding as these men were essentially working twenty-four hours a day while residing on hospital property. The hospital staff was told they needed to be careful of their own mental health due to the long works days and the daily strain that they had to endure.

Dr Campbell had been a prominent superintendent at the Garlands Lunatic Asylum in Carlisle since 1873. But in 1898, his excellent record and high standing at the hospital were ruined by his assault on a female patient. He was a mere three weeks away from retiring. According to a laundry maid, in 1898, Campbell was seen taking a female patient by the name of Janet Mooney into a coal cellar where he had sex with her. The door to the cellar had been left wide open, and the act was witnessed by several other workers. It was believed that the patient did comply, though only after she had accepted a form of payment from Campbell.

Campbell was in breach of the 1890 Lunacy Act, and so he was prosecuted. Several witnesses stated that Campbell was under the influence of alcohol when he committed the act. Following an investigation into the case, Campbell threatened to kill himself with a laudanum overdose. He was then put under constant supervision at his home.

Campbell's trial included the testimony of several of his colleagues who claimed he had had a problem with alcohol for some time. But it was also discussed that his length of time as superintendent, along with an inadequate number of staff, may have begun to complicate matters regarding his own mental health. During the trial, evidence began to surface that Campbell had been boastful of several illusions of grandeur. He insisted that one of his patients was a member of the royal family and that he would be moving to London to serve wealthier clients. Collectively these characteristics of Campbell that had begun to surface were the same as other hospital staff throughout the country who had to suffer from mental health problems of their own. Ironically, Campbell was found guilty and insane at his trial and was sent to Broadmoor Insane Asylum to spend his days as a criminal lunatic.

Throughout the twentieth century, tales of patient abuse were much more documented. A charity by the name of Mental Health Media recorded the stories of several patient cases of abuse from 1925 to 1985. These documents now sit in the National Sound Archive at the British Library as an essential piece of English history.

In 1923, Edna Martin was born and was being raised by her grandfather. Her own mother had been sent away to the asylum for having children out of wedlock. Edna's grandfather treated her no better, and before the age of eighteen, she was declared an imbecile and transferred to Calderstones Asylum, the same place her mother had been sent.

Ms Martin claims the abuse was never-ending. She speaks of being put in a straitjacket on the isolation ward, with no clothes underneath, and given a chamber pot to do her business in. She sat in total darkness and had to eat her food off the floor of her cell.

> They used enemas for punishment. I was once sitting with my legs up under me, and a nurse pulled out the chair from underneath me, so I fell on the floor. I asked what she'd done that for, and she marched me to the bathroom.

Edna was transferred to Rampton Asylum at the age of twenty-one. She said the abuse there was worse. Coldwater baths were given as a form of punishment. Nurses would ridicule the naked bodies of the patients and beat them with towels soaked in cold water.

After post-war Britain, the push towards mixed-sex wards in the asylum would become more prevalent, and significant changes began to take place inside the walls of the psychiatric hospitals. Patients were still being abused but in more subtle ways, almost in plain sight in some cases.

It should be stated here that most staff and doctors of the asylums in the twentieth century had the right intent and wanted to help, not hurt, their patients. But that doesn't mean these things did not happen.

The move to create mixed-sex wards during the 1950s would be one that, if not intentionally, would benefit both male patients and staff. Women would now be greatly subjected to abuse from their male counterparts. It should also be noted that male patients were subject to sexual violence as well. Sexual abuse can be described as harassment through touching, staring, exposing, and also through sexual remarks. It is also described as forcible rape or other coercive sexual acts. Abuse in the asylums is also recognised as other forms as well, such as abuse of power by staff.

As we know, since the first asylums were established in the early nineteenth century, segregation of the sexes was seen through almost every aspect of life. Different working practices, daily routines, and different wards aimed to keep men and women apart. One of the primary purposes of segregation was keeping the female patients safe. Into the middle of the century, there was some relaxation around the rules as more female nurses were permitted to work with male patients.

Over one hundred years later, following the Second World War, things progressed ever further towards mixed-sex wards. In a 1953 report by the World Health Organization, it was stated:

> The life within the hospital should, as far as possible, be modeled on life within the community in which it is set. In a western country where men and women mix freely at work and in recreation, it is obviously desirable that they should do so when in the mental hospital.

In the 1950s though many hospital wards still remained segregated, they were left unlocked, which gave both male and female patients the freedom to move about freely. This often led to secret meetings in covert parts of the hospital. Patients were able to sit together during meals or when participating in activities. It was noted by staff at Shelton Hospital that the mixing of sexes was a positive thing. According to team psychiatrist, J.C. Baker, men were said to:

> smarten themselves up in the presence of females, and many patients who for years had hardly spoken to members of the opposite sex began to take an active interest in each other and in their hospital.

It's certainly easy to appreciate that folks of any mental capacity would react positively to people of the opposite sex taking a friendly or endearing interest in them. A charge nurse at Moorhaven Hospital in Devon reported similar effects. He explained that spitting and acts of aggression in patients had decreased.

> The decrease in noise was noticeable, likewise the eternal pacing and general restlessness of the men. The presence of women moving among them and helping them in their ward routines acted as an inspiration and a spur to improving their behaviour.

And yet, despite these obvious positive observations, there is also historical evidence of the inevitable consequences of mixing male and female staff, increasing the potential of sexual assaults.

In the 1960s, asylums had begun to adopt more of a revolving door policy regarding admissions. This meant that selecting the most suitable patients for admission, especially in an asylum that now had unlocked wards, was crucial to the safety of patients and staff. There was an abundant amount of anxiety surrounding the issues of criminals who were being admitted to Britain's asylums. An increase in the number of male patients, many of them sex offenders, were being admitted to hospitals where they could freely mix with men and women. Understandably, these patients, who had little interest in treatment, were not overly popular among both patients and staff. They were often disruptive and made the staff nervous. And yet, in several asylums, too much emphasis was put on having one or two locked wards for misbehaved woman patients.

Superintendent Denis Martin, at Claybury Hospital, kept one locked ward for unruly women, while male patients were given no locked ward at all. The argument, which I suppose in some way makes sense, is that the female wards were more closely monitored to prevent pregnancy or the fear that female patients would be manipulated.

However, this still left most women vulnerable to abuse and violence. At Severalls Asylum in Essex, the underground passages of the hospital were a perfect meeting spot for patients. While some of the sex was consensual, much of it was not.

It was the male nurses who were often given the most respect as their presence added a strong sense of stability to the wards throughout the asylums in the 1960s. Many of these nurses firmly disagreed with mixing the patient wards and even accused physicians of overlooking patient safety.

At the 1965 Confederation of Health Service Employees conference, many male nurses spoke out against the mixed-sex wards, calling them haphazard and nothing but a vanity push by psychiatrists.

Jack Charles, a member of the Confederations executive committee, made a passionate speech on his view of the mixed wards and the psychiatrist that facilitated them.

> most of you have wives and daughters, and none of them is immune from having a mental breakdown. They may have to enter a psychiatric hospital for treatment, and

while there, they will be exposed to the risk of being seduced by that type of person (a deadbeat, layabout psychopath).

Mr Charles also reported:

> blatant cases of sexual intercourse ... and of the pregnancies which have been terminated', adding 'I know of a situation where a known prostitute was practising her profession inside the hospital'.

At Storthes Hall in Yorkshire, rumours of sex orgies on the wards were spread. There was also great concern regarding the mixture of violent patients with those who were vulnerable due to schizophrenia. Women patients, especially, could easily be persuaded to perform undesirable acts if they were suffering from a lapse in reality.

The public also felt some trepidation around the idea of mixed wards, as those who had spouses staying at an asylum felt they could be subject to a threat in the marriage.

The demand for more nurses was a direct result of the mixed-sex wards and open-door policy of the 1960s asylums. Male nurses were hesitant to work with female patients, as they had a genuine concern about unfounded charges being brought against them by irrational patients. Because of this, male nurses were instructed not to find themselves alone on a woman's ward. Understandably, male nurses wanted to avoid any possibility of prison time because of false allegations.

In the 1950s, so-called psychopathic women were seen as 'higher grade' patients needing control rather than support. According to the 1957 Royal Commission report, psychopathics were among the most problematic of female patients, presenting a particular threat to male staff. Male staff was taught to be aware of women who would wrongly accuse men of rape and those who in their minds would conjure up events that never took place.

Of course, there was also the fact that male staff could pose a threat to female patients, but it seemed as if it was a matter that was tiptoed around. Because of the high demand for nurses, asylums certainly didn't want to deter men from choosing a career in nursing. However, the reality remained that women patients were abused by both male and sometimes female staff and patients.

At Fulbourn Hospital in 1967, a social worker remarked that:

> There were occasions on which friendships ... between staff and patients, which were highly inappropriate, could develop. And I think patients were sometimes very confused—even more, families were very confused

What remains remarkable is that superintendents appear to have either turned the other cheek or had just been totally oblivious when it came to the dangers of unlocked wards. To the point of the furious arguments by male nurses, perhaps it really was a case of professionals simply looking to attract attention to their facilities.

It's also possible that superintendents may not have considered that woman patients were vulnerable as they just weren't viewed as sexual beings. Many patients had been prisoners to the walls of the asylum for decades, leaving them almost as empty souls. Many of these women suffered simply from being in the asylum and now lacked interest in anything, had no individuality, and were completely submissive.

However, these decades of patient abuse in the asylum didn't go unfounded. Incidentally, one of the most eminent reformers for patient abuse began her fight in the mid-nineteenth century.

Dorothea Dix, an American, made her mark not only in the United States but in the United Kingdom as well. Dorothea was born and raised in New England. She began work as a teacher in central Massachusetts and, in 1821, opened her own school in the capital city of Boston. She was less than twenty years old at the time and would write several textbooks for school teachers over the next few years.

Despite her brilliance and success, Ms Dix had long suffered from both tuberculosis and depression. In 1836, she sailed to Liverpool to rest under the care of William Rathbone. Rathbone was a friend of a former client of Ms Dix and a well-known advocate of social reform. While recovering in England, she met others who sparked her passion for the proper care of the mentally ill. She met with Dr Phillipe Pinel, where she then visited several of Britain's asylums. She then made it her mission to devote herself to the movement of lunacy reform.

When she returned to the United States in 1840, Ms Dix began to investigate American prisons, where she found the same horrible conditions she had discovered in Britain. She was appalled to see people being treated as less than human. Many were kept in dark, cold cells with no ventilation or were locked up in shackles. The sanitary facilities were abhorrent, and the patients were given less than adequate food and water.

Beginning in 1845, Dorothea would visit close to 1,000 poorhouses, prisons, and jails throughout the United States and Canada. She lobbied state and federal officials to earmark money to aid the mentally ill. Her push for national reform was stopped at the desk of President Franklin Pierce. He became concerned that the federal government would end up being responsible for all of the poor in the United States, and not just the mentally ill.

Ms Dix would return to Europe, where she was far more appreciated for her reform work. Perhaps the appreciation of the Europeans was what ultimately grounded her efforts in her own country. In 1860, she finally got a bill passed to fund New Jersey State Lunatic Asylum in Trenton, a hospital that she founded.

Ms Dix would continue to work for mental health reform up until the day she passed, at age seventy-nine. Both the United States and the United Kingdom pride Dorthea Dix on her efforts to change life in the insane asylum.

While the people that lived through the Victorian era have all passed on, their legacy is left to us through harrowing stories and old hospital records. And while atrocities no doubt took place, I do believe that the great asylum once stood as a beacon of hope for so many who had nowhere to turn. I picture it as the grand estate it was, set deep the countrysides of England, with the promise of understanding and compassion that it was meant to be.

Chapter Eight

Nineteenth and Twentieth Century Treatments for Mental Illness and the Breakthrough of Psychopharmacology

By the late nineteenth century and into the early twentieth century, thanks to Sigmund Freud, medical doctors now had an understanding of psychoanalysis, even if it was in its primitive state. With the turn of the century came new alternatives in treating mental illness. Many were revolutionary and downright dangerous, but there was an outstanding level of desperation in the field of psychiatry. With asylums filling up to overcapacity, there was even more of a need to better understand the disorders of the mind. And while hospitals were growing in size, they failed in therapeutic powers. During the 1920s in England, the recovery rate for a patient in the hospital was only 31%. Those that tended to patients could do little more for them than make them comfortable and try to return them to the community.

Nonetheless, psychiatrists were persistent in their drive to help the mentally ill. The advancement of psychiatry was made possible by experimentation on patients, as was much of the progress in the world of medicine. That still holds true today with new medications to treat cancer and other life-altering conditions. Chronic psychosis was still a fairly broad term, and under that umbrella fell schizophrenia and manic depressive orders, and doctors were on the fast track to finding a remedy. It's fair to say that with the cure to neurosyphilis in 1917, doctors were well on their way to grasping a better knowledge of the workings of the brain.

During his 1883 residency at the Vienna Asylum, doctor Julis Wagner-Jaureg (1857-1940) noted that a female patient of his who had contracted syphilis experienced a remission of her psychosis after being plagued with high fevers. This spiked the doctor's interest in the relationship between fever and insanity. He contemplated the idea that psychosis could be treated with fever and injected several of his patients with the newly discovered tuberculin, a glycerine extract of tubercle bacilli that was developed to remedy tuberculosis. His objective was to give his psychotic patients a tuberculosis fever, with the notion that fever would stop the progression of neurosyphilis in much the same way. This treatment went as planned until it was discovered that tuberculin was toxic. However, Dr Wagner-Jaureg was intent on using fever to cure syphilis. He found that a malaria fever could be controlled with the anti-parasite, quinine, so he experimented with blood from malaria patients. After admitting a patient with neurosyphilis who presented with weak memory and fits, Wagner tried his malaria blood theory, and the patient slowly began to recover.

Wagner-Jaureg's work in treating neurosyphilis was so successful that he was presented with the Nobel Prize in 1927. However, his treatment was cumbersome and expensive. At the beginning of the second world war, researchers at Oxford University recognised that it was penicillin that was helpful in treating the bacteria that caused neurosyphilis. By 1944 doctors throughout Europe and the United States understood that it was a huge success. Physicians now had the knowledge that the insanity caused by neurosyphilis was curable.

But neurosyphilis was caused by a bacterium, which was easy to control with medication. The same could not be said for the other causes of mental illness that remained somewhat of a mystery for doctors. The late nineteenth and twentieth centuries would be remembered as a time of pure experimentation on patients suffering from mental disabilities.

The use of water, as mentioned earlier, was and still is used in the treatment of patients with mental illness. Even in those of us who are entirely sane, there is no denying that a warm bath or a cool dip in the pool during the summer can work wonders both mentally and physically. Since ancient times, humans have sought out the healing properties of water in natural springs and other bodies of water. Water is not only essential for life physically, but it has long been symbolised in legend for its therapeutic powers.

In some form or another, bathing has been a suggested method of treatment since ancient Greece. While bathing in the luxurious spas of the time may have been relaxing, they also treated the mad.

Many medieval and renaissance pilgrimages were often made to holy sites containing water that was believed to have healing powers. Cathedrals were often built around water, and they became a great source of comfort to many. In 1326, the mineral springs of Spa, Belgium, were discovered and used for centuries, as were the hot sulphur springs of Bath, England. People seeking healing for disease frequented these places, as did those who simply enjoyed the warmth of the water.

Flemish physician and chemist Jean Baptiste Van Helmont (1580-1644) spoke about water therapy in his work, *Ortus Medicinae.* He recommended that patients be fully immersed in cold water to the point of near-death to 'kill the mad idea' that caused derangement. In a treatment known as the ducking treatment, Van Helmont's patients were often suspended headfirst underwater until they slipped into unconsciousness. They were then quickly revived, God willing, and apparently cured.

Throughout the next several centuries, it was believed that many conditions were treatable by bathing, such as leprosy, plague, female hysteria, and numbness, and this belief quickly made its way into the asylum.

The bath of surprise, or *bain de surprise*, originated in the seventeenth century and was much like the dunk tank we see today at amusement parks. Without warning, a patient was submerged into a vat of ice-cold water without notice. It was the element of shock that was believed to calm agitated patients.

Dr William Cullen (1710-1790), a physician at the Royal College of Physicians, Edinburgh and personal physician to the King of

Scotland from 1773 until his death in 1790, wrote extensively on the use of cold bathing as a method of treatment for several ailments. In the letter to a husband regarding his wife, who was a patient of Dr Cullen's being treated for female problems, he writes:

> I expect much benefit from the cold bathing and the best way of using it is by the bathing machine got from this place. In using it, the coldness should be brought on by degrees, by adding to the cold water every day until she comes to take the water quite cold.

During the nineteenth century, with the construction of municipal water systems in European cities, more and more asylums had the infrastructure needed to supply the use of water for therapy, which had become known as hydrotherapy. In Phillipe Pinel's Bicetre Hospital in Paris, elaborated rooms for hydrotherapy were established. Hydrotherapy had become a way to coerce patients without having to restrain them physically. Because of Dr Pinel's appreciation of it, France became a leader in the procedure. However, Pinel may have used it more as a form of punishment than for treatment.

Hydrotherapy using cold water could take the form of full-body bathing, head bathing, or bathing of the appendages. Many European and American doctors followed Pinel's example in the treatment of the insane. Dr William Handy, a physician at a New York hospital, said that the 'shower-bath', 'was explicitly used to punish infractions such as the tearing of clothing, silly behaviour, and laughing, soiling a cell or room, striking attendants, and attempted escape'.

By the middle of the nineteenth century, using water to cure, or at least treat, mental illness was becoming increasingly popular throughout Great Britain and the United States. It offered an alternative for patients looking to avoid other more orthodox treatments. It was also seen as effective at warmer temperatures too. Whether cold or heated, one of the main benefits of hydrotherapy was that it worked quickly. Warm, continuous baths became popular in the early twentieth century, where a patient was strapped into a tub and covered with a canvas sheet, allowing only the patient's head to stick out. These baths tended to last several hours to several days and were often used to treat depression or suicidal thoughts and calm excited or agitated behaviours. Asylum doctors felt that continuous baths were most effective in quiet rooms with very little light or sound, where a patient could relax. Water temperatures usually ranged between 92 to 97 degrees but often got as high as 105 to calm especially restless patients.

Water treatment could also be in the form of wrapping an agitated patient up mummy-style in soaking wet sheets and keeping them like this for several hours. This method of water treatment was considered effective in managing manic depression.

Hydrotherapy in the early 1900s was also delivered in the form of a spray. Patients who suffered from manic depressiveness or those who exhibited too much excitement or movement were believed to benefit from being strapped inside a shower and hosed down violently with cold water varying in temperatures from 48 to 70 degrees. These showers were thought to cool the heat of madness and calm nerves by cold-shocking a patient into sanity. Physically, the cold water slowed blood flow to the brain, which decreased the patient's mental and physical activity.

Although Wagner-Jaureg's work on treating neurosyphilis was a medical breakthrough, the use of certain drugs to treat psychotic illnesses was not new at all. Since before the days of Bedlam, laxatives were given for almost every type of ailment, including insanity, as it was believed that toxins in the colon made one go mad. The use of laxatives would persist through the early nineteenth century. Dr John Haslam, who treated patients at Bedlam, called laxatives an indispensable remedy in cases of insanity. The use of laxatives continued into the early 1920s, as English physicians used croton oil as a laxative until realising that it was highly poisonous. Even a drop of croton oil led to severe abdominal pain and diarrhoea and often resulted in bloody stool and even death.

Hyoscyamus niger, known as henbane or belladonna, was a plant derivative used to sedate patients through the early modern period. The uses of henbane can be traced back to 4000 BC throughout Europe. The drug's physical and psychological reaction was the loss of muscle control, dilated pupils, heart palpitation, hallucinations, delirium, coma, and even death. Known as the *Plant of Apollo*, it was used to communicate with the divine during ancient Greek times. During Anglo-Saxon times, it was used for toothache or what would have been labelled worm of the tooth. In the Middle Ages, it was known as *Witches Herb*, as it gave one the sensation of flying.

Henbane was reintroduced to British pharmacology in the late eighteenth century by Austrian doctor Baron Storck (1731-1803), who was considered one of the leading authorities in herbal medicine. Storck gave the extract of henbane to patients in cases of epilepsy and other nervous disorders. In the second half of the nineteenth century, the drug hyoscyamus, also derived from henbane extracts, was used to calm maniacal delirium in patients. Another medicine with active components in the Hyoscyamus niger family, Scopolamine, was one of the earliest alkaloids used as a presurgical anaesthetic in the late nineteenth century. Scopolamine was used to induce what would become known as twilight sleep, and it was also used for its calming and sedating effect on patients.

In the late nineteenth century, alkaloids and their compounds were mainly used as sedatives or sleep-inducing medications on patients suffering from mental health issues. Apomorphine, manufactured under the name Apokyn, was a form of morphine composition, and it was made by boiling morphine with concentrated amounts of acid. The resulting medication didn't actually contain morphine, nor did it bind to the opioid receptors in the brain. Instead, Apokyn was used to relieve anxiety and ease vomiting in patients in the mid to late nineteenth century. Historically, apomorphine, or Apokyn, has been used to reduce cravings in alcoholics and treat repeated behaviour in farm animals.

Francis Hare (1858-1928) was a Dublin-born physician working in a London asylum. He was a firm believer in the use of Apokyn, and in 1905, he wrote 'In the Sanitorium, it is used in three different sets of circumstances. In maniacal or hysterical drunkenness, during the paroxysm of dipsomania and in essential insomnia of a special variety'.

Apokyn has proved its worth and is still used today in the treatment of Parkinson's disease.

The use of Hyoscyamine cocktails was a true beginning to asylum psychopharmacology. Hyoscyamine is a tropane alkaloid similar to the Hyoscyamus niger that today is used to provide relief of several abdominal ailments. When combined with opioids, an increased level of pain relief is reached. Hyoscyamine cocktails made up of hyoscine, morphine, and atropine became the basic lore of treatment through the late nineteenth-century asylums. They eased the aggression of headbanging as well as the rubbing and pulling of hair or skin. These cocktails became vital for patients who were agitating themselves to the point of significant harm or even death. But while hyoscyamine cocktails were a step in the right direction, they only cured the symptoms of insanity, not the insanity itself.

In the 1850s, a doctor from Scotland would invent something that would not only lead him to notoriety but change the world of medicine as we know it - the first hypodermic needle.

In 1817, Alexander Wood was born in Fife and enrolled in the University of Edinburgh, where he took up the study of medicine. He became particularly interested in administering anaesthesia and finding better ways of pain relief.

In 1853, Wood's research led him to improve on the idea of a hollow needle by adding a plunger. His ideas resulted in the first glass syringe with a needle, allowing doctors to estimate the dosage of liquid medication administered to their patients. The actual term 'hypodermic' would not be used for several decades, and Wood referred to his invention as treatment by subcutaneous. He further described his work as using his needles to inject morphine directly into the bloodstream of agitated patients to calm them, and it worked. The method soon became wildly popular in Britain.

One unfortunate side of Wood's discovery is that history tells us his wife, Rebecca, suffered from intravenous morphine addictions and would later die due to an overdose delivered by her husband's invention.

The idea of sedating patients to ease agitation or mania was becoming more popular, especially with the discovery of Bromide Sleep. Bromide Sleep, also called Deep Sleep Therapy, or Prolonged Sleep Treatment, was developed by Scottish psychiatrist Neil Macleod at the end of the nineteenth century. Using sodium bromide, which was effective as an anti-convulsant and sedative, Macleod began to induce sleep in a few of his patients suffering from drug addiction. Using large doses of the bromide would cause his patients to sleep for days on end and lose all ability to stand, walk or speak.

Unfortunately, Macleod's experiment would cause the death of one of his patients. Monitoring Bromide Sleep was difficult because of bromide's rapid accumulation in the blood. Past the early manifestations of sleepiness and mental dullness, a toxic aspect is delivered if bromide levels rise above a certain level in the body.

Macleod spent time practising medicine in Shanghai, China, where he would administer doses of sodium bromide to his female patients in the hopes of curing their morphine addictions. In most cases, it played a large part in the recovery of these patients. Around the year 1900, it was soon discovered that Macleod's Bromide Sleep could also be used as a potential treatment for acute mania, and his success was written about in the *British Journal of Medicine*.

Historian Edward Shorter said 'For the first time in the history of psychiatry, here was a drug therapy that seemed to alleviate major psychiatric illnesses with a physical procedure'.

Macleod's Bromide Sleep would often last anywhere for five to nine days. During this period of sleep, the 'higher nerve centers arrested to an extent that cannot be attained in any other way'.

After patients rose from their death-like slumber, a gradual recovery period included a slow awakening and regaining of mental capacity.

Macleod's method of sleep therapy would soon be abandoned as it may have been considered too risky. It wasn't under the 1920s that Swiss psychiatrist Jakob Klaesi (1883-1980) would bring the treatment back to popularity in the field of mental health.

Klaesi was known for his contributions to sleep therapy by combining two barbiturates in the treatment of schizophrenic patients. Barbiturates are a class of drugs that slow the central nervous system and are used as anti-convulsants and hypnotics. Swiss pharmaceutical company Roche, founded in 1896, marketed Klaesi's combination of barbiturates as a drug called Somnifen. Somnifen would become popular in mental hospitals throughout the 1930s and 1940s and was wildly promoted in the United Kingdom by psychiatrist William Sargant. Sargant was a massive advocate for deep sleep therapy and other methods of treating mental illness. By using Somnifen, doctors were able to block out all stimuli through the deep period of narcosis.

Deep Sleep Therapy became even more popular, and it made its way to Australia, where it was practised by Dr Harry Bailey in New South Wales at Chelmsford Private Hospital. Bailey used the treatment for patients with not only schizophrenia but premenstrual syndrome in women, depression, and drug dependence.

Unfortunately, it was at Chelmsford Private Hospital where disaster would strike. During the 1960s and 1970s, twenty-five patients would die as a result of deep sleep therapy. Despite this, the treatment would continue until 1979.

It wasn't that the use of barbiturates was dangerous; they were just safer in and of themselves. Around the time that Somnifen was being marketed, Barbital, one of the first commercially available barbiturates, was being used as a sleeping aid in Germany.

German chemist and 1902 recipient of the Nobel Prize in Chemistry, Emil Fischer (1852-1919), understood barbiturates on a deeper level. He knew they were sedatives, but he also knew they were not toxic if used properly. They also didn't share the same unpleasant taste that many of their predecessors did.

By 1904, barbiturates were heavily marketed by the German pharmaceutical company, Bayer Company, founded in 1863, under the name Veronal. Veronal, a soluble salt of barbital, was being used for insomnia and nervous excitability in patients.

Though expensive, barbital was considered a significant improvement over the existing hypnotics used to treat agitation and anxiety. Side effects were slim, and its effective dosage was nowhere near the toxic level of bromides. Barbital directly affects the central nervous system, causing mild sedation to coma in some cases. Bayer Company's Veronal quickly became the drug of choice in private clinics.

Bayer Company would also bring to market a drug called Luminal in 1912. Luminal was the drug phenobarbital, which was also synthesised by Emil Fischer. While the drug's sedating effects were well known, it was not yet discovered that Luminal was also a remarkable anti-convulsant. When German psychiatrist and neurologist Alfred Hauptmann used it to tranquillize his epileptic patients, he found that it affected their seizures. At the time, most of Hauptmann's patients were being treated with bromide, with little effect along with its undesirable side effects. Hauptmann was delighted to see that even his worse patients suffered fewer and less severe seizures after being treated with phenobarbital. Some even became free of their seizures altogether and could return to everyday life outside the asylum. Luminal was quickly adopted as the first safe and effective anti-convulsant medication, and it is still used today in both human and veterinary medicine.

With the transformative success of barbiturates came the first attempt of psychiatrists at curing mental illness. Doctors seemed to be making sense of the fact that changing a patient's brain chemistry could improve or reverse symptoms of certain mental health conditions, but they were still far from understanding exactly how. With the brilliance of Germany's medical establishments, the embarkment of these therapies gave psychiatrists of the early twentieth-century new hope.

In 1925 Berlin, a psychiatric graduate student named Manfred Sakel (1900-1957) would further change the world of psychiatric medicine. Sakel, who had studied medicine at the University of Vienna, specialised in neurology and neuropsychiatry.

While working at a private clinic, Sakel worked predominately with patients suffering from morphine addiction, an unfortunate result of Alexander Wood's invention of using the hypodermic needle to administer the drug. Part of Sakel's work was to ease the withdrawal symptoms of discontinuing morphine, which was highly unsettling. Patients would typically experience flu-like symptoms, such as headaches, nausea, and fever. Body chills, anxiety, depression, and diarrhoea were also common and could result in severe dehydration, which could be fatal at times.

Sakel discovered that the side effects from withdrawal could be eased by giving his patients small doses of insulin.

The discovery of insulin started in 1889 when two German researchers discovered that removing the pancreas gland from dogs would cause symptoms of diabetes and eventually death. Fast forward to 1910, where Sir Edward Albert Sharpey-Shafer (1850-1935) discovered that one chemical was the missing link for those with diabetes. He called that chemical insulin. Fast forward again to 1921, where a young surgeon named Frederick Banting discovered how to remove insulin from a dog's pancreas, and it was later used to save a fourteen-year-old boy from Canada with diabetes from dying. A simple injection brought the boy's high glucose levels to normal, and the news about insulin spread worldwide.

Not only would the discovery of insulin in 1922 mark the beginning of a significant breakthrough in therapy for diabetic patients, but, as

Sakel discovered not long after, it offered some hope in the treatment of morphine addiction. He also found that insulin could help treat the mentally ill. He knew that insulin was produced naturally, worked by causing the muscles in the body to use glucose in the blood. If the body created an overabundance of insulin and too much glucose was withdrawn, then the body would suffer from hypoglycemic shock and coma. Hypoglycemic shock is the opposite of high blood sugar in diabetics but can be just as dangerous.

Through his research with addiction patients, Sakel had learned that measured doses of insulin could cause tranquillity in those suffering from the discomforts of withdrawal. When using his insulin treatment on a patient in 1927, he accidentally gave the gentleman too much, causing him to slip into a coma. When the patient recovered from that coma, there was a noticeable improvement in his mental state. Seeing this caused Dr Sakel to ponder whether or not insulin-induced comas could do the same for patients suffering from schizophrenia

While practising as a young doctor in Vienna, he began to test his insulin therapy on his mentally ill patients. After positive results, he ultimately believed that a coma could safely continue for up to several hours until it was interrupted by giving the patient glucose in various forms. After publicly announcing his theory in 1933, the methods were quickly adopted by other psychiatrists throughout the world. British psychiatrists who had visited Vienna were impressed, and by 1938, thirty-one hospitals throughout the United Kingdom were using insulin treatment for psychiatric patients.

Insulin treatment wards became standard in most asylums and usually presented as two rows of patient beds on either side of the room kept in semi-darkness to promote relaxation. Insulin Coma Therapy, or ICT, was a treatment that often required a specially trained staff assigned to the insulin ward and was usually the line of treatment for those suffering from schizophrenia.

Most hospitals followed a fairly standard routine when it came to insulin treatment. The patient was denied anything to eat or drink after midnight and would typically be woken around 6 am, where they were dressed in a short sleeve cotton shirt and long cotton drawers. The patient was brought to the specific treatment ward where a nurse would take their vital signs, which they would be paying close attention to throughout the procedure.

The patient would then be given an intramuscular or subcutaneous injection of pre-dosed insulin in the shoulder or buttock. The patient would fall asleep gradually before slipping into a coma. This was known as the pre-coma stage. Two different kinds of comas were recognised, a 'dry' and a 'wet' coma. During a dry coma, the patient's skin was often hot and dry, and their muscles twitched in a specific sequence that began with the face and worked its way down to the legs. These twitches were often small, but it wasn't unheard of for a patient to violently move an arm and leg. During a wet coma, the patient would begin to sweat uncontrollably, and goosebumps often erupted over their skin. The patient's salivary glands would go into overdrive to the point that nurses often had to sop up any drool. Patients in a wet coma often shivered from being cold and could often become restless or excited. To protect them and the staff from physical harm, bedsheets were usually tucked around the patients as a gentle form of restraint.

When the patient slipped into a deep coma, they would no longer respond to voice or touch. Their breathing would become slow, and the eyes might wander about, though the pupillary response to light was still on point. The patient's muscles would spasm, and if sweating were profuse, often a temperature would present.

Most patients stayed under direct observation of the staff as close attention needed to be paid to the various coma stages throughout the treatment. Some patients fell into a coma more quickly than others, and if the doctor was concerned about the patient's vitals in any way, a time of rest was ordered.

Low blood sugar, or hypoglycemia, which was achieved with the insulin injection, triggers the release of epinephrine, which causes symptoms such as increased heart rate, sweating, and anxiety. When the blood sugar levels continue to drop, the brain does not get enough glucose and ceases to function as it should. Starving the brain of glucose for too long leads to comas, but it can also cause death.

Patients were watched closely to ensure their body temperature didn't drop lower than 92 degrees. They were also closely monitored for excessive salvation as it could cause fluid in one's lungs, requiring the need to be aspirated. The patient's breathing would eventually become irregular and their pulse rapid, and the pupillary response would become absent.

Convulsions were an expected part of the therapy and appeared in the second and third stages of coma, particularly during periods of dry coma. Seizures called for the protection of the patient and staff. In addition to sheet restraints, the patient's teeth and tongue needed to be protected during tonic spasms, which were brief but painful, unilateral muscle contractions. In the ICT ward, each bed had a table next to it with mouth guards, usually made from wooden tongue depressors covered with gauze making the device soft against the patient's teeth. Besides protecting the patient's teeth from breakage, the idea of the mouthguard was to prevent the patients from biting off their tongues.

Patients often experienced laryngospasms, which was a sudden spasm of the vocal cords brought about by the stress of the procedure. During these spasms, the patient was unable to speak or breathe effectively and would sometimes slip deeper into the coma.

The stages of the coma were monitored every ten minutes or so and generally ended anywhere from 30-60 minutes later, depending on the physician's orders. After remaining in their death-like state for an extended time, the patient would be given a sugar solution to reverse the effects of the insulin. The solution, usually dextrose or corn syrup, was administered depending on how awake the patient was. If a patient were coherent enough, they would be asked to sit up and drink the solution. But if the patient remained in the comatose state, a nurse would often insert a gavage tube up through the nose and into the stomach with 50% glucose solution. If the nasal infusion wasn't effective, the glucose would be given intravenously at 10% glucose solution. Both methods would cause the patient to awaken almost immediately.

When a patient awakened from an insulin-induced coma, their speech would often be slow and drunken-like, but they would slowly regain awareness of their surroundings and usually ask for something to eat. It was not uncommon for a patient to soil the bed, so a shower and clean clothes would be in order.

After treatment, the patients often appeared calm and void of delusions and could communicate with others in a friendly and relaxed manner, though weakness in their speech was not uncommon. The patients were encouraged to spend the next day relaxing with a book or tending to light hospital routines.

Doctors were hopeful that after a series of treatments, the patient's mental illness would vanish in what was called a 'lucid period' where all abnormal behaviour would be displaced. Treatments could go on for months, sometimes bi-weekly, until the patient achieved the desired outcome. There were some wonderous achievements along this path to modern psychiatry. Several very ill patients were relieved of their symptoms, which allowed psychiatrists to feel like they were genuinely medical doctors able to help their patients. Kark Dussik (1908-1968), a Viennese neuroscientist and colleague of Sakel, said 'The personality of the patient can often be changed so entirely during the hypoglycemic reactions that it seems as though the glycogenic treatment has created a new beginning'.

In 1934, when Sakel broadcasted his ICT results throughout Europe, he claimed a complete remission of schizophrenia in 70% of patients. While his results were entirely favoured in many parts of Europe, his coma therapy was especially accepted in Switzerland and England. The Munsinger Asylum in Switzerland would soon become the mecca of insulin therapy.

Author JD Ratcliff, a prolific writer in science and medicine, said in 1938:

> Insulin shock, the new violent method of dealing with certain forms of insanity, is as dramatic as medieval magic. And it really works. Dr. Manfred Sakel, its inventor, has brought hope to hundreds of thousands of people otherwise condemned to a life of constant nightmare.

German physician, Pullar Strecker, is essentially responsible for bringing the idea of insulin therapy to England. After receiving a research grant, he was put in charge of the insulin unit at Royal Edinburgh Hospital for Mental Disorders, where he first initiated insulin therapy in 1936. British doctors were hooked and saw insulin therapy as heaven-sent.

Dr Eliot Slater (1904-1983), a British physicist who was a pioneer in the field of mental disorders, spoke highly of insulin therapy. He said it was the first therapy that helped his severely ill patients. A Canadian physician, who practised in Warwickshire, said:

> This 1400 bed hospital of block type has a staff of six physicians, all under age 35 and all are keen. Our trust is not in the extra staff but in the drugs and barbiturates in particular. And now, of course, insulin shock for the schizophrenic group is giving us a chemical procedure for the other great biogenic group. How the heart of the druggist has been gladdened these past four years. Dr. DN Parfitt, our chief, spent six weeks in Vienna, and we started cases 5 weeks ago. Only three or four places in Great Britain have started, and no literature of importance has appeared here. I expect to spend August and September in the insulin shock clinic.

In 1934, Sakel's insulin therapy had made it to the United States with great success, and by 1939, every self-respecting hospital throughout the Western world had an insulin unit. Patients began to report some improvements after several insulin-induced comas, and at Maudsley Hospital in London, recovery rates among patients were reported to have doubled.

Despite its success, some physicians found the process of ICT to be too lengthy as patients needed to be monitored for several hours. ICT was also required to be administered several times a week and put high demand on already understaffed hospitals.

Ladislaus Von Meduna (1896-1964), a Hungarian psychiatrist and neuropathologist who worked at the Brain Research Institute in Budapest, had developed a great interest in treating patients with schizophrenia. He observed the neurological differences between schizophrenics and epileptics during autopsies. He came up with a theory that the two conditions were not compatible, and he proposed helping schizophrenic patients by deliberately causing them to have epileptic fits. His fellow scholars had also reported that epileptic patients who later developed schizophrenia seemed to experience fewer epileptic fits. Meduna wondered if that meant schizophrenic patients might improve after developing epilepsy. His objective was to effect specific psychosis by artificially and carefully controlling convulsive attacks.

After practising on guinea pigs, in January of 1934, Meduna gave the terpenoid, Camphor, to a delusional patient of his at the Royal State Mental Hospital in Budapest. His patient had a history of hearing voices and began hiding in his bed and refusing food.

Camphor is a crystalline compound that is derived from camphor tree bark. Administered by injection, camphor was thought to be an effective medication at producing convulsions. Meduna treated his patient for two weeks with painful camphor injections, which brought on epileptic attacks. Slowly the patient began to improve. He got out of bed and started to speak normally, asking for food. The patient seemed almost entirely coherent, and after four years of being committed to the hospital, he was able to go home.

While camphor did appear promising and had helped other patients recover, it was still unreliable in producing the kind of fits doctors were looking for. It was also a painful injection that instilled tremendous trepidation in patients before their treatment.

Max Muller, director of the Munsingen Asylum in Switzerland, had this to say on the Camphor injections he witnessed. He said:

> The sight of the artificially produced attack of epilepsy, especially of the contorted blue faces, was so awful to me that I sought to get away from the room whenever I could. I realize now the inadequacy of my excuse that I could have achieved nothing with my presence and that my colleagues were more robust and not so squeamish. But it was my responsibility.

After experimenting further, Meduna settled on the synthetic drug cardiazol, or metrozol as it was called in the United States, as the perfect trigger for convulsions. The discovery of using cardiazol, a potent central nervous system stimulant, to induce comas was very promising to Meduna.

The medication was similar to camphor and had fewer side effects. It was also easily soluble in water, making it easier to inject. Cardiazol treatment was also based on the observation that schizophrenia rarely existed in patients with epilepsy. However, when it did occur, epileptics had a recovery rate of almost sixteen times higher. It was also noted that schizophrenics of the catatonic type found their symptoms to disappear after epileptic seizures. Meduna was curious if inducing artificial seizures in patients would cause them to recover from schizophrenia. He had confidence in his treatment and believed it to be safe and ready to carry out.

Patients receiving the cardiazol treatment would have a complete exam by a physician and sign a consent waiver in most cases. Cardiazol was given intravenously, and the dosage would fluctuate depending on the patient. This method was preferred over muscular injections as it reached the body's central nervous system more rapidly, usually in mere seconds. In several cases, the patient would begin to have a seizure before the needle was even withdrawn.

In a 1937 edition of the *Journal of Mental Medicines*, Assistant Medical Officer of West Park Hospital in Surrey, Alexander Kennedy, described cardiazol treatment in detail.

> a wide bore needle was pushed 2 cm into the vein to avoid leakage resulting from the high pressure at which the solution was injected. Almost immediately, colour was drained from the patient's face, which became stiff and motionless.

The medication was administered roughly three times a week, as doctors believed that the more convulsions the patient had, the higher the success rate. Seizures lasted anywhere from 30 seconds to a minute and a half and consisted of three phases; clonic, tonic, followed by another clonic stage. The physical presentation of the seizure must have been distressing as the patient could go into coughing fits, have flushing of the skin, and frozen facial muscles, which were most likely from fear. The patient would then fall unconscious and clonic movements would present, which included the hands and feet used in a fight or flight way. Due to this natural reaction of the body, the patient may try to sit forward in an attempt to escape. However, the tonic phase followed next. This would cause the patient to become rigid and fall back on the table. A gag was often inserted into the mouth so the patient didn't accidentally bite their tongue or damage their teeth. During the tonic phase, the patient often stopped breathing and took on a blueish appearance before the clonic movements would begin again. The patient then fell into a comatose state, where they were exhausted and confused and often fell asleep.

Severe reactions could be had, including nausea, vomiting, and headache, along with back soreness. It wasn't unheard of for the patient's jaw to become dislocated from the rigid yawning movement of the tonic phase. Dislocation of the humerus or scapula, though rare, was not unheard of. Although there was much anxiety from the patients before the treatments, it was believed that favourable changes were seen. Disturbed or restless patients became calmer and more cooperative. Often mute patients began to talk and become more alert and responsive. They also seemed to become more receptive to the help offered by hospital staff.

Meduna was quite optimistic about the cardiazol treatments, and he felt they were best done in the early stages of mental illness. He also stated that he saw remissions in over 80% of his patients.

The late 1930s brought about much talk of new physical therapies for mental illness that were different from anything else that had been attempted. Barbiturates, insulin, and cardiazol certainly extended the promise that there may be a cure. Talk of what would be known as electroconvulsive therapy or ECT began. However, this wasn't exactly a new idea. History tells us that Galen used a form of shock from electric eels to ease gout in several patients. Richard Lovett (1692-1780), an English lay amateur scientist, claimed to treat mental illness while experimenting with sparks and currents of electricity, following its discovery by Benjamin Franklin in 1752. Only a few years later, in 1759, John Wesley (1703-1791), founder of the Methodist Church, spoke in favour of the use of electricity towards treating the mentally ill. He said 'I doubt not, but more nervous disorders would be cured in one year by this single remedy than the whole English medica will cure by the end of the century'.

The early part of the nineteenth century witnessed widespread use of static electricity, and German scientist Robert Remark held a private practice primarily based on electrotherapy. His patients were treated with Galvano therapy, a form of electrotherapy used on those afflicted with diseases of the brain and spinal cord.

But it wasn't until 1938 that actual electroshock therapy, or ECT, was first used. Italian physician Ugo Cerletti (1877-1963) was working at the time as director of the Neuropsychiatric Clinic in Genoa. While researching epilepsy, he wondered if lesions in the brain may be the cause or the effect of an epileptic attack. He attempted to use electricity in dogs as an experiment; however, most of the dogs died as a result. For almost a year, once a week, a local dog officer would bring a group of stray dogs to Cerletti's lab for experimentation. Initially, Cerletti and his colleagues placed electrodes in the mouths and in the anus' of dogs, which almost always caused them to die. The configuration of this process crossed the heart, causing cardiac arrest in the unfortunate animals. The team was using around 125 volts to induce convulsions in the dogs. However, death in humans by only 40 volts had been reported. So it's not hard to understand why these animals died.

While working closely with one of his students, Lucio Bini (1908-1964), Cerletti attempted to research further into the experiments. He discovered that if electrodes were placed on the dog's temples rather than their tongues, the pulse of electricity produced convulsions without death. The pair continued their experiments while simultaneously performing autopsies on the brains of the canines. They soon brought their experiments to a local slaughterhouse to study the boundaries between successful convulsive therapy and killing an animal with a lethal dose of electricity. As they grew more proficient in their work, Bini began to ponder whether or not the treatment could be used on people. They used the same concept in that using one disease to treat another could be successful, much like Meduna and his cardiazol treatments. But while Meduna's patients had to wait for the onset of a seizure, they waited in terror for what was known to be an extremely unpleasant procedure. Cerletti and Bini wondered if there was a better way.

It was Lucio Bini who built the first electroshock device, which was initially used to research epilepsy.

On the morning of 11 April 1938, at the Clinic of Mental and Nervous Diseases in Rome, Cerletti and his team gathered around a bed in an isolated room. In the bed lay a middle-aged man who had been wandering through a Rome train station. Police brought the unnamed man in after he was picked up, walking around in a confused state. The man did not know his name or where he was from, and his speech was hardly recognisable. Assuming he was another mentally ill hobo, the authorities brought him to Cerletti's clinic. He would be the first human being to undergo ECT.

With his hair already shaved off for the procedure, a circular device made of metal was placed on the man's head. Several wires branched off of the device to a machine that sat on a nearby table.

With the go-ahead from Cerletti, Lucio Bini switched on the bedside machine to send 80 volts of electrical current to the patient's temples. The patient's body contracted, and he jerked, but he then relaxed again on the bed with no understanding of what had just happened to him. Cerletti saw that he was still very much alive and had tolerated the voltage of electricity. But because he was looking for a full seizure, Cerletti ordered another shock of electricity to be administered. This time at 90 volts. After a brief moment of asphyxia, the patient sat up on the bed and began to sing. Cerletti was relieved that the patient was still alive, but he was still intent on inducing a seizure.

With some apprehension to move forward from his team, another shock of 110 volts was delivered. The patient's muscles began to contract, only this time he did not relax afterwards. He started to shake in the undeniable rhythm of a total seizure. After a 48 second convulsion, with questionable breathing at times, the patient exhaled, relaxed, and fell fast asleep. All of his vital signs were normal, and Cerletti declared the first successful run of ECT on a human being.

Cerletti's patient received regular electroshock treatments over the next several months. The patient then began to speak clearly and not with the unintelligible babble he first presented with. The patient was not homeless, and in fact, his wife had been frantically searching for him. The man's treatment remained successful, the couple was reunited, and he returned to everyday life. Cerletti saw it as a tremendous breakthrough.

Around the same time that Ugo Cerletti discovered ECT, another doctor was also taking up an interest in the procedure. Lothar Kalinowsky (1899-1992) was born in Berlin in December of 1899 and went to medical school in Heidelberg and Munich. After an internship at a psychiatric hospital in Hamburg, he decided to pursue a psychiatry career.

Kalinowsky left Germany for Rome in 1933 after losing his academic position because of Nazi influence. He passed Italy's medical boards and met up with Cerletti in 1935. He found him to be brilliant and very inventive. Kalinowski also met the young and enthusiastic Lucio Bini. The three of them were in the same room together as the first patient ever received ECT.

Kalinowsky became a strong advocate for ECT and later introduced it to France, England, and the Netherlands. While working at the Maudsley Hospital, he pioneered in sparking the interest of English doctors in using ECT. Based on the original machine Bini had constructed in Rome, the Solus Electrical Company in London built the first one in the country.

It was found that ECT did greatly alleviate the symptoms of insanity, allowing most of the patients to function somewhat normally again. The idea spread throughout the world of psychiatry, partly thanks to Kalinowsky, and everywhere the ECT machine was introduced, it was greeted by enthusiasm. Upon its arrival at Bethlem, one doctor said 'ECT produced instant unconsciousness, no dread, no physical upset after the convulsion, no vomiting'.

Another said:

> Without ECT, I would not have lasted out in psychiatry as I would not have been able to tolerate the sadness and hopelessness of most mental illness before the introduction of convulsive therapy.

Before receiving treatment, the patient was not allowed to eat or drink for roughly six hours. They would also be expected to use the bathroom, and any jewellery would be removed from their person.

The patient was then brought to a treatment room where they were asked to lay on a bed and were given some form of barbiturate to sedate them, though sedation wasn't always offered. The medication atropine was often given to maintain the patient's heart activity and to dry any secretions in the mouth. Muscle relaxants were often given alongside this to reduce the risk of fractures. Much like the cardiazol treatment, a gag would have been placed in the patient's mouth for protection. After vitals were taken and the electrodes were placed on the temple, the physician would administer a shock by pressing a button on the shock device. Between 100 and 150 volts of electricity could be delivered, inducing a seizure that lasted several seconds. The idea was to produce a grand mal convulsion that could continue for up to one minute. Immediate complications would include lack of breathing, reduced oxygen, or cardiac arrest. If done successfully, convulsions were followed by a brief coma before the patient would awaken. It was reasonable to expect the patient to experience disorientation and dizziness, followed by headache and nausea. In some cases, the patient could experience amnesia that lasted for months and was sometimes permanent.

Doctors estimated that the effectiveness of ECT could be as high as 90%, and by 1944, in England, ECT had completely overcome cardiazol in producing fits. The therapy grew in popularity, and soon, journals were being written worldwide. In 1941, an American doctor by the name of Lucie Jessner published a piece called *Shock Treatment in Psychiatry: A Manual*. At the Maudsley hospital in 1944, William

Sargant and Eliot Slater wrote *An Introduction to Physical Methods of Treatment in Psychiatry*. And in 1946, along with Lothar Kalinowsky, Dr. Paul Hoch wrote *Shock Treatment and Other Somatic Procedures in Psychiatry*.

By the 1950s, ECT was standard practice in asylums throughout the United States and Western Europe. A patient hospitalised for mental illness stood an excellent chance of not only receiving ECT but benefitting greatly from it. Clementine, the wife of Winston Churchill, received ECT in 1963. American actress, Judy Garland, was treated with ECT at the age of twenty-six, after years of battling depression.

Doctors didn't understand how ECT worked then, and they still don't today. But they saw their patients being shed of the horrible symptoms of catatonia, mania, severe depression, and even suicide. Patients who had spent months, even years, in a deep slumber of mental illness were seen interacting with others, enjoying food again, and often returning to everyday life outside the asylum.

But there were also dangers to the use of ECT. As the patient thrashed on the table, they were at risk of broken limbs and vertebrae. At the Horton Hospital in England, nurses had to drape themselves over the patient, holding their feet and pressing down on their pelvis and shoulders, and holding the head and jaw to try to keep them from breaking a bone. Though rare, bone fractures were a severe complication of ECT, and physicians experimented with different medications to modify the patient's convulsions. The use of suxamethonium, a derivative of the paralytic poison curare, led to more widespread use of what was deemed modified ECT. It was given along with a short-acting anaesthetic and a muscle relaxant to calm patients before the procedure. In 1949, ECT was changed more by placing the electrode over the brain's right hemisphere to avoid the areas that affected speech.

Aside from headaches and muscle pain, psychiatrists weren't immune to the fact that patients often had unfavourable reactions to

ECT, including confusion, which could last several hours to several days. Retrograde amnesia, when patients had trouble remembering events that led up to the procedure, was also seen.

Dr Paul Hoch said that the brain damage caused by ECT was beneficial. He said 'Is a certain amount of brain damage not necessary in this type of treatment?' Still, not all professionals were convinced, and several spoke out about it.

Dr Peter Breggin, an American psychiatrist, who is still alive today, states that the only effect of ECT was from the brain damage it caused. ECT may do the same damage as a severe head injury, resulting in amnesia and extreme mood swings. However, Breggin said that early twentieth-century psychiatrists may have seen the symptoms of brain injury as those of recovery.

A 1984 United States article reported that in fifty years of research on ECT, no study found the procedure's benefits to last longer than four weeks. Part of this conclusion was that mental disorders are irreversible and chronic. Studies published on the death rate of ECT seem to vary as one study in 1985 claimed that the death rate was between 0.01-0.03%, while other similar studies suggest the death rate was as high as 2%.

Italian-born neuropsychiatrist David Impastato (1903-1986), who pioneered the use of ECT in the United States, suggested that the death rate among the elderly was even higher. He said that cardio failure among patients was to blame for almost half the deaths resulting from ECT. This isn't an unreasonable assumption, as we know that the current passed into the brain from ECT would have been fatal if the same amount had been applied to the chest.

While commenting on the extent of brain damage caused by ECT, neurosurgeon and renowned professor at Radford University in Virginia, Karl Pribram, said 'I'd much rather have a small lobotomy than a series of ECT shocks. I just know what the brain looks like after a series of shocks, and it's not very pleasant to look at'.

Regardless of the opinions of medical professionals, by 1959, ECT had become the treatment of choice for manic depressive illness and major depression. ECT is the only physical treatment for mental illness from the early twentieth century to survive. Today ECT is practised with patient consent and using only the highest standards of medical care. It is believed to be entirely safe, especially for patients who don't respond to traditional methods of care.

Sam, a former asylum patient who resides in Cardiff today, had ECT to treat her severe depression. During the 1970s, she had a psychotic episode after childbirth, and a series of ECT treatments significantly improved her state of mind. Over the next several decades, she had a few relapses, but it was ECT that once again essentially saved her life.

'ECT has saved my life a number of times,' said Sam. 'There are side effects, I get some short-term memory loss, but for me, that's far outweighed by the benefits.'

Despite the stigma it has today, the idea of operating on patients to cure mental illness was not unreasonable. Medical practitioners have always wondered if surgical intervention might put an end to psychosis. We know that a long history of trepidation was used to alter undesirable behaviour and mental illness. Aside from the use of puncturing the skull in ancient Greek and Roman times, as well as the Middle Ages, Medicine men of the Pre-Inca Civilisation would incise the scalp of their patients with a surgical knife and apply his tumi, or ceremonial knife, to the skull to relieve headaches or supposed possession. It's hard to believe that people could survive an operation that was undoubtedly gruesome, even if well-intended. But the survival of patients is evident in the skulls of people who underwent trepidation, as the edges of the bone showed apparent healing when discovered by archaeologists.

Because of insufficient medical data in history, we don't know if the patient's maladies ever actually improved through the first trials of psychosurgery.

Gottlieb Burckhardt (1836-1907) was a Swiss psychiatrist and is regarded as having performed the first psychosurgical operation of the modern era. He was born in the city of Basel and attended medical school at the Universities of Basel, Berlin, and Gottingen and received his degree in 1860. Burckhardt formed an illustrious career over the next several decades, including being elected president of the Basel Medical Society in 1873. He lectured extensively on nervous and mental disorders and contributed to several medical publications.

In 1822, Dr Burckhardt became the medical director of a small but up-and-coming psychiatric clinic in the Swiss Canton of Neuchatel. At the clinic's laboratory, he deepened his research into neuroanatomy.

Six years later, in December of 1888, having minimal experience in surgery, Burckhardt performed the first series of psychosurgical operations. He had six patients under his care whose conditions were particularly problematic, including chronic mania, paranoid psychosis, and dementia. Recordings in his case notes tell us that his patients suffered from severe hallucinations, delusions, aggression, and violence, all of which stemmed from the brain's cerebral cortex. Burckhardt's operations removed specific parts of the cerebral cortex, including sections of the frontal and temporal lobes, using his 'T' shaped trepanning tool that had a bladed cylinder at one end. He also used a Hey's saw.

The results of the surgeries were less than promising as one patient passed after five days, one later committed suicide, two became somewhat quieter, and the other two showed no change whatsoever. However, Burckhardt stood behind his theories—one being that the basis of mental illness is physical and came from disordered brains. He believed that each cognitive module of the brain could be linked to a particular location. By severing the connecting system, problems with communication might be fixable without damaging the input and output of the nervous system.

He presented his findings at the Berlin Medical Conference of 1889, but they were received with much negativity, as there was a lot of uncertainty about the procedures he had performed. He also published his results of the procedure but received nothing but scathe and ridicule from his colleagues. Due to this, Burckhardt ended his career in psychiatry.

Gottlieb Burckhardt's impressive and lengthy career ended in somewhat of a disaster, but I feel that it's important to reflect on his attempts at treating his patients. His methods may have been radical, but without them, I wonder if the advancements made in psychosurgery would have come as far as they did.

As it became known in the United States, the American Crowbar Case may have helped develop the early concept of true psychosurgery. Ideas were derived from the study of brain pathology and the changed behaviour of a Mr Phineas Gage. Mr Gage was a railroad foreman living in Vermont in 1848. On the afternoon of 13 September, an event would occur that would change his life forever. As he turned around to speak to one of his workers, a tamping rod used in a blast hole would find its way through his head when he opened his mouth. The rod, which was 1.25 inches in diameter, over three feet long, and weighing over thirteen pounds, rocketed up from the blasting hole and bore its way through the left side of Gage's face through his lower jaw. The rod continued through his upper jaw, passed behind his left eye, and exited through his skull's frontal bone. It propelled roughly 80 feet away where it landed point down, covered in blood and brain matter.

Phineas Gage was thrown onto his back and began to convulse, but he spoke within a few minutes and shockingly got up to walk away with little assistance from his men. Upon meeting up with physician Edward H Williams, he was astonished at what he saw.

> I first noticed the wound upon the head before I alighted from my carriage, the pulsations of the brain being very distinct. The top of the head appeared somewhat like an inverted funnel, as if some wedge-shaped body had passed from below upward. Mr. Gage, during the time

> I was examining this wound, was relating the manner in which he was injured to the bystanders. I did not believe Mr. Gage's statement at that time, but thought he was deceived. Mr. Gage persisted in saying that the bar went through his head. Mr. G. got up and vomited; the effort of vomiting pressed out about half a teacupful of the brain [through the exit hole at the top of the skull], which fell upon the floor.

Gage was then presented to a surgeon, Dr Harlow, later that evening, upon which he remarked:

> You will excuse me for remarking here, that the picture presented was, to one unaccustomed to military surgery, truly terrific; but the patient bore his sufferings with the most heroic firmness. He recognized me at once, and said he hoped he was not much hurt. He seemed to be perfectly conscious, but was getting exhausted from the hemorrhage. His person, and the bed on which he was laid, were literally one gore of blood.

Dr Williams and Dr Harlow would embark on a surgery that would change the face of history. Together they removed bone fragments and over an ounce of blood and parts of Gage's brain. The wound was closed with bandage strips.

Remarkably, Mr Gage survived but not without noteworthy mental and behavioural changes. He went from being motivated, capable, and outgoing to a man filled with irresponsibility and social ineptness. His injury was later deemed frontal lobe syndrome. The American Crowbar case received a great deal of notoriety in the medical community, and Gage's doctor kept in touch with him throughout his life. Today, his skull and tamping iron remain in the museum at Harvard Medical School in Cambridge, Massachusetts.

In 1890, Doctors Claye Shaw and Harrison Cripps wrote about one of their patients in the *British Medical Journal*. They had a male patient at Banstead Hospital in the village of Belmont Sutton, who had been suffering from some sort of fluid build-up in the brain that was causing a considerable amount of pressure and severe headaches along with paralytic insanity.

In order to find relief for his patient, Dr Cripps felt that a means of relieving the intracranial pressure was needed. He intended to do this by removing a small piece of bone from the skull. During the late 1880s and early 1890s, the *British Medical Journal* printed several articles giving opinions of using trepanation to treat mental illness. Both Dr Shaw and Dr Cripps were hopeful about the operation as they read data that spoke of the 'increased arterial tension in the early stages of general paralysis'.

The desired response to the surgery depended on early diagnosis, and both doctors were convinced that the patient would benefit if the operation were performed as soon as possible.

The patient was given chloroform, a powerful anaesthetic used for surgery before Dr Cripps performed the trepanation procedure. Two one-inch trephine holes were made, one of them revealing the bulging of dura mater, the outer layer of tissue that covers the brain and spinal cord, which was removed.

The operation was deemed a success as only a few days later, the patient's delusions and headache seemed to have eased. 'The present state of the patient is a great improvement upon what it was; in fact, he is no longer insane, and I propose to discharge him'.

Dr Shaw was triumphant in the success of the operation. The patient's delusions and headaches seemed to have eased, though temporarily. Later, the patient's wife wrote to the doctor to say that her husband could not keep his job and that he had become increasingly irritable. But Shaw and Cripps still saw the operation as a success because their patient no longer suffered from debilitating headaches, despite the change in his personality.

Much like Burkhardt, Shaws, Cripp, and even Phineas Gage's surgeons are sometimes forgotten in the history of psychosurgery. These men deserve recognition for their fearless bravery in attempting to go into the uncharted areas of the human brain. Even with today's modern medicine, neurosurgeons still don't know as much as they'd like about the human brain. Kailash Narayan MD, programme director for neurosurgical residency at Doctor's Hospital in Columbus, OH, said:

> What propels us is that neurosurgery is technically very challenging and intellectually very challenging. In spite of how far we've come, there is still so much more to know about the brain and how it functions.

It now seemed reasonable that operating on the cerebral cortex may offer promise. There was no doubt a willingness among doctors to meddle surgically in the brain, and it would just require time and new findings for it to be successful. The early nineteenth century saw several doctors who had dabbled with psychosurgery. Still, it wasn't until the 1930s that the Western world would embark on the true emergence of surgically trying to eliminate mental illness.

In 1935, in London, the 2nd International Neurology Congress in London was held and would prove to be a landmark for psychosurgery. The congress was a gathering of several doctors of neurology and psychiatry who were all further exploring the brain's functions.

It was here that American Physiologist John Fulton (1899-1960) presented the findings of his experiment with two chimpanzees. Along with his colleague, Carlyle Jacobson, Fulton tested the brains of two chimps to determine their level of intelligence. They then removed sections of the animal's frontal lobes and discovered that the intelligence of the chimps was not affected by the operation. Fulton did notice, however, that the chimps' temperaments were affected. They grew frustrated and began pulling at their hair and throwing their bodily stools around. Experimenting further, the two doctors removed the entire frontal lobes of the animals and noticed that they now presented as more docile. It was reported that the chimps were now devoid of any emotion and didn't seem to have the frustrating behaviour that was initially plaguing them.

The Neurology Congress was also attended by other doctors who would leave their marks on psychosurgery, including Dr Egas Moniz (1874-1955) and Dr Almeida Lima (1903-1985) from the University of Lisbon. Moniz was greatly interested in the emotional changes of the chimps after hearing about the ablation of their frontal lobes.

Moniz was born in 1874 in the coastal village of Avanca, Portugal, and attended medical school at the University of Coimbra, Portugal. He later studied in France, where he received training in neurology and psychiatry. He concentrated his career on experimenting with brain imaging and didn't consider psychosurgery before seeing Fulton's presentation at the Congress of Neurology in 1935. He was also influenced by the ideas of Richard Brickner, a neurologist who removed a sizeable frontal meningioma from a patient. Prominent sections of the patient's frontal lobe had to be removed during the procedure, but Brickner noted that the patient had no change in intellect. However, Brickner's patient, who had once been shy and withdrawn, now presented as boastful and full of energy after the surgery.

Moniz began to consider that there may be the presence of abnormal neural connections coming from the frontal lobe in mentally ill patients. He believed that patients suffering from melancholic personalities could be helped if their frontal lobes were altered. He wondered if frontal lobe removal would be feasible to relieve the anxieties felt by many of his own patients. When speaking about Dr Fulton's chimps, he remarked 'Those are just like my patients. I think that might be done in man'.

Upon returning to Lisbon, he teamed up with Dr Lima, who also had an interest in the procedure, calling it the leucotomy, the surgical cutting of white nerve fibres in the brain. In his earlier methods, Moniz gave his patients a series of alcohol injections after drilling holes into the skull near the frontal lobe. This was done to seven patients before Moniz and Lima worked closely to develop a needle-like device with a retractable wire loop. The instrument allowed the wire to move through the posterior aspect of the brain's frontal lobe, slicing through the white matter fibres. They called their invention the leucotom.

On 12 November 1935, only months after attending the International Neurology Congress in London, Dr Moniz performed his first psychosurgery. His patient was a sixty-three-year-old woman who suffered terribly from paranoia, depression, hallucinations, and insomnia. The patient's former doctor, who had evaluated her before surgery, said 'the patient's anxiety and restlessness had declined rapidly with a concomitant marked attenuation of paranoid features'.

Moniz and Lima went on to perform a total of twenty leucotomies together. Moniz reported that seven of his patients were cured, seven were better, and six had no change at all. But Moniz had almost no detail to support his apparent success, and he was known for taking inadequate documentation and poor patient follow-up. Still, his conclusion was 'Prefrontal leukotomy is a simple operation, always safe, which may prove to be an effective surgical treatment in certain cases of mental disorder'.

Moniz would go on to be quite successful and, in 1949, was awarded the Nobel Peace Prize for his work in leucotomies, specifically the white matter connections between the prefrontal cortex and thalamus.

Perhaps most importantly, the 1935 Neurology Congress was attended by American psychiatrist, Walter Freeman who would leave the most significant impact on psychosurgery the world had ever seen.

Freeman was born in November 1895 in Philadelphia and studied neurology at the prestigious Yale University as well as the University of Pennsylvania Medical School. While working in Washington DC, he was moved by the pain and upset suffered by his patients. It encouraged him to pursue medicine further, and he earned his PhD in neuropathy at George Washington University.

Freeman became fascinated by the success of Dr Egas Muniz and decided to modify his procedure and called it the lobotomy. He felt confident that his modification would lead to great success. Moniz preferred the prefrontal lobotomy or leukotomy. This procedure was done in an operating theatre, and the patient was sedated with general anaesthesia. The surgeon then drilled two burr holes in each side of the patient's skull above the prefrontal lobes. Moniz would go in through the burr holes with his leucotome and cut the white matter in the oval centre of the brain's two frontal lobes in a whisk-like manner. This movement would destroy nerve fibres, which Moniz believed gave him desired results among his patients.

Freeman's procedure was different in that he preferred going through orbital cavities to sever the connection between the thalamus and the frontal lobes. But Freeman was not a trained neurosurgeon, so he teamed up with Dr James Watts at George Washington University Hospital.

In less than one year after Muniz performed his first leucotomy, in September 1936, Dr Walter Freeman and Dr James Watts performed the first prefrontal lobotomy in the United States on a housewife from Kansas.

During the following two months, the team would perform twenty more lobotomies, and by 1942, they had completed over 200, claiming success in 63% of their patients. But Freeman believed he could further perfect the procedure.

Dr Freeman got word of an Italian doctor who operated on his patient's brain through their eye socket, a much less invasive procedure as there was no need to drill into the skull. After much experimentation, Dr Freeman developed a new technique called the transorbital lobotomy, which soon became known as the 'icepick lobotomy'.

Freeman also intended for the procedure to be done in the office instead of the operating theatre. He felt that operating in the theatre was too long of a process as you had to sterilise the environment and wait for the anaesthesia to take effect. Instead, Dr Freeman used electric shock therapy to knock his patients out, making it much easier for the procedure to be done in his office because an anaesthesiologist wasn't needed.

Freeman's modification of the lobotomy included using an ordinary household ice pick to insert into the corner of the patient's eye sockets. He would lift the patient's upper eyelid and point his instrument against the top of the eye socket. Using a rubber mallet, Freeman hammered the ice pick 7cm at the base of the frontal lobe and moved it back and forth with a sweeping motion 15% laterally until he had severed the connecting fibres of the prefrontal cortex and frontal lobes of the brain. His very first transorbital lobotomy was again performed on a housewife, this time from Washington DC.

Because Freeman's new procedure required no neurosurgeon and could easily be performed without the use of an operating room or anaesthesia, it would allow the process to be completed in psychiatric hospitals across the United States, Canada, and Puerto Rico.

However, Freeman's assistant, Watts, was not entirely convinced of the procedure, and he was considerably put off by the lack of sterile equipment and the cruel overuse of the operation. In 1950 James Watts left Freeman's practice.

One of Freeman's earliest and most notorious cases was Rosemary Kennedy, sister of American President John F. Kennedy. From her earliest years, Rosemary experienced severe seizures and mood swings, and at the age of twenty-three, in 1941, she would undergo a prefrontal lobotomy. James Watts, who was still working with Freeman at the time, describes the procedure as such:

> After Rosemary was mildly sedated, we went through the top of the head. I think she was awake. She had a mild tranquilizer. I made a surgical incision in the brain through the skull. It was near the front. It was on both

sides. We just made a small incision, no more than an inch. We put an instrument inside.

Watts explains that as he made the incisions, Dr Freeman asked Rosemary to answer some questions, such as reciting the Lord's Prayer or counting backwards. The doctors judged how far to cut based on how Rosemary responded to the questions. When she began to show incoherence, they stopped the procedure. The procedure was so unsuccessful that her mental capacity lessened to the point that she resembled a toddler. Rosemary could no longer walk or speak and also had problems with incontinence.

Nonetheless, the American doctor's lobotomy also got the attention of British physicians. Freeman's lobotomy became known as the standard Freeman-Watts prefrontal leucotomy in Britain. William Sargant, the British psychiatrist, who was already a huge advocate for finding psychical ways to treat mental illness, met Freeman on a trip to the United States. He was impressed with Freeman's ideas after watching a handful of his operations.

Sargant himself suffered from mental illness and, in 1934, had a nervous breakdown and spent time in a mental hospital. He was born in 1907 in London and studied medicine at St John's College in Cambridge. After his recovery from his illness, Sargant decided to favour his career towards psychiatry and was later awarded a position at Maudsley Hospital, where he studied insulin shock therapy.

In 1938, after spending time at Harvard Medical School in Boston, he arranged to meet Walter Freeman in Washington DC to observe his lobotomies.

Upon returning to England, he encouraged doctors with enthusiasm in the country to begin a programme using psychosurgery. Sargant persuaded Frederick Golla, director of the Buren Neurological Institute, to start experimenting with the surgery. Working with surgeon F. Wilfred Willway, Golla operated on patients at Barnwood House in Gloucester and Brislington House in Bristol. All of these patients were volunteered by hospital staff and used as test subjects for Golla and his ideas.

The first operation was performed in December 1940, and over the next few months, another eight were performed on incarcerated patients. The results of these operations were presented in a July issue of the *Lancet* the following year, except for one. This case involved the death of a young woman who bled to death during the operation, and her case was omitted from the report. The results of the other operations were deemed successful enough for a complete lobotomy programme at the Burden Institute, along with the introduction of the procedure at Belmont Hospital.

After the success of psychosurgery at Burden, doctors at Warlingham Park Hospital in Surrey began experimenting with the procedure. James McGregor, the senior psychiatrist on staff, designed his own leucotome in the early 1940s. The instrument was meant to make the lobotomy more precise, and it was tested in a series of operations by Dr John Crumbie, a visiting surgeon from Corydon General Hospital.

It was created after the innovations of British neurosurgeon Wylie McKissock (1906-1994), who operated with a radioactive radium needle knowns as Cushing's Brain Needle. McKissock used the needle much in the way a whisk would be used, greatly influencing McGregor's design. McKissock was a fan of the Freeman-Watts leucotomy and developed his own technique called the rostral leucotomy, in which the frontal lobes were approached from the top of the patient's head. He explained that 'The actual bilateral prefrontal leucotomy can be done by a properly trained neurosurgeon in six minutes and seldom take more than ten minutes'.

The results of the operations at Burden and Warlingham were published and looked at as a great success. Other mental hospitals in Britain caught on, and the use of psychosurgery spread throughout the country. Women seemed to be a particular target amongst lobotomists, with the age range between twenty to sixty years old. The procedures were often done on promiscuous housewives.

One hundred and forty-two patients at Crichton Royal Hospital in Dumfries were labelled as doomed to a life of invalidity and elected for surgery by the end of 1945. In Surrey, at Belmont Hospital, under the direction of William Sargant, disturbed patients were operated on for things such as eating disorders and skin afflictions. The leucotomy was introduced to North Wales Hospital in Denbigh in 1942. A hand-selected group of patients who failed to respond to ECT was operated on. But not by a neurosurgeon. They were operated on by a general practitioner. By 1943, fifty patients at Netherne Hospital in Surrey underwent the procedure. Eric Cunningham Dax (1908-2008) described in the April issue of *Journal of Mental Science* how he selected his patients:

> The operation was carried out with the primary object of relieving the most disturbed patients in the hospital quite independently of their poor prognosis. They formed a large proportion of the most violent, hostile, noisy, excited, destructive, or obscene cases in the hospital; the type who distress their relatives upset the other patients and consume the time and energy which could be put to so much better purpose by the staff.

In March 1944, at St Lawrence's Hospital in Surrey, a lobotomy programme began on 'mental defectives'. Forty-four patients in total were operated on under the programme by Crumbie, McKisssock, and his assistant, Dr McCall. Nine of the patients were under the age of twenty-one. Five patients died, perhaps from bleeding in the brain caused by the rotating blade on the leucotome. The majority of the patients operated on showed slight improvement, if any, and twelve patients got worse.

Similar disasters occurred at Rampton Hospital when doctors there turned to the lobotomy in 1947. In less than a year, twenty patients were operated on, including a girl of only fourteen. But with only one death, the hospital superintendent felt the results were sufficient enough to extend the programme.

By mid-1945, Dr Wylie McKissock was operating an ambulatory psychosurgery business, much like Walter Freeman's in America. McKissock travelled throughout the south of England, visiting hospitals to perform lobotomies. Because of McKissock, more lobotomies were done in the United Kingdom, per population, than in the United States.

In 1944, the Board of Control in Great Britain published the result of over 1,000 lobotomies in a thirty-page booklet.

> Crudely described the purpose of the operation is to break the connection between the patient's thoughts and his emotions. It is to relieve the connection between the patient's thoughts and his emotions. It is to relieve mental tension, to take the sting out of the experience and thus to favour improvement or to hasten recovery from mental disorder.

By the mid-1950s, the leucotome was deemed cumbersome, and its use began to cease. The decline of the lobotomy was seen more in Great Britain but not before over 10,000 in total were done throughout the country. And while it may have declined, the procedure was far from over.

Neurosurgeon Henry Marsh took a job as a medical student in the 1970s at a psychiatric nursing ward. He described the ward as being 'the end stage ward where the burnt-out cases went to die'.

In this ward Dr Marsh witnessed the horrific effects of the lobotomy on patients, all of who had been operated on by McKissock and his assistants.

'It was painfully apparent to me that there was no proper follow-up of the patients at all. The patients who were the worst, most apathetic, sort of ruined patients were the ones who had been lobotomised'.

The procedure had become quite popular throughout the world, everywhere from India to Japan and Germany. In West Germany, the lobotomy was done to cure sexual deviation. In a 1969 edition of the *British Medical Journal*, the Germans were praised for destroying part of the hypothalamus of 3 homosexual male patients. Apparently, it was a success as the men lost most of their sex drive. But sadly, they also lost the drive to do much of anything.

Doctors in the United States have performed almost 20,000 lobotomies since 1936, and Boston Psychopathic Hospital was called the fortress of the lobotomy. Many doctors eventually became disappointed with the results of Freeman's procedures, as several patients developed complications or even died. However, many of Freeman's patients did improve, with many of their severe symptoms going away, and patients in the hospital became more manageable.

American, Howard Dully, was lobotomised by Walter Freeman at the age of only twelve. Dully was an active boy who didn't get along easily with his stepmother, who brought him to see Dr Freeman. Mr Dully can still remember the operation in detail:

> They lifted up the eye and went into the corner and tapped it through and wiggled it around with this egg beater thing. To me, it's insane. I mean, you're talking about a brain. Shouldn't there be some precision involved?

Freeman claimed to have a success rate of 85%, but he also had a fatality rate of 15%. One-third of his patients were reported to have improved, but the other one-third were much worse off than when they started.

Though it's hard to grasp the notion, I still believe that most lobotomists wanted to help their patients. At its time, it was a new and promising procedure that offered hope to many who had been suffering their entire lives. Still, we know that the lobotomy did tend to tranquillize patients. It deprived them of their judgment and social skills. These people became disinhibited. And irreversible damage was done to their brains and personality. I think today, we can all agree that no mental illness was so bad that it was worth having parts of the brain surgically destroyed.

The struggle to treat the mentally ill would decrease dramatically with the birth of modern psychopharmacology in the 1950s. A series of medications would emerge and change the course of psychiatry forever.

Today, lithium is used as a mood stabilizer approved to treat bipolar disorder. It is now the standard treatment for mental illness and has remained one of the most effective medications in the world of psychiatry. However, like most advances in the mental health field, the rise of this psychopharmaceutical drug had its stutter steps.

Bipolar disorder was known as manic depression until the 1980s and is still often referred to this way today. Doctors in the mid-twentieth century had more of an idea of how the disease was a ruthless cycle of emotional mood swings, and while they may have found ways to mask its symptoms temporarily, there still was no solid treatment. But this would all change with the discovery of the silvery metal called lithium.

During the Second World War, Australian psychiatrist John Cade was being held in Singapore at a Japanese prisoner of war camp. It was there that he noticed a direct correlation between certain diseases and food deficiencies in his fellow prisoners. He saw, for example, that a lack of Vitamin B seemed to cause symptoms of beriberi, a thiamine deficiency.

After the war had passed and Cade was released, he was working in Bundoora Repatriation Mental Hospital in Melbourne when he decided to further investigate his findings. While doing his research in an abandoned kitchen pantry at the hospital, he collected urine samples from patients suffering from mania, depression, and schizophrenia. Cade wanted to find out if something in their urine may be directly related to the mental health symptoms. He injected the urine directly into the abdomens of guinea pigs and raised the dosage until they died. It was clear to him that the urine of patients affected with mania was especially deadly to the animals. But he also noticed that giving one large dosage of lithium tended to calm the guinea pigs. The rodents, which usually protested to being held, were completely lucid once they were given a substantial dosage at one time.

The use of lithium carbonate was not new and had been used since the nineteenth century to treat gout. In 1847, London physician Alfred Baring Garrod used lithium as an antigout treatment after discovering uric acid in his gout patients' blood. After a publication in the 1859 journal, *The Nature and Treatment of Gout and Rheumatic Gout*, lithium was being used widespread.

Psychiatric references were made to lithium in 1870 by American neurologist Silas Weir Mitchell, who was using lithium bromide as an anti-convulsant at Bellevue Hospital in New York. In 1871, the use of lithium was also recommended by Dr William Hammond at Bellevue Hospital. But so little was written about it that lithium treatment was soon forgotten as there were virtually no other references to it before Cade's discovery.

Through further experiments, Cade discovered that lithium also reduced the toxicity in the urine of his patients. Cade wondered if lithium's calming effect on the guinea pigs would be the same on his patients.

After trying it on himself to be sure he was using a safe dosage, he started to treat ten of his patients suffering from mania. The results floored him. In the September 1949 *Medical Journal of Australia*, Cade reported that his ten patients had been institutionalised for years. Still, with the lithium treatment, five had such an improvement that they were able to be discharged.

But Cade's milestone was not without setbacks. His continued experiments with other salts, such as cerium and rubidium, were unsuccessful. And after one of his patients died from lithium poisoning, he gave up on his experiments with that as well. The therapeutic dosage of lithium was so dangerously close to the toxic dose that Cade felt it wasn't worth the risk.

Around the same time that Cade was experimenting with lithium, Danish psychiatrist, Mogens Schou, had also been trying to get lithium accepted as a treatment for manic depressive patients. Schou had a personal connection with the disorder as his brother suffered from it, which gave him the determination to move forward. Along with a colleague, Poul Baastrup, he began a series of experiments with lithium, using stringent conditions. He used a double-blind, placebo-controlled clinical trial, which helped him prove that lithium, when used safely, was absolutely effective for people with manic depressive disorder. He knew this because he had seen a dramatic change in his own brother.

Schou's results were published in the *British Journal of Medicine*, where it was concluded that 'Lithium therapy appears to offer a useful alternative to electroconvulsive therapy since many patients can be kept in a normal state by administration of a maintenance dose'.

However, despite Schou's success, lithium was a challenge to administer, and getting accurate blood levels was almost impossible. Schou's publication in the journal was dismissed by eminent British psychiatrist Eliot Slater. But with the introduction of the Coleman Photometer in 1958, a device that used a micro method for determining sodium, calcium, and potassium levels in the blood, the future of lithium changed forever.

Yet, acceptance in the United Kingdom was hindered by a dispute between Schou and several doctors at Maudsley Hospital. In *The Lancet*, Schou's methods were called 'shoddy and unconvincing'.

As a result, the use of lithium to treat the mentally ill remained underused in the United Kingdom until the mid-1970s. It was eventually granted a go-ahead for use, but thousands of patients who were denied the treatment likely suffered as a result.

How lithium works is still somewhat of a mystery today, but it has helped stabilise the moods of millions of patients who suffer from bipolar disorder. We know that it effectively treats both acute manias and works for the long-term care of mood disorders. Lithium also has a unique way of positively affecting suicidal patients. It is thought that lithium may reduce cognitive decline when it comes to cognition, and it also appears to increase the number of brain structures that are involved in emotion.

The dosage must be carefully monitored, and there are some unpleasant side effects, the most common being feelings of nausea, dry mouth, metallic taste, and diarrhoea.

Still, there is no doubt that lithium was a game-changer in treating the mentally ill.

The discovery of lithium was followed by another game-changer in treating mental illness; the world's first antipsychotic drug, Chlorpromazine, otherwise known as Thorazine. Though there are now many other similar medications, no antipsychotic since has been more effective in treating schizophrenia.

Thorazine was first manufactured in 1950 by Rhone-Poulenc, a French pharmaceutical company, but not as a psychiatric drug. They were developing a range of antihistamines when surgeon Henri Laborit spoke with Rhone-Poulenc about creating an antihistamine that would be useful as a pre-anaesthetic before surgery. Thorazine was one of several compounds being developed, and Laborit noticed that it induced calmness in patients prior to surgery but without sedation. He considered if it would be effective in treating those with mental illness.

Two psychiatrists at St Anne's Hospital in Paris began using Thorazine to treat some of their patients with mania and schizophrenia and concluded that it was highly effective. They noticed that it worked exceptionally well at calming agitated patients. Thorazine was initially known as a tranquillizer, especially in the United States.

News of Thorazine spread over the following years, and publications about its effectiveness began to appear in medical journals.

Thorazine entered into psychiatry in 1952 and with it brought a new treatment for the mentally ill. Doctors were amazed by its benefits and felt the promise that a new treatment era was starting.

By 1956, Thorazine was being prescribed throughout North America and Western Europe. After clinical trials were conducted in the United States, Thorazine and other up-and-coming antipsychotics, it was determined that these medications were highly effective in treating the symptoms of schizophrenia.

The introduction of Thorazine also had a significant impact on how doctors and scientists viewed mental illness. It was essentially the start of research into the biological nature of psychiatric illness. Thorazine reduced hallucinations and delusions in schizophrenic patients and slowed the swing of extreme emotions.

However, Thorazine did come with a lengthy list of side effects. One of the most commonly seen side effects of Thorazine is tardive dyskinesia, which is characterised by jaw swinging, facial grimacing, repetitive chewing, and tongue thrusting.

Other side effects include confusion, drooling, extreme tiredness, and a shuffling walk. It wasn't uncommon to hear Thorazine referred to as a chemical lobotomy. However, it kept mental patients quiet and manageable. Thorazine also changed the public's perception of the mentally ill and helped reduce the often cruel stigma associated with them.

Valium was invented by a chemist in New Jersey in 1963 and skyrocketed to be the top-selling pharmaceutical in the United States from 1969 to 1982. Though Valium was the second benzodiazepine to be discovered, it would be an absolute victory in psychiatry. Valium was used to treat anxiety, alcohol withdrawal, and insomnia, among several other ailments. Valium created a calming effect which was typically felt in a little as fifteen minutes after ingestion. Though the use of Valium along with other benzodiazepines has been criticised for being addictive, they are still incredibly effective against several conditions.

Aside from the early forms of medications to treat different conditions of mania came the discovery of imipramine, the world's first antidepressant.

Throughout the early 1950s, competing drug companies were looking for something to mimic Thorazine. Swiss psychiatrist Roland Kuhn was researching new compounds but was more interested in treating depression than schizophrenia.

After initiating the proper compounds to form imipramine, Kuhn began giving it to his patients who suffered from depression. To his astonishment, after only a few weeks, his patients were starting to crawl out of the fog of misery they had been in for so long. They began to regain a sense of motivation and purpose and life and found themselves being filled with hope. Kuhn's chronically ill patients had responded extraordinarily to imipramine.

With Kahun's discovery of imipramine, the world of psychiatry had finally found the biological fundamentals to treat depression. The discovery of imipramine led to the use of SSRIs such as Prozac and SNRIs in the early 1980s, marking the unofficial beginning of the end of the asylum as it had been known.

Chapter Nine

The Eugenics Movement and the Mentally Ill

It's easy to say that the treatment of the mentally ill certainly didn't improve during the pre-Second World War era, and many would argue that it worsened. We often associate the word eugenics with Nazi Germany and Hitler's atrocities. And while this is true, the history of eugenics goes deeper than that.

I felt it was important to write a chapter on the history of eugenics when it comes to the mentally ill because there is so much more to the story. The mentally ill have always had to face the notion that someone, somewhere, was trying to get rid of them. True, it was often in the asylum, but society as a whole has a very long history of creating ways to eliminate those with mental disabilities from the human race.

In laymen's terms, eugenics is the act of trying to improve upon the human species, in many cases race and those who hold desirable hereditary traits. The general thought behind those who support eugenics is that it improves upon the human race by breeding out disease, disabilities, or any undesirable characteristics. Early supporters felt that people with disorders, inherited mental illness, and even poverty could be washed out of the gene pool over time.

And while the negative association with eugenics is mainly derived from Hitler's crimes, it was not Germany who initially encouraged the production of a superior race or the discouragement of any mentally ill person to reproduce.

The term eugenics comes from ancient Greece and means 'good creation.' In *The Republic*, one of Plato's best-known works, he speaks of breeding high-class people together to achieve a superior society. He also writes of trying to discourage those from the lower class to procreate. He suggested a series of mating rules that he felt would help achieve a perfect society.

While Plato may have been one of the first people to consider the idea, eugenics didn't truly gain recognition until 1833 AD. British scholar Sir Francis Galton first used the term in his book, *Inquiries into Human Faculty and its Development*, though he gave little if any credit to Plato for his ideas.

Galton, born in 1822 in England, was well known for his studies in human intelligence and eugenics. As a cousin of Charles Darwin, he also studied the theory of evolution, and his interests lay with selective mating. The Birmingham native showed great intellectual promise at a young age and studied medicine at Birmingham's General Hospital and King's College in the late 1830s. But it was eventually mathematics and world geography that he would pursue.

Galton went on to develop theories on inherited human traits. He also studied identical twins and spent much of his life studying hereditary and his coined phrase, *eugenics*. His cousin, Charles Darwin, is perhaps a name we are all more familiar with. The British naturalist is famed for his theory of evolution based on natural selection, which remains controversial today.

Born in the tiny town of Shrewsbury, England, Darwin came from a long line of scientists. His father and grandfather were both renowned doctors. But after attending the University of Edinburgh and Christ's College, Darwin felt drawn to study natural history over medicine.

After a trip around the world and throughout the Pacific Islands that lasted several years, Darwin wrote extensively on his findings upon returning to England in 1836. He had developed a theory about the origin of living things that was contrary to those of other naturalists of his time.

Darwin believed that living things survived through natural selection, meaning that those species adapted to their habitat would thrive. And those that failed to adapt and reproduce would eventually die off. His theory would later become known as Darwinism. But other naturalists felt that species more or less remained the same over time.

Emerging in the late 1800s was a collection of ideas called Social Darwinism, an adaptation of Darwin's theory that was used to explain more social and economic matters. While Darwin himself rarely commented on any connection his theories had with human society, the term Social Darwinism has been used as the rationalisation behind poverty, racism and eugenics.

It was Darwin's cousin, Galton, who felt that he could improve humankind by trying to impress his ideas upon the British elite. However, it was in America, where it was enthusiastically embraced.

In the state of Connecticut in 1896, eugenics made its first rendezvous through the state's marriage laws. Connecticut made it illegal for any American who had epilepsy or was considered feeble-minded to marry. This, in turn, led to the creation of the American Breeder's Association in 1903, a group formed to study eugenics.

In 1911, John Harvey Kellogg, of the Kellogg cereal family, created the Race Betterment Foundation, along with a pedigree registry. The foundation would go on to hold conferences on the theory of eugenics in 1914, 1915, and 1928. Interestingly enough, Kellogg was a medical doctor who ran the Battle Creek Sanitarium in the state of Michigan for several years

Slowly the idea of eugenics began to get the attention of the American elite, and both scientists and socialites embraced the causes. The Eugenics Record Office, or ERO, was soon created to keep track of American families and their genetic components. The ERO claimed that those considered unfit were either poor, minorities or immigrants. The ERO was convinced that it was unfavourable genes that caused any negative family traits.

Beginning in the year 1909, in the state of California, eugenics in America took a very dark turn that would eventually influence other parts of the world. Under the pretence of protecting society from those with mental illness, California began to mandate forced sterilisations. The 1909 Asexualization Act gave authorisation for state hospitals to involuntarily sterilise certain groups of people. Aside from those deemed mentally unfit, the law also allowed prisoners with life sentences and repeat sexual offenders, to undergo sterilisation. But the majority of the procedures took place in the state's mental hospitals.

Dr Leo Stanley, head surgeon at San Quentin Penitentiary, was especially interested in ridding society of those deemed unfit. Dr Stanley was hired by the prison in 1913 with no surgical experience. A staunch eugenist, Stanley was disturbed about the lack of racial separation among the prisoners. He was also remarkably in favour of the recent law passed by the state that allowed for forced sterilisations.

Throughout the prison, radical surgeries were performed by Stanley on the genitals of men. The testicles were removed and replaced with the testicles of a corpse who was seen fit for society when he was alive.

Any patients that Dr Stanley could not sterilise by force were talked into the procedure through propaganda posters. One such sign put up in the prison yard claimed 'This simple operation prevents the man from producing children, but it does not interfere with his normal pleasure. In fact, it is claimed that sexual vigor is increased'.

Aside from being bizarre, Stanley's procedures were highly unsuccessful. Throughout his time at the prison, he sterilised over 600 prisoners before serving overseas at the start of the Second World War.

Thirty-three American states would eventually legalize involuntary sterilisation, and in 1927, the US Supreme court withheld the ruling, stating that it did not violate the US Constitution.

Forced sterilisation in the United States may have been terrible. Still, it wasn't until the idea spread to Europe during the Second

World War that the real horrors began to take place for not only the mentally ill but people of all creeds and backgrounds.

After the movement was well established in the United States, California eugenicists began to promote it overseas. Through eugenics promoting literature, the idea was spread to medical professionals and German scientists. California alone had sterilised more people than any other US state, and it was their programme that partly inspired the Nazi Party.

The Kaiser Wilhelm Institute for Anthropology was founded in 1927 in Berlin with financial support from the American Rockefeller Foundation. The director of this organisation, who studied human genetics, was German professor Eugen Fischer. Fischer was a professor of medicine and a well-known proponent of eugenics, whose work would help provide the foundation for the eugenics policies of the Nazi Party.

His earlier work began in 1906 when he conducted field research in German southwest Africa, which today is known as Namibia. He studied the offspring of German men and the native women in the area, known as Basters, and decided that preventing a mixed-race was best. His ideas on racial purity greatly influenced the Nazis.

Before joining the party in 1940, Fischer examined over 600 children descended from French-African soldiers, and those children were eventually sterilised. His work, *Principles of Human Hereditary and Race Hygiene*, would greatly influence Hitler's book, *Mein Kampf*.

Before becoming chancellor of Germany, Adolf Hitler served time in Landsberg Prison after being arrested during the Beer Hall Putsch, a failed takeover of the Bavarian government. While in prison, Hitler began reading American textbooks on eugenics, and he was especially interested in the opinions of Leon Whitney, President of the American Eugenics Society. Whitney was an influential voice in decisions that would lead to the sterilisation of thousands of Americans. He referred to those deemed undesirable as 'human debris' and 'a cancer on the body politic'.

Whitney spoke of the corruption of the Nordic race by negroes, Jews, and others who did not possess the trademark blonde hair and blue eyes.

So while he wrote about it in his book, *Mein Kampf*, Hitler did not entirely come up with the idea of a perfect race on his own. He wrote much about his knowledge and admiration of American eugenics and also spoke of the US National Origins Act, which in part says:

> In the US Model, an effort is made to consult reason at least partially. By refusing immigrants on principle to elements in poor health, by simply excluding certain races from naturalisation, it professes in slow beginnings a view that is peculiar to the People's State.

On 30 January 1933, Adolf Hitler was sworn in as chancellor of Germany. He would do everything in his power to ensure that his ideas on the superior Aryan race were put into action. As he wrote in *Mein Kampf*, racial hygiene, 'will appear as a deed greater than the most victorious wars of our present bourgeois era'.

In July 1933, only six months into Hitler's political career, the Law for the Prevention of Genetically Diseased Offspring was passed. Based on the American Eugenical Sterilization Law, the law allowed for the sterilisation of people with detrimental hereditary conditions. The law stated that:

> Any person suffering from a hereditary disease may be rendered incapable of procreation by means of a surgical operation if medical science shows that his descendants would suffer from some serious physical or mental hereditary defect.

The law considered hereditary diseases to be not only deformity, blindness, and deafness but congenital mental deficiency, schizophrenia, manic depressive insanity, and epilepsy. The introductory provisions of the 1933 law stated that:

> Any person suffering from a hereditary disease may be rendered incapable of procreation by means of a surgical operation (sterilization) if the experience of medical science shows that it is highly probable that his descendants would suffer from some serious physical or mental hereditary defect.

The law applied to anyone in Germany's general population, but those in psychiatric hospitals were especially targeted. Special Hereditary Health Courts (HHC), under the direction of the interior ministry at the time, Wilhelm Frick, examined those in nursing homes, special schools, prisons, and asylums, to determine whether or not they should be sterilised. The basic provisions of the law were built on the ideas of Emil Kraepelin, who had outwardly opposed the works of Freud, and who believed that Jews were predisposed to mental illness. Despite his pioneering works in psychiatry, Kraepelin eagerly promoted his agenda of racial hygiene throughout Nazi Germany.

Swiss psychiatrist Eugen Bleuler also favoured the idea of eugenic sterilisation of those who were considered 'mental and physical cripples'. Born in 1857, Bleuler studied medicine at Burgholzi University in Switzerland and became a professor of psychiatry at the same university hospital in which he was schooled. It was Bleuler who would come up with the term schizophrenia while making many contributions to the world of psychiatry. He introduced the term at a lecture in Berlin in April 1908 as a way of explaining a psychiatric illness in which the patient suffered from rapid cognitive breakdown, starting in the late teens or early adulthood. He explained that the patient might suffer from delusions, and he believed there was no cure for the disease. Bleuler thought there would always be some long-lasting deficiency in the patient's cognitive ability. Bleuler was confident that heredity played a big part in whether or not someone would suffer from schizophrenia. In his book, *Textbook of Psychiatry*, he advocated that:

> The more severely burdened should not propagate themselves, and the healthy stocks have to limit the number of their children because so much has to be done for the maintenance of others. If natural selection is generally suppressed, then unless we will get new measure, our race must rapidly deteriorate.

Advocacy of eugenics steadily began to take hold in Germany around the time Hitler's sterilisation law was passed. The Great Depression had caused cuts in state funding for the insane, which led to overcrowding and less than desirable conditions. Several of Germany's eugenicists were also anti-semites who welcomed the new Nazi regime. Many were given positions in the Health Ministry, where their ideas were readily adopted by much of the county's medical professionals.

When the law granting sterilisation was passed in 1933, Hitler already favoured the murder of those unable to be cured of mental illness, but he also knew the German people might not accept this. Hitler knew that carrying out the solution to such a programme would go much smoother during wartime, and he fully intended to put an end to the problems going on in mental hospitals.

Jewish or communist doctors found working in Germany's hospital were terminated as the Reich began to spread their propaganda, hoping to sway the country's citizens. The National Socialist Racial and Political Office, also known as NSRPA, was established to overlook all propaganda works in the areas of controlling population, began to produce pamphlets and short films explaining to German citizens the high cost of keeping the mentally ill in asylums.

The indoctrination of the NSRPA fell in line with the regime's policy of racial hygiene. Policies stated that German people needed to be clean of racial enemies and any who who suffered mental illness or had been confined to an asylum. Those people should be shown a *Gnadentod*, or mercy killing.

German physician and SS officer Karl Brandt joined the Nazi Party in 1932 and became Hitler's personal physician in mid-1934. Like several of his like-minded colleagues, Brandt believed that the health of German society should be considered over that of the individual. Under the 1933 law for the prevention of hereditarily diseased offspring, Brandt terminated the pregnancies of many women who were seen as genetically deficient. He favoured the idea that a Gnadentod was one of the best ways to deal with those who infringed on the Regime's idea of a perfect society.

In September 1939, Brandt was appointed to head the T4 Aktion programme, along with Philipp Bouhler, a high-ranking SS administrator. The T4 programme was a programme of involuntary mass murder of the mentally disabled.

In an order written on his own personal letterhead, Adolf Hitler wrote:

> Reichleiter Bouhler and Dr Brandt MD are charged with the responsibility of extending the authority of specially designated physicians so that patients, who after a very thorough review of their condition, are judged incurable, can be granted a mercy killing.

This short text, though not a written law, was taken as an 'enabling act by the Fuhrer' to legalise a procedure that, at the time, was still a crime. Preparations for getting patients registered had already begun to take place before the order was drafted, and the search for extermination centres was already underway.

During the initial planning stages of the programme, Brandt discussed with Hitler the different techniques in which to administer euthanasia. The decision was made for carbon monoxide gas, and

Brandt was instructed to recruit other physicians to take part in the programme. Patients were taken to one of six centres for the *Secret Euthanasia Dept at Tiergarten Street Four in Berlin*, giving the programme its name, T4, for four Tiergarten. It was in the latter part of 1938 that the programme truly began.

Soon after the programme had been initiated, Brandt was asked to look over a petition sent in by the parents of a boy who was blind and had both mental and physical disabilities. In 1938 and 1939, there were several requests from the parents of handicapped children, asking to have their own children euthanised. Clearly, the propaganda of the T4 programme had already begun to take effect.

The subject of one of the first mercy killings in the summer of 1939 was a baby boy named Gerhard Kretschnar. He was born blind and had deformities in one leg and one arm. His parents believed strongly in the Nazi race and felt it was better if their child did not live.

Gerhard's father brought him to Leipzig Children's Clinic when he was only a few months old to have him admitted. The head of the clinic, Weiner Catel, said that the baby's father wanted him to be put to death right away. Catel, however, refused on legal grounds. The child's parents were not accepting of that answer, so they petitioned Hitler himself. Hitler then sent Dr Brandt to examine the child. After seeing that he was indeed blind and deformed, Brandt authorised the killing of the child, and he was 'put to sleep'. He was just five months old.

After only a few short weeks, the Reich Committee for the Scientific Registering of Hereditary and Congenital Illnesses was founded. The case of five-month-old Gerhard was significant in launching the programme.

The committee was set up to register sick children and even newborns, to identify them as flawed in some way, or as Hitler said, judged as 'Life Unworthy of Life'.

Hitler gave his top advisors examples of what he believed the mentally ill to be. He deemed them ones that could only be 'bedded on sawdust or sand' because they had 'perpetually dirtied themselves and put their own excrement into their mouths'.

Both Dr Brandt and SS Officer Bouler were authorised to go forward with the killing of children who met this description.

At six of Germany's psychiatric hospitals, the extermination of children began to take place. As the Interior Ministry registered children with deficiencies, doctors and midwives were required by law to report all cases of disabled newborns to the Reich. All children under the age of three who had the following serious hereditary diseases would be killed; Down Syndrome, idiocy, hydrocephaly, microcephaly, malformations, and paralysis. Each case was examined by a group of doctors, who gave their approval before a child's life could be ended.

However, the Ministry used a great deal of deceit when dealing with the parents of a child approved to be euthanised. Parents were informed that their children were simply being sent away to receive proper treatment for their ailment. But children sent for 'treatment' were usually killed by an injection of phenol, and their deaths were recorded as pneumonia. The consciences of any persons involved were quickly eased as they believed that their work was a part of medical research, especially during autopsies when tissue samples were extracted.

After being annexed by the Nazis, Austria soon became one of the hotspots for the abuse and murder of children during the T4 programme. The Steinhof Hospital in Vienna was a compound of thirty-four different buildings, and thirteen of them would be used for a children's psychiatric clinic called Am Spiegelgrund. The children admitted were selected through the T4 process, along with the children of anyone showing resistance to the Regime. The ward, which opened in July of 1940, would serve as one of the largest killing centres during the span of the war.

Heinrich Gross, psychiatrist, neurologist, and one of the head physicians of the ward, personally selected admitted children to be used for deadly experiments. Like the other senior directors at the facility, Gross saw the children as a research opportunity.

In one of the hospital's pavilions, doctors conducted horrific experiments on thousands of living and breathing children before being ultimately murdered. Many children were subjected to an excruciating procedure known as pneumatic encephalography. During this procedure, most of the cerebrospinal fluid was removed from the brain through lumbar puncture and replaced with oxygen, helium, or air to allow certain brain structures to appear on x-ray.

Many children died from the procedure, and those who didn't were usually transferred to another building. If they weren't outright murdered, they were generally starved, given sedating drugs and experimental vaccines, or allowed to freeze to death.

Whether killed by lethal injection, gas poisoning, or abuse, 789 children in all lost their lives at Am Spiegelgrund. The brains and spinal cords of the children were preserved and stored in the hospital's basement as a part of Gross's private collection.

Only a few months before the opening of Am Spiegelgrund, the standards for assessing children from mental illness loosened considerably. The approval process also became quicker and began to include children with a growing list of conditions. Any parents who refused to cooperate in their child being sent away were threatened with loss of custody. By 1941, over 5,000 children had already been killed.

Around the same time the T4 programme began to progress, both Dr Brandt and SS Officer Bouhler had already planned to expand the programme to include adults. A meeting held with the SS Medical Department head, Professor Werner Heyde, determined that a national register of all adults with mental illnesses who were institutionalised was needed. The Nazis believed that the Volkskorper, or body of the people, needed to be cleansed of inferior socially unfit or genetically diseased people.

Patients of Polish descent were initially targeted through the Nazi regime for their mass killing of the mentally ill. The earliest liquidations of patients took place in Pomerania, at Kocborowo and Swiecie State Psychiatric Institutes. In September 1939, twenty-two patients at Kocborowo were told they were being transported to a better hospital but instead were taken into the forest and shot. This continued through January 1940. Patients from Swiecie were also taken by truck to their execution.

The gassing of mentally ill patients in Warthegau at Owinska Hospital was seen under the direction of SS Office Herbert Lange. One hundred and fifty patients of German descent were taken by bus to an asylum in Gniezo, where they were told they were being relocated. Many patients thought they were going to a better institution. If patients became upset, they were beaten or given sedatives. Trucks came day and night to Fort VII camp, and patients were sent for gassing on the South Courtyard in 7m, 2.5m wide, and 2.5m high bunkers.

A physician from the centre in Hadamar describes the scenario:

> The process lasted a few minutes. There was also a built-in window. I looked through this window once. It was co gas. It is a peaceful death. It is simply sleeping in the true sense of the word. The people become tired and lose all touch with the outside world and fall asleep. A doctor had to operate the apparatus, and only a doctor was legally authorized to carry out the killing.

However, another witness account tells a very different story.

> Did I ever watch a gassing? Dear God, unfortunately, yes. Downstairs on the left was a short pathway, and there, I looked through the window. In the chamber, there were patients, naked people, some semi-collapsed, others with their mouths terribly wide open, their chests heaving. I saw that. I have never seen anything more gruesome.

I could not imagine that this was completely without pain. A few were lying on the ground. The spines of all the naked people protruded. Some sat at the bench with their mouths wide open, their eyes wide open, and breathing with difficulty.

Other Polish prisoners often had to remove the corpses from the bunkers and move cylinders containing carbon monoxide next to the bunker doors once a new set of prisoners was inside. They would then seal the door shut before the SS members would turn on the gas. Patients would die within twenty-five to thirty minutes after being exposed to the deadly poison. Corpses were then taken to forests, where other prisoners were ordered to dig graves and remove the bodies from the transport pickup trucks.

For those patients who were cremated, any gold teeth, or bridges, were removed beforehand. Those who operated the crematoriums often had to do so intoxicated to do the job.

In January 1940, Koscian Hospital had 612 patients, most of whom had a severe mental deficiency. By mid-January, all had been killed, using gas chambers built into the chassis of a cargo van. Like at other hospitals, patients were often told they were getting a vaccine but were instead drugged with morphine and scopolamine until they died.

In the annexe of Wartheland, all mental asylums were emptied by the Nazis. In the city of Danzig, seven thousand mental patients of Polish descent were executed. In the Gdynia area, that number reached ten thousand by shooting alone.

The atrocities of killing mentally ill patients continued, and patients followed a protocol before going to their death. They were registered and then asked to undress and remove all their valuables. A medical inspection was done as well as a review of the patient's medical record. The made-up cause of death was then documented. Photos of the patient were taken after a number was stamped onto the chest. Death notices were staggered over time to prevent large numbers of letters from going out at once. However, the T4 programme continued to collect health fees for several weeks before informing the patient's family of their death. By doing so, millions of Reichs were accumulated.

The idea of ending the lives of adults with mental disabilities began to spread from Poland to areas of Germany. To make room for wounded German soldiers, The Gauleiter of Pomerania, Franz Schwede-Coburg, sent 1,400 mental patients from five Pomerania hospitals to locations in Poland, where they were shot. More than 8,000 mentally ill Germans were also killed.

The legal basis for the killing programmes derived from a letter drafted by Hitler, not a formal decree with written law. Hitler intentionally bypassed the country's health minister as he feared they might question the legality of the programme. Aktion T4 was then entrusted to Officer Bouhler and Dr Brandt. Both were given the ability to extend the authority to kill the doctors whom they appointed. Those patients deemed incurable could be granted a merciful death.

The 'Charitable Foundation for Cure and Institutional Care,' or Tiergarenstrabe 4, was under the authority of SS Officer Viktor Brack. His officials included Dr Herbert Linden, who was involved in the killing children programme, Ernst-Robert Grawitz, chief doctor to the SS, and August Becker, an SS chemist. These officials selected the doctors who were to carry out the part of the programme meant for the execution of adults, as most of these doctors had already proved their worth in the killing children programme.

In January 1939, a paper from Joseph Mayer, professor of Moral Theology at the University of Paderborn, was received by SS Officer Brack. Being a euthanasia advocate himself, he reported that the churches would not oppose the programme as they saw it as part of Germany's national interest. When Hitler saw the letter in July of that same year, he grew confident that the programme would be acceptable to German citizens under the protection of national interest.

The 'inner mission' movement was one reason that Hitler was confident that church leaders would not object to his programme. The Inner Mission was a movement of German Evangelists (primarily Protestants) developed by theologian Johann Hinrich Wichern in the mid-nineteenth century. The Inner Mission was meant to be a rebirth of Christianity through social services. Protestant theologians argued that God had created supra-individual nations and races that overrode the rights of the individual. Though they were against eugenic abortions and the destruction of 'life unworthy', the group claimed that:

> The artificial prolongation of life which is in the process of being extinguished can represent as much of an interference in God's creative will as euthanasia that is the artificial curtailment of physical dissolution.

The leaders of the T4 programme easily translated this into support for their cause.

The National Protestant Church accepted measures introduced by National Socialists, but they believed that sterilisation of the mentally ill should be voluntary, not forced. Yet in Protestant asylums, in the year 1934, 2,399 patients were sterilised. Many authorities of the Inner Mission Asylums applied for permission to have their patients sterilised. The staff tried to persuade patients to be accepting of the idea with the promise of special privileges or early discharge.

Some opposed the programme, including Lothar Kreyssig, a district judge who argued that there was no legality in the programme as Hitler had written no formal law on it. Franz Gurtner, the Minister of Justice, responded 'If you cannot recognise the will of the Fuhrer as a source of law, then you cannot remain a judge'.

Kreyssig was then condemned.

In early October 1939, all nursing homes, hospitals, and sanitariums were required to report any patients they had who had been in their care for more than five years. These people were deemed incurable and criminally insane if they met the following conditions: epilepsy, schizophrenia, Huntington's Chorea, dementia, syphilis, paralysis, encephalitis, and any other 'terminal, general neurological conditions'.

Many hospitals administrators believed that these reports were used to find inmates capable of being used for the labour service of the Nazis. Some hospitals would not comply, and so a team of T4 doctors would visit the facility, compile their own lists, and remove the patients themselves.

As was done with children, the adult patients were looked at by a panel of experts working for the T4 programme. These experts were asked to make a judgment not based on any medical history or physical exams but on a written report. Each report was either given a +, which meant death, or a -, which meant life.

By January 1940, the first gassings of patients took place at the Brandenburg Euthanasia Centre, which Officer Brack headed. He said 'the needle belongs in the hand of the doctor'.

Pure, bottled carbon monoxide gas was used, Brandt described it as a significant advance in medical history. This method became standard and was used at several centres throughout Germany under the supervision of Officers Widmann, Becker, and Christian Wirth, who also played a role in the Final Solution, or extermination of the Jews.

Other killing centres included Grafeneck Castle, Schloss Hartheim, Sonnestiein, Bernburg, and Hadmar. Patients were transferred to these new centres by T4 charitable ambulances, called community patient transports, run by teams of SS men wearing white lab coats to give the illusion of a medical atmosphere.

The patients were often sent to transit centres to prevent their families from contacting them. They were then sent to Sonderbehandlung (special treatment) centres, and families were sent letters explaining that it was impossible to visit them due to wartime regulations.

However, most of these patients were killed within twenty-four hours of arriving, soon before a letter arrived at the family's dwelling. Each patient killed was then cremated, and a death certificate was written up with a false but possible cause of death. These were sent to the family along with a jar of random ashes.

During 1940 alone, the centres at Brandenburg, Grafenekc, and Hartheim killed 10,000 patients, and several thousand more were killed at other facilities.

However, the people who lived in the towns where the euthanasia centres were located were not oblivious. Many saw folks arriving by buses and saw the mass amounts of smoke in the air from the crematorium chimneys. The townspeople then noticed that those same buses were leaving empty.

Rumours began to spread about what people believed was taking place, and many Germans who had loved ones suffering from mental illness were appalled. Though it was with great expense and difficulties, many families attempted to have their loved ones withdrawn from the asylums. Many physicians also began to question their actions, and some rediagnosed their patients in the hopes that they would no longer meet the Nazi's criteria for the T4 programme.

Protests were now occurring throughout Austria as the rumours spread about the killings at Hartheim and Am Spieglegrund.

In August 1941, Hitler ordered the suspension of the programme. By mid-August 1941, protests in Germany had begun to mount. Several doctors and clergy wrote to Hitler and described the programme as barbaric, while others voiced their opinions in secret. Bishop Count Clemens von Galen had officially denounced the killings. Hitler, fearing too much publicity, suspended the programme.

Heinrich Himmler, chief commander of the SS, spoke of his regrets about the programme's suspension. He said, had the SS been directly in charge of the entire programme, things would have been different. 'We know how to deal with it correctly without causing useless uproar among the people'.

Roughly 35,000 patients were killed in the T4 operation that year. Another 35,000 were killed by mid-1941 before Hitler shut the programme down. The centres were then used to kill concentration camp victims.

Franz Stangl, SS Officer and commandant of the killing centre in Hartheim, gave detailed accounts of the atrocities after he was arrested for his crimes. He said inmates of various asylums were removed and brought to Hartheim by bus. Some were in no state to know what was happening to them, but many were relatively sane. For these patients, different forms of deception were used. They were told they were going to a clinic to be given better treatment after a short medical examination. They were then told they would take a shower, where they were instead gassed with carbon monoxide.

It is estimated that from 1939-1945, over 300,000 patients were killed in the T4 programme.

However, the end of T4 didn't end the desire to do away with the mentally ill. Although it was no longer centrally organised, it now depended on the initiatives of individual doctors. Instead of ending the lives of the mentally ill through gas chambers or shootings, they were now forced to die slowly by starvation. The diets of asylum patients were reduced over time until they eventually led to weakness and death.

In November 1942, a letter to the medical directors of a Bavarian Psych Hospital explained that too few patients were dying, and perhaps not treating their infections would help to change that. Dr Valentin Falthouser gave his patients that would have been in the T4 programme a completely fat-free diet. He stressed that it was totally fat-free because, within three months, most died of famine oedema and fluid retention resulting from severe malnutrition.

This 'starvation diet' was recommended for all institutions and was soon in psychiatric hospitals nationwide. Eichberg Asylum, which was part of T4 in 1939, was spending only 0.4 Deutschmarks a day per patient, yet they were still charging families between 1.8 and

2.5 Deutschmarks a day per patient. Any disabled patients who could not feed themselves were simply not provided for.

Ninety thousand people died in German asylums as a result of starvation diets or indirectly from illnesses arising from malnutrition.

Post liberation, deaths at asylums still rose for several years due to ineffective treatment for illness. People were also dying from the damage from prior starvation, leading to low resistance to disease. Food was still scarce, there was very little coal for heating, and in some places, the staff simply abandoned the facilities, leaving patients to fend for themselves. Starvation was usually a side effect of famine, a consequence of pure inattention, or worse, it was wanted to eliminate those who were 'worthless eaters.'

While the atrocities of the Nazi's Eugenics programme is close to eighty years ago, it has left a massive damper on the treatment of the mentally ill. The eugenics programmes of both the United States and Western Europe helps to understand that there will always be a targeted group of people that someone wants to destroy using the most horrible methods imaginable. It has happened several times since the Second World War, and it still happens today in some parts of the world.

Chapter Ten

The Closure of the Asylums

Things would change drastically for the insane asylum in Britain starting in the 1950s. With new, life-altering medications available to treat mental illness, along with the move towards reform, the era of the asylum was about to come to an end.

The birth of an anti-psychiatric movement and the theory of deinstitutionalisation would lead to a more progressive approach to caring for the mentally ill. Many of Britain's hospitals were run by rather ambitious superintendents, who introduced many changes meant to rehab patients by creating what they deemed a typical environment. The social and therapeutic experiments of the past were now considered cruel. However, the move towards reform also felt that locked wards and excessive medication were cruel as well.

The Mental Treatment Act of 1930 allowed patients to be admitted to the hospital on a more voluntary basis. The act also permitted patients to move more freely around the hospital. But in September 1939, with the outbreak of war, patients were once again locked inside due to overcrowding and short staff. And post-war, the overcrowding of the facilities was a growing problem. Many suffered from the pure shock of war, so there began a push to make hospitals humble places for their patients, and both Conservative and Labour parties were quick to endorse a therapeutic way to help patients

One of the post-war innovations was a return to an open-door policy, where patients would be allowed to move freely throughout the hospital. Since the early nineteenth century, every aspect of asylum life, from working practices to a daily routine, had been segregated. This applied not only to patients but to staff too, as female wards were off-limits to men, except for doctors. It wasn't until the late nineteenth century that female nurses were allowed into male wards. In post-war Britain, there was also a move towards mixing male and female wards.

In 1953, a report issued by the World Health Organization stated that:

> The life within the hospital should, as far as possible, be modelled on life within the community in which it is set. In a western country where men and women mix freely at work and in recreation, it is obviously desirable that they should do so when in the mental hospital.

Many people agreed that patients who had spent particularly long periods in institutions suffered from 'institutional neurosis' and that if the environment of the institution was changed or removed, these patients could return to everyday life and reside in the community. For a start, changes needed to be made to prepare male and female patients for being in a mixed ward.

In the 1950s though many wards remained single-sex, they were now unlocked in response to the WHO's report. But the mixing of wards had mixed results. Some patients claimed that their illness was better when they began to be noticed by the opposite sex, and they felt a sense of pride and self-worth in knowing that the spark of human attraction was not lost. Nurses noticed that male patients seemed to smarten up near female patients, and the two began interacting more.

Hospital staff also observed that mixing the sexes resulted in less violence and aggression. The presence of women among men helped them to change their behaviour. However, it is not surprising that patients began to meet in unsupervised areas to have sex.

As some of the boundaries between the two wards disappeared, there was anxiety about patients who were criminal psychopaths. Many patients were sex offenders from the courts or prisons that were being admitted to asylums. In mixed-sex wards, this became a big concern, especially for women. These criminal patients were often disliked as their presence was disruptive and threatening. There was also the struggle of trying to control them without restraint. Some doctors argued that allowing male and female patients to roam increased the use of sedating drugs.

Some hospitals kept locked wards for the more troublesome patients, many of them women. Some of these women were promiscuous by their illness alone. The female wards were now being closely monitored in fear of pregnancy, with more and more patients meeting in private places.

While male nurses were often more respected because they tended to be older with longer tenure, many weren't fans of the mixed ward because it was more work for them. A large group of male nurses saw mixing the sexes as frivolous and said it felt more like an experiment with the patients.

In order to make all the changes for not only mixing patient wards but preparing them for life outside the asylum, several things needed to be done. Ward doors were purposely left unlocked, and bars were removed from the windows. Fences in the airing courts were also being taken down.

Dingleton Hospital in Melrose, Scotland, was a pioneer in the open-door policy, and by 1949, there were no locked wards at all. Mapperley Hospital in Nottingham introduced the open-door policy in 1952 with the removal of locks on all wards and gates. Other hospitals would soon follow with the arrival of pharmaceuticals that could control psychotic symptoms.

The open-door policy of the 1950s was one of the most radical post-war changes, and it was hard to convince staff and surrounding communities that allowing patients free rein in and around the asylum was a good idea. If we take a step back and look at the history surrounding the progressive movements, we can get a better grasp on why there was such a debate on whether or not the closing of the asylums was a change for the positive.

The Second World War had taken from Britain almost all of its financial resources from foreign countries, and the nation was in debt by several billion pounds. The economy was in complete disarray, and the railways and coal mines were in desperate need of repair. The end of the war had also created a housing crisis. The New Towns Act, passed in 1946, allowed the government to plan for areas as new towns, handing building control to development corporations. This act, along with the rebuilding of existing war-torn cities, led to new centres of a booming population, predominately in the southeast. And with the housing shortage, food rationing, and an alarmingly high rate of death from tuberculosis. The New Towns Act, along with the NHS act of 1946, came at a much-needed time for the post-war country.

The National Health Service Act was brought before parliament in 1946 as part of a new welfare policy that aimed to provide free and universal health benefits to all British citizens in need. The NHS was seen as one way to not only help Britain recover from the war but to help stop the spread of disease and poverty.

On 5 July 1948, the NHS took control of almost half a million beds throughout hospitals in England and Wales. In the urban areas, nearly 200,000 belonged to patients in mental hospitals, and many of these residents were considered to have an irrecoverable mental illness.

It was essentially the establishment of the NHS and the development of antipsychotic drugs that were the main factors in the closing of the mental institutions throughout Great Britain. The social and political climate of the country also greatly influenced the move to close the asylums with what became known as deinstitutionalisation. Deinstitutionalisation was the act of moving the care and support of those with mental illness from asylums into community-based settings. The agenda behind it was one of public and moral necessity. There was a growing emphasis on human rights and philosophies that criticised psychiatry and what constituted mental illness. Increased awareness was put on whether or not keeping patients in the hospital after they recovered from their illness was taking away their rights.

In October 1953, the appointment of the Royal Commission on the Law Relating to Mental Illness and Mental Deficiency, to be chaired by Baron Percy of Newcastle, was announced. The Commission (also known as the Percy Commission) was to inquire into all existing laws regarding those patients who were said to be suffering from mental illness.

The work of the Commission was then published in 1957, with the May Report of the Royal Commission on the Law Relating to Mental Illness and Mental Deficiency. They brought the issue of mental health reform under public scrutiny. The commission's view was that the care of the mentally infringed did not need to be in special hospitals that only further socially isolated the patients. They also argued that the hospitals were overrun with large numbers of chronic patients, putting a tremendous strain on hospital staff. The Royal Commission recommended that 'no patient should be retained as a hospital inpatient when he has reached the stage at which he could go home'.

And:

> The law should be altered so that whenever possible, suitable care may be provided for mentally disordered patients with no more restriction of liberty or legal formality than is applied to people who need care because of other types of illness, disability, or social difficulty.

The commission also recommended that folks with mental disorders be treated in their community whenever possible instead of in large institutions. By 1957, it was more common to see psychiatrists working in outpatient cases as the concept of the 'day procedure' or 'day hospital' was being introduced. But to achieve the commission's recommendation, there would need to be an expansion of community services. The commission also felt that mental health treatment should be handled primarily by the NHS. Local authorities were required to provide accommodations to patients under the National Health Service Act.

Following the recommendations made by the Royal Commission came the Mental Health Act of 1959. This act would give the legislative groundwork to carry out those recommendations. The act aimed to dispel the separation of psychiatric hospitals and general hospitals, ensuring that patients with mental illness could fair in a home setting or a social service facility. The law required local authorities to see that mentally ill patients received the proper after-care on an outpatient basis. This included providing and maintaining residential homes, training centres, and supplemental sources.

The Mental Health Act of 1959 stands out as it was the first legislation to specify why patients may need to be admitted to the hospital involuntarily and clarify the distinction between involuntary and voluntary care.

A member of the Royal College of Psychiatrists, Dr. John Wing, observed that folks who spent long periods of time in institutions developed a syndrome known as institutionalism. Institutionalism was seen in patients as a withdrawal from society, an unwillingness to initiate ideas, apathy, and absolute dependence on the institution. These patients had spent so long being committed that it was as if they knew no other way of life.

The general consensus was shared among medical authorities throughout Britain and the United States.

American sociologist Erving Goffman spoke of what he called total institutions. These places, many being mental hospitals, removed any and all dignity a patient may have by way of impersonal treatment. He believed that patients could foster regression as they were set in the ways of a deviant. Both Dr Wing and Dr Goffman thought that the environment found in mental hospitals strongly influenced the rise of psychotic behaviour. It was their thinking that began the political movement to ultimately close down the asylums.

Minister of Health, Enoch Powell, who was also in favour of closing the asylums, spoke to the National Association for Mental Health in 1961. He explained his desire to see the community come together to support mental health patients. He was enthusiastic about the recent advancements in psychiatric medicine and felt that with successful community care, the number of psychiatric beds could decrease by 75,000 within fifteen years. Clinically, the developments in medical treatment with antipsychotic drugs and antidepressants said that people with severe mental illness could be treated outside the asylum. Powell felt that asylum care might even be harmful. He also thought that the existing buildings were deteriorating and should be closed indefinitely. It was also likely that asylums were not financially sustainable and offered prime real estate for contractors.

Powell's speech to the National Association for Mental Health, which became known as the Water Tower Speech, said:

> This is a colossal undertaking, not so much in the new physical provision which it involves, as in the sheer inertia of mind and matter which it required to be overcome. There they stand, isolated, majestic, imperious, brooded over by the gigantic water tower and chimney combined, rising unmistakable and daunting out of the countryside - the asylums which our forefathers built with such immense solidity to express the notions of their day. Do not for a moment underestimate their powers of resistance to our assault. We have to strive to alter our whole mentality about hospitals and about mental hospitals especially. Hospital building is not like pyramid building, the erection of memorials to endure to a remote posterity. We have to get the idea into our heads that a hospital is a shell, a framework, however complex, to contain certain

processes. When the processes change or are superseded, then the shell must most probably be scrapped.

The Hospital Plan for England and Wales, developed by Enoch Powell, set out to establish a programme for building hospitals with two general purposes. The plan's goal was to configure the sizes and types of hospitals needed to support both general care and home care. The programme also called for a rebuilding plan. Enoch's plan announced that all large area hospitals would be the mainstay of hospital provision over the next several decades. These district general hospitals were to provide almost all of the care a patient would need, including inpatient and outpatient care.

New programmes were set up to manage everything and deliver services. There were a lot of existing charities and different groups like the district health authority, local authority, and the voluntary sector. The goal was to make sure that no one organisation had sole ownership. There were aspects of patient transformation, like understanding the needs of the patients in the hospital and what funding would be available over time. They needed to identify setting, care, and staff.

Between 1960 and 1970, the number of beds being used fell from 136,000 to 103,000 throughout Great Britain as day programmes rose from 708,000 to almost two million by 1970. It was predicted that the eventual end of the 'extended stay' at mental hospitals was greatly affected by the growth of the outpatient clinic, more effective treatments, and better rehabilitation of patients who required lengthy care.

During the 1960s, there was a considerable effort to deinstitutionalise patients, along with vigorous attempts to discharge them all together. There was a rising sense of overoptimism in British psychiatry along with growing criticism of the asylum. Doctors felt confident that with the introduction of new medications, they could now treat the acute stages in their patients, preventing a chronic situation.

There was also a rise of considerable protest against the routine of the mental hospital, along with the distribution of documents that attacked the way institutional care was being used. The speculation regarding the effects of the asylum on its patients also contributed to the influential ideas that reinforced deinstitutionalisation.

The result of Powell's plan caused a noticeable change in psychiatric services throughout the country. Essentially, the mental hospital was completely abandoned as all services were now being performed at the district hospitals. There was also a shift in planning community-based programmes for those with mental illness, such as day services and home-based care, which essentially fell in with the newly initiated community care policy.

The model adopted by the district general hospitals for the organisation of psychiatric services was the same as for other hospital disciplines, namely, inpatient and outpatient facilities within the hospital building. Outpatient clinics became an essential part of psychiatric service provision and moved from having a triage function to becoming a resource for both evaluation and follow-up.

Not surprisingly, these new models for patient care would prove disastrous for many. Those who had lived in asylums were now given inadequate community care, sparking much debate which lasted almost fifty years. There soon became increased numbers of people with untreated mental illness that were now on the streets due to the closure of the asylums. Many stated this was evidence that community care had failed miserably. Thousands of patients, who knew no other way than what the asylum provided for them, were now expected to acclimate to everyday life.

But some longer-term studies did show the outcome for people who had been in the asylums to be favourable. Many patients increased their social skills and gained independent living skills, improving their quality of life.

In 1962, Ken Kesey published his famous book, *One Flew Over the Cuckoo's Nest*, at the height of the anti-psychiatry movement. The collective view was that mental illness did not exist, and if it did, it was the result.

While the end of institutional care was slowly in the works, Kesey's book then made into a film gave the public a very intimate look at the treatment of psychiatric patients, albeit through a somewhat defunct cinematic lens. This was somewhat of an eye-opener of the pros and cons of the newly emerging psychiatry drugs.

As we know, most historians would agree that it was the introduction of antipsychotics that brought about the most significant change in psychiatric care. These medications could treat the symptoms of such illnesses as schizophrenia and reduce the risk of the patient relapsing. Most countries throughout Europe saw a dramatic decrease in the number of inpatient psychiatric patients as the shift to community care began to unfold.

Antipsychotics played an essential role because they offered hope in the treatment of schizophrenia and gave doctors the confidence to discharge their patients. These medications also impacted how doctors viewed their patients, and they helped stimulate further research into the treatment of mental illness, what we know today as psychopharmacology. With more of a biological understanding of psychosis, physicians could better understand how medications helped patients.

With the introduction of Thorazine came a more scientific way of finding out the effectiveness and safety of these medications. Clinical trials soon began and are now regarded as the golden standard in getting medicines approved. Clinical trials allowed for research studies in patients trying out a new drug, allowing doctors to determine if a medication was safe and effective.

These medications also helped change the way the public viewed the treatment of psychiatric patients. It gave families hope that there was now a serious alternative to treat mental illness instead of the unfavourable therapies used in the past. The possibility of having to lock your loved one away for years at a time now seemed like ancient history. This hope was shared collectively by patients and physicians alike.

While the goal of deinstitutionalisation was to begin the closing of asylums in the 1960s, it only decreased admission. While the idea of community care was certainly not new, it wasn't until 1983 that Prime Minister Margaret Thatcher implemented a new policy after a report by the Audit Commission, called 'Making a Reality of Community Care', was published. The report exposed the lack of progress in moving patients from long-stay hospitals to community care.

British businessman Sir Roy Griffiths was asked by PM Thatcher to produce a report outlining the problems of the NHS in regards to community care. Thatcher admired his prior work as a businessman, and he was asked to create a so-called 'Agenda of Action' for community care. Griffiths believed that there was a grey area between health and social services in the care of several dependent groups, including the mentally ill. He firmly believed that community care was not working because no one wanted to assume responsibility for such a vast undertaking. Griffiths Agenda of Action called for the Minister of State to ensure the policies of community care were carried out. Specific grants from the central government would help fund community care development. The idea was to have community care facilities viewed as a transitional phase for patients to return to society.

However, the notion that many patients may require no less than lifelong support was either being denied or ignored. While some may have responded favourably to rehabilitation measures, others were not cut out for community care services. There was still a large number of patients that needed that lifelong care that only the asylum could provide.

Many patients who still needed long-term care really challenged the idea of community care, and its attempts seemed to imply a rejection of staying in the hospital. Would the support services offered by the community be able to provide the adequate care that the asylum did? Asylums provided shelter, food, support, treatments, and a sense of order that many patients desperately needed. The asylum had truly been the framework of a life that would have been if its patient was well enough to live independently.

Many community care facilities had staff that was not equipped to handle patients who presented with significant difficulty. These patients often ended up in prisons when they could have remained in long-term care. Short-term care facilities were unable to provide adequate support, and as a result, the prison population and the number of destitute were overwhelmed with ex-mental hospital patients.

The actual start of the closings of the asylums took place almost twenty-five years later, in 1986. Banstead Asylum, which opened its doors in 1877, was the first asylum to close entirely in 1986. It was built with accommodation for 1,700 patients when it opened that continually increased throughout the years. In 1948, Banstead had over 2,500 beds when it came under the control of the NHS. The hospital was seen as outdated and in need of a facelift. Within a few years, several wards were given updated equipment, and the hospital entrance was improved. The hospital was also given a library and reading room. The hospital thrived throughout 1967 but by 1968 was down to only 1,600 beds. After a reorganisation of the NHS in 1974, Banstead Hospital would pass through several hands before it ultimately closed in 1986 and was demolished in 1989.

The East Riding Asylum, located in the parish of Walkington, opened in 1871. It was designed by Charles Henry Howell, a well-known architect who had been involved in developing other asylums. Like Howell's other designs, East Riding followed the corridor plan and featured beautiful archways and brickwork. The facility expanded throughout the years to include new cottages on the property to house attendants. As with most of Britain's asylums, after the Care in the

Community act, the number of beds dwindled at East Riding. The hospital closed for good in April 1989, and the site was demolished.

Aside from Banstead and East Riding Asylums, around 100 asylums throughout Great Britain closed in the 1980s and 1990s. British society initially saw the closing of the asylums as a charitable concern for the welfare of the mentally ill. But events in the 1990s brought about an increasing fear of the insane now that they were not behind the asylum walls.

In December 1992, while he waited at the Finsbury Park Tube Station with his brother, musician Johnathan Zito, was stabbed to death. The accused, Christopher Clunis, had a long history of psychiatric illness. A report that inquired into Clunis's past found that both hospitals and social services did not attempt to contact his doctor or family after several mishaps. Authorities also discharged him from the hospital before he was healthy to save either money or beds.

The inquiry also established that Clunis had a history of several violent attacks over the past several years involving knives. Just a week before lethally stabbing Mr Zito, Clunis attacked another man with a screwdriver in North London. He was also seen later that day terrorising a group of children as he chased them with a screwdriver.

Throughout the span of the six years that he was unwell, Clunis did not keep any of his outpatient appointments but was admitted to several psychiatric hospitals.

The ruthless murder of Mr Zito highlighted what could very well happen to mental patients who were trying to transition to everyday life.

In 1991, the Care Programme Approach (CPA) was created to act as a form of case management for the community care of mentally ill folks. The CPA was based on a programme in the United States that targeted care for those who were most in need. Community care was failing terribly, and an influx of disturbed and unkempt individuals were seen sleeping on the streets of Britain.

The government still insisted it wanted to prioritise mental health but faced great difficulty doing so. Psychiatrists saw the CPA as an encroachment on their better judgment and their private practices, and they also believed that the CPA was far too bureaucratic.

Nonetheless, the CPA had devised a plan that called for a supervision register for high-risk patients. But it was seen more as a way to control patients instead of care for them, and it was seen as nothing more than a different set of restrictions.

A form of supervised discharge was put into the Mental Health Act of 1995, requiring patients to agree to a care plan after their release from the hospital. Psychiatrists saw this too as just another modification. The act stated that:

> An Act to make provision for certain mentally disordered patients in England and Wales to receive after-care under supervision after leaving hospital; to provide for the making of community care orders in the case of certain mentally disordered patients in Scotland; to amend the law relating to mentally disordered patients absent without leave or on leave of absence from hospital; and for connected purposes.

Politicians also criticised the CPA for its poor coordination and lack of detail. Any attempts to develop joint records systems failed as significant computer problems were encountered. There were very few agreed-upon procedures for risk assessment, and any plans that were put in place were ineffective. Any written information for the public about the CPA programme was rarely available. The CPA was essentially dismissed as an ineffective approach for helping Britain's mentally ill population.

The general consensus seemed to be that community care had failed entirely. The Zito Trust, which the widow of Jonathan Zito established, argued that community care had been a negligent disaster.

Many others agreed that it wasn't more supervision that was needed; it was care and support of the patients. The asylum should be no less part of the community than alternative sources.

Over 110 asylums throughout Great Britain have closed, leaving it to be an era gone. There are very few places for long-term psychiatric patients to go, and most are treated for five to seven days and then put back into the community - often without a place to live.

While many state mental hospitals in Great Britain have now been closed and demolished, their history remains a remnant of the psychiatry of years past.

Bibliography

(n.d.). From Britannica: https://www.britannica.com/biography/Sigmund-Freud

(2015). From Good Therapy: https://www.goodtherapy.org/famous-psychologists/emil-kraepelin.html

Andrews, J. (2001). *Undertaker of the Mind John Monro and Mad-Doctoring in Eighteenth-Century England*. University of California Press.

Arnold, C. (2003). *Bedlam London and It's Mad*. London: Simon and Schuster.

Arnott, J. (2008). *The Genius of Erasmus Darwin*. Burlington: Ashgate Publishing.

Arnott, R. (2003). *Trepanation History Discovery Theory*. Taylor and Francis.

Austin, M. (1922). *The Use of Luminal in Epilepsy*. Ohio Dept of Pulic Welfare.

Bachrach, S. (2004). *Deadly Medicine Creating the Master Race*. National Holocaust Museum.

Bartlett, P. (1999). *The poor law of lunacy : the administration of pauper lunatics in mid-nineteenth-century England*. Bloomsbury Acedemic.

Bean, P. (2008). *Madness and Crime*. Abington: Taylor and Francis.

Beatty, H. (2012). *Nervous Disease in Late Eighteenth-Century Britain: The Reality of a Fashionable Disorder*. New York: Pickering and Chatto.

Bedell, G. (2002). The Guardian. From https://www.theguardian.com/society/2002/apr/07/mentalhealth.observerreview

Bennett, A. (1995). *The Madness of King George*. Fabor & Fabor.

Bentall, R. (2003). *Madness Explained Psychosis and Human Nature*. Penguin Books Limited.

Bogousslavsky, J. (2014). *Hysteria: The Rise of an Enigma*. S Karger.

Brown, W. (2019). *Lithium: A Doctor, a Drug, and a Breakthrough*. Liveright.

Burt, J. (2017). *Lunatics, Imbeciles and Idiots*. Yorkshire: Pen & Sword.

Carlise, L. (2010). *Elizabeth Packard A Noble Fight*. University of Illinois.

Cherry, C. (1989). *Moral Treatment Quakers, Moral Treatment, and Asylum Reform*. University of Michigan.

Cherry, S. (2003). *The Norfolk Lunatic Asylum/St. Andrew's Hospital c. 1810-1998*. Bodell Press.

Colt, S. (n.d.). *Bridewell, Palace. Prison, School*.

Connolly, J. (2013). *The Treatment of the Insane Without Mechanical Restraints*. Cambridge University.

Conroy, M. (2017). *Nazi Eugenics Precursors, Policy, Aftermath*. Columbia University.

Ctlin, A. (2009). *An Intellectual History of Cannibalism*. Princeton University Press.

Cummings, J. (2021). *Medicine in the Middle Ages*. Yorkshire: Pen & Sword.

Davis, M. (2013). *West Riding Pauper Lunatic Asylum Through Time*. Amberley Publishing.

de Young, M. (2015). *Encyclopedia of Asylum Therapeutics, 1750-1950s*. Jefferson: McPharland.

Dobbing, C. (2021). *Sexual abuse by superintending staff in the nineteenth-century lunatic asylum: medical practice, complaint and risk*. NCBI.

Dully, H. (2007). *My Lobotomy A Memoir*. New York: Random House.

Earl, P. (1851). *American Journal of Psychiatry*, 16.

El-Hai, J. (2005). *The Lobotomist A Maverick Medical Genius and His Tragic Quest to Rid the World of Mental Illness*. Hoboken: Wiley.

Elmer, P. (2004). *Health, Disease and Society in Europe, 1500-1800*. Manchester: Manchester University Press.

Flemming, J. (1960). *Clitoridectomy - the Disastrous Downfall of Isaac Baker Brown, F.R.C.S.* (1867). Headly Brothers.

Foucault, M. (1961). *Madness and Civilization*. Knopf Doubleday Publishing Group.

Fox, F. (1836). *History and Present State of Brislington House Near Bristol*. Light and Ridler.

Fried, S. (2018). *Rush Revolution, Madness, and Benjamin Rush, the Visionary Doctor Who Became a Founding Father*. New York: Random House.

G, H. (2018). *The Direct Action of Atropine, Homatropine, Hyoscine, Hyoscyamine, and Daturine on the Heart of the Dog, Terrapin, and Frog*. Creative Media Partners, LLC.

Gaskell, E. (1857). *The Life of Charlotte Brontë*. Oxford University.

Gass, W. (2001). *The Anatomy of Melancholia*. New York: New York Publisher of Books.

Goc, N. (2013). *Women, Infanticide and the Press, 1822-1922*. Taylor and Francis.

Hassink, J. (2006). *Farming for Health Green-Care Farming Across Europe and the United States of America*. Dordrecht: Springer.

Healey, D. (1997). *The Antidepressant Era*. Cambridge: Harvard University Press.

Health, U. D. (1967). *Tuberculosis Beds in Hospitals and Sanatoria*.

Ingram, A. (2013). *The Madhouse of Language Writing and Reading Madness in the Eighteenth Century*. Taylor and Francis.

Larry, H. (1994). *First Among Friends George Fox and the Creation of Quakerism*. Oxford: Oxford University Press.

Lawlar, C. (2012). *A History of Depression From Melancholia to Prozac*. Oxford: Oxford University Press.

Longrigg, J. (1998). *Greek Medicine From the Heroic to the Hellenistic Age: A Source Book*. London: Gerald Duckworth and Co.

MacCoullagh, D. (2010). *Christianity: The First Three Thousand Years*. New York: Penguin.

Maines, R. (2001). *'Hysteria,' the Vibrator, and Women's Sexual Satisfaction*. John Hopkins University Press.

Mansell, J. (1996). *Deinstitutionalization and Community Living*. Springer.

Markler, B. (1968). *Philippe Pinel, Unchainer of the Insane*. F. Watts.

Marland, H. (2004). *Dangerous Motherhood Insanity and Childbirth in Victorian Britain*. New York: Palgrave McMillian.

Matyas, J. (2020). *Famous Case Histories in Neurotrauma*. Routledge.

McDonald, C. (2008). *The Maudsley Family Study of Psychosis*. East Sussex: Taylor and Francis.

McGettrick, C. (2021). *Ireland and the Magdalene Laundries*. Bloomsbury.

Medical Review Volume 3 1900. (1898).

Medicine, M. a. (2018). Hadass, Offer. Park, PA: Penn State University.

Melling, J. (1997). 'A Proper Lunatic for Two Years': Pauper Lunatic Children in Victorian and Edwardian. University of Exeter.

Melling, J. (2006). *The State, Insanity and Society in England, 1845–1914*. Taylor and Francis.

Mitchell, S. (2016). *Freud and Beyond A History of Modern Psychoanalytic Thought*. New York: Basic Books.

Morrison, K. (1999). *The Workhouse A Study of Poor-law Buildings in England*. Royal Commission.

Moses, B. (1997). *A Tudor Medicine Chest*. Wayland.

Muckenhoupt, M. (2003). *Dorthea Dix: Advocate for Mental Health Care*. New York: Oxford University Press.

Murdoch, L. (2013). *Daily Life of Victorian Women*. ABC-CLIO.

Ourselves, F. H. (2002). *Race and Membership in American History: The Eugenics Movement*. Facing History and Ourselves.

Parkes, J. (1988). *Neurological Disorders*. Springer London.

Patel, D. (2020). *The Age of Enlightenment*. Lulu.

Pavão Martins, I. (1999). *Egas Moniz: 50 years after the Nobel Prize*. Tecnimede.

Payne, M. (1995). *Social Work and Community Care*. Hampshire: MacMillan.

Poorman, P. (2007). *Medieval Islamic Medicine*. Edinburgh: Edinburgh University Press.

Porter, R. (2013). *George Cheyne: The English Malady (1733) (Psychology Revivals)*. Taylor and Francis.

Pressman, J. (1998). *Last Resort Psychosurgery and the Limits of Medicine*. Cambridge: Cambridge University Press.

Publications, C. (2000). *Dingleton Hospital Melrose: The Story of a Community*. Cheifswoods Publications.

Rappaport, H. (2003). *Queen Victoria: A Biographical Companion*. ABC-CLIO.

Roelcke, V. (2010). *International Relations in Psychiatry*. Rochester: University of Rochester.

Rushdan, A. (2018). *Talking Back against the Nazi Scheme to Kill the Handicapped Citizens of Germany 1933-1945*. Newcastle: Cambridge Scholars.

Saltz, G. (2017). *The Power of Different*. New York: Flat Iron Books.

Schaler, J. (2017). *Thomas Szasz A Man and His Ideas*. New York: Taylor and Francis.

Schmidt, U. (2007). *Karl Brand:t The Nazi Doctor Medicine and Power in the Third Reich*. Bloomsbury.

Schweizerischer, V. f. (1938). *The Treatment of Schizophrenia Insulin Shock, Cardiazol, Sleep Treatment*.

Shields, L. (2014). *Nurses and Midwives in Nazi Germany: The Euthanasia Program*. New York: Taylor and Francis.

Shorter, E. (2007). *A History of Electroconvulsive Treatment in Mental Illness*. Piscataway: Rutgers University Press.

Slack, P. (1990). *The English Poor Law 1531-1782*. Cambridge: Press Syndicate.

Stevens, M. (2014). *Life in the Victorian Asylum*. Yorkshire: Pen & Sword.

Steward, K. (1992). *The York Retreat in the Light of the Quaker Way*. University of Michigan.

Taylor, J. (1991). *Hospital and Asylum Architecture in England, 1840-1914*. Mansell.

Taylor, S. (2016). *Child Insanity in England, 1845-1907*. Palgrave McMillian.

Tomes, N. (1994). *Thomas Story Kirkbride and the Origins of American Psychiatry*. University of Pennsylvania Press.

Weikart, R. (2004). *From Darwin to Hitler Evolutionary Ethics, Eugenics and Racism in Germany*. Hampshire: Palgrave Macmillan US.

Weitz, D. (2004). *Insulin Shock A Survivors Tale of Psychiatric Torture*.

Welch, E. (2018). *The NHS at 70 A Living History*. Yorkshire: Pen & Sword.

Winokur, G. (1996). *The natural history of mania, depression, and schizophrenia*. Washington: APP.

Wright, T. (1850). *Cholera in the Asylum*. Longman Brown, and Green.

About the Author

Juliana has been writing for over thirty years. From her first publication in her junior high school newspaper to her current writing on Tudor and Medieval History, writing has always been Juliana's passion in life. While she's always been interested in history, she discovered that her family lineage led to Tudor Royalty, which pursued her to learn even more.

Juliana's interests also lie strongly with other aspects of medieval history, particularly medicine and the macabre.

She continues to write for various publications throughout the United Kingdom and the United States. Her work has been published in History is Now magazine, Matt's History Blog, A Tudor Writing Circle, and Tudor Dynasty.

Juliana also has self-published on Amazon.com, and you can find her through Facebook and Twitter under The Savage Revolt. You can also visit her website, https://thesavagerevolt.com

Her books can be found on Amazon, including *Sleeping with the Impaler* and *Medicine in the Middle Ages*. She writes both non-fiction and historical fiction and is currently working on her next novel.

Index

Age of Enlightenment 63, 65, 66, 69, 78
Al-Razi 15, 16
Aretaeus 6, 7, 10, 11
Aristotle 4, 10
Asclepius 2, 3, 5
Astrology 40, 49, 50
Avicenna 14, 15

Battie, William 78, 79, 144
Bedlam 21, 22, 29, 30, 31, 32, 33, 34, 43, 59, 62, 73, 78, 85, 144, 162
Bethlem Hospital 30, 145, 146, 180
Blair, Patrick 74, 75
Bloodletting 11, 39, 51, 71
Bridewell Palace 30, 31, 32, 33, 46
Bright, Timothy 41, 42, 43
Burton, Robert 52, 53, 54, 55, 56, 57, 58

Calvinism 49, 63
Catholic Church 12, 29, 38, 65, 66, 67, 68
Cheyne, Geroge 77

Chiarugi, Vincent 78, 79, 80
Christianity 11, 12, 220
Church of England 38, 49, 62, 134
Cicero 8, 9
Cox, Joseph 72, 73
Crooke, Heikiah 32, 33

Darwin, Charles 70, 206, 207
Dementia Praecox 17, 144, 145
Depression 8, 9, 14, 17, 23, 27, 50, 53, 54, 93, 103, 106, 113, 120, 122, 156, 162, 166, 168, 184, 191, 199, 204, 212
Dymphna 12, 13, 132

Edward VI 30, 31, 46, 61
Elizabeth I 41, 47
English Malady 77
English Poor Laws 31, 43, 46
English Poor Laws 31, 46
English Revolution 48, 62
Epilepsy 6, 9, 29, 36, 37, 112, 117, 127, 128, 129, 139, 163, 174, 175, 178, 179, 207, 211, 221
Exorcism 12, 22, 25, 62

Foucault, Michel 20, 21
Four Humours 4, 11, 23, 66
Freud, Sigmund 1, 17, 18, 19, 20, 158, 211

Galen 4, 11, 15, 23, 35, 39, 64, 177
Geel 12, 13, 14, 84, 132
George III 75, 76, 85

Hallucination 7, 36, 28, 104, 122, 144, 163, 185, 191, 203
Henry VI 59, 60, 61
Henry VIII 30, 38, 44, 45, 46, 69
Hippocrates 2, 4, 5, 10, 11, 23, 25, 36, 39
Hume, David 69
Hysteria 9, 10, 11, 112, 113, 114, 115, 119

Islamic 14, 15, 21, 36

Jesus Christ 12, 13, 23

Kraepelin, Emil 16, 17, 18, 19, 144, 211

Laxatives 33, 39, 162

Madhouse Act 81
Mania 1, 4, 7, 8, 11, 14, 23, 35, 37, 54, 79, 85, 94, 103, 115, 117, 120, 121, 122, 127, 128, 133, 142, 165, 182, 185, 199, 200, 202, 204
Melancholia 14, 127, 133
Melancholy 4, 5, 6, 7, 8, 11, 14, 15, 23, 35, 39, 41, 42, 43, 48, 49, 51, 52, 53, 54, 55, 56, 57, 58, 59, 60, 74, 106, 135
Mercury 71
Middle Ages 22, 23, 24, 25, 26, 27, 28, 29, 38, 40, 64, 68, 84, 100, 103, 131, 163, 184
Moral Treatment 72, 76, 80, 82, 85, 89, 90, 96, 97, 110, 116, 131, 143, 146
Mozart, Wolfgang 52, 53, 54, 56, 107

Napier, Richard 49, 50, 51
Nerves 74, 77, 78, 79, 102, 131, 162
Newton, Isaac 67

Pinel, Philippe 78, 80, 81, 144, 155, 161
Plato 7, 10, 205, 206
Poe, Edgar Allen 54, 56, 107
Pool of Bethesda 3
Possession 11, 12, 22, 23, 25, 26, 27, 33, 36, 38, 51, 60, 61, 69, 76, 184
Protestant 38, 50, 62, 220
Psychoanalysis 17, 19, 158

248

Psychosurgery 24, 184, 186, 189, 190, 191, 194, 195, 197
Purging 11, 33, 39, 40, 71, 119

Quakers 62, 82, 90, 99

Reil, Johann 79, 80
Renaissance 36, 48, 49, 52, 64, 66, 68, 84, 100, 115, 160
Restraints 72, 76, 82, 91, 97, 99, 146, 171
Rochford, Lady Jane 44, 45
Rousseau 69
Rush, Benjamin 70, 71, 72

Schizophrenia 8, 17, 144, 145, 158, 166, 169, 172, 174, 175, 199, 202, 203, 204, 211, 212, 221, 234
Seizure 26, 36, 37, 167, 171, 175, 176, 178, 179, 181, 193
Soranus 8, 10, 11
Spinning Chair 70
Straightjacket 70, 72, 83, 97, 98, 139, 150

Stuart 39, 40, 41, 47, 58, 63
Swing Chair 72, 73, 75
Szasz, Thomas 19, 20

Townshend, Thomas 81
Tranquillizer Chair 70
Trepanation 24, 25, 188
Tudor 30, 31, 35, 38, 39, 40, 41, 44, 46, 58, 62, 63
Tuke, William 76, 79, 81, 82, 83, 97

Uterus 9, 10, 11, 77, 105

Vagabonds Acts 43, 46, 47
Voltaire 68
Vomiting 40, 72, 73, 74, 94, 163, 177, 180, 187

Wandering Womb 10, 11, 38, 112
Water Treatment 74, 75, 162
Willis, Francis 75, 76

York Lunatic Asylum 82
York Retreat 82, 83, 85, 90